THE MAKING OF A WOMAN SURGEON

Elizabeth Morgan was raised in rural Virginia. She went to Harvard University at the age of sixteen, moving on to become one of the seven women in a class of ninety-seven students at Yale Medical School. She did her professional training in New England and two years of research at Somerville College, Oxford. After eleven years of training and surgical work she moved to Washington DC to practice as a plastic surgeon. She has written many articles on problems in surgery and is also the medical correspondent for *Cosmopolitan* magazine in America.

Critical acclaim for *The Making of a Woman Surgeon*:

'An extremely well-written account of surgeon/writer Morgan's 11-year odyssey through medical school and general and plastic surgery residences. The reader quickly becomes caught up in Morgan's struggle to survive in the male-dominated world of surgery'
Library Journal

'The book is almost like a diary of her experiences – a medical student's intimate journal, except in dialogue form. It is exciting to read and moves quickly from chapter to chapter; clearly, the author is as skilled with the pen as with the scalpel'
South Bend Tribune

'An absorbing story of one woman and her profession. Reading it is one way to learn about the people, good and bad, who take knives and with our permission cut into our bodies and hold our lives in their gloved and sometimes trembling hands'
Atlanta Journal

THE MAKING OF A
WOMAN SURGEON

Elizabeth Morgan, M.D.

Star
A STAR BOOK
published by
the Paperback Division of
W. H. ALLEN & CO. LTD

A Star Book
Published in 1981
by the Paperback Division of
W. H. Allen & Co. Ltd
A Howard and Wyndham Company
44 Hill Street, London W1X 8LB

First published in the United States
by G. P. Putnam's Sons, 1980

Reproduced, printed and bound in Great Britain by
Hazell Watson & Viney Ltd, Aylesbury, Bucks

ISBN 0 352 30891 5

Acknowledgments

I should like to thank the doctors who spent so much time, teaching me about surgery so gladly, and with such devotion to the highest ideals in medicine. I am especially grateful to the few surgeons in both general and plastic surgery who went out of their way to advise and to help me during the three most difficult periods of my residency.

There is great pleasure in helping one's own patients, and in working in a team with other residents. I am grateful to the patients and the residents it was my privilege to help and to work with.

Helen Gurley Brown, Roberta Ashley and Barbara Hustedt at *Cosmopolitan* helped to keep me writing about medicine through six years of residency. I could not have begun, or kept at it, without their approval, help and encouragement.

Phyllis Stohl and Clare Ring have typed this manuscript. I am grateful for their superb help, particularly in detecting those errors of mine that made nonsense out of an otherwise sensible sentence.

This book is dedicated to my parents.

Introduction

I spent eleven years training to be a plastic surgeon. I enjoyed my surgical training, but it was very hard. I want you to know what it is like. I started when I was twenty. I finished a month before I turned thirty-one.

It is often easier to be a woman in surgery during the internship and early residency years, because the men think it is sweet for a woman to try to be a surgeon. Later on it is harder, because most men don't like to be subordinate to a woman surgeon, who is telling them what to do, or who is right on a diagnosis when they are wrong. On the other hand, several surgeons have helped me so much that I doubt if I could have finished my training without their support.

Medicine is an ancient and honorable profession. It attracts men and women who dedicate their lives to helping other people. Medicine aims to cure disease when possible, and to relieve pain and suffering when cure is not possible. A tiny fraction of doctors are more interested in medicine as a business than in the care of their patients. Unfortunately these few attract public attention and create ill will against the profession. Most doctors are interested only in helping their patients, by treating them directly, and through teaching and research.Ever since Hippocrates, good physicians have struggled to protect the sick by keeping medical standards high, and by keeping charlatans and quacks out of the profession. This book is written as a tribute to the doctors who trained me, who spend their lives not in seeking money or publicity, but in caring for the sick and suffering.

To protect the privacy of patients I have cared for, their names and the names of their attending surgeons have been changed.

Starting Out

Medical School

On Call on New Year's Eve

It was New Year's Day, about 12:30 A.M., when I got into bed. I was the chief resident in surgery. It was snowing heavily and the streets looked beautiful. The wards were quiet. The few patients who had stayed in the hospital for the holidays were tucked in for the night. I had been asleep for two wonderful hours when the telephone at my bedside rang. I was sleeping in an empty bed on the ward, because it was too much trouble to stagger to my on-call room in another building.

"Dr. Morgan," said the hospital operator, on the phone, "they need you in the emergency room STAT!" In a thick voice I tried to ask what time it was. When at last she understood me, she said it was 2:30 A.M. Reluctantly, I struggled out of bed. I didn't have to dress, because I would always sleep in an operating-room gown when on call. I may look rumpled and unprofessional but I'm ready for an emergency. The hospital is in the Danger Zone, the center of drugs, crime and prostitution. I walked very quickly, almost running, to the emergency room, taking an outside shortcut through the snow.

A stat call means you are needed for a life-and-death emergency, but an experienced doctor never runs at top speed. The last time I sprinted to an emergency was during my first year of surgical residency. I had had no sleep for a week, and I was eating breakfast in the cafeteria with Mark, a fellow surgical resident. That stat page came just as I finished a second cup of coffee. I ran to the "code," or emergency, at top speed up seven flights of stairs. The elevators were much too slow, and besides, they were filled with nurses and secretaries coming to work. I arrived on the seventh floor with Mark barely ahead of me. I dashed to the dying patient's bedside, took a deep breath and fainted from extreme fatigue and exercising on a full stomach. A nurse and Mark had to drag me out of the room because everyone was stumbling over me, trying to reach the patient. He had had a heart attack, but other people saved his life, and I learned not to run to an emergency.

Now, as chief resident, I walked very quickly and arrived in the emergency room from the outside shortcut, which was not the most comfortable way to reach the E.R., but it saved a ten-minute walk in hospital corridors. I walked in shivering from the biting Boston wind and covered with snow, but awake and in control. The emergency room secretary waved me on to the "code room," where all possible surgical emergencies are brought. It is old, with faded green paint, but its battered shelves stock everything from arm restraints to heart surgery instruments. Jim, the junior surgical resident on call in the emergency room, shouted to me as soon as I reached the doorway. He was from Vermont, and he had recently grown a full beard which made him look like a wild man of the mountains. The room was crowded with nurses, policemen, ambulance drivers and junior residents who had helped bring the patient into the code room. I couldn't see the patient because of the crowd, but I saw a medical resident putting in an intravenous line and the anesthesiology resident giving him oxygen.

"Hey, Elizabeth," called Jim, "this is a John Doe, stabbed in a bar. It's some stabbing—it must be his liver or something big. They tried for his heart, too, but the knife skidded off the ribs. His son is over at City Hospital, stabbed in the lung. There are two others, but they were dead when the ambulance got to the bar. This guy's heart stopped on the way over in the ambulance. He's got to go to the O.R."

I really did not want to spend New Year's Eve night operating, but I had expected it. I had operated every night that I was on call during December, and I had been on call in the hospital every other night. On top of that I had worked every one of those days from 6:30 A.M. to 7:30 P.M. or later. I was tired. I snapped at a policeman to please move aside. He stared at me, but jumped out of the way. I got to the stretcher and saw the patient for the first time. His skin was mottled blue, cold because his blood was not circulating. He stank horribly, covered with vomited red wine. There was a stab wound just under his right ribs. It wasn't very large, but it clearly had been effective. It was probably a lacerated liver or vena cava, but now wasn't the time to chat about the possibilities. Whatever the damage, he was obviously bleeding to death, and his only possible chance was for me to operate and stop the bleeding. I stood by the head of the stretcher and pumped in blood that had just arrived from the blood bank. His heart stopped for the second time and an orderly pounded on his chest. The night nursing supervisor herded the crowd out of the room while Jim and I pumped in blood and unbraked the stretcher to move the patient to the O.R. around the corner. The anesthesiologist squeezed oxygen into his lungs through a tube.

"He really needs more blood," I said. "Have you given him all we have down here?" I turned to the nursing supervisor. "We must have more blood," and to the orderly, "Keep pumping his heart. Don't stop now. We can't operate on cadavers."

"I'm going to shock him! Everyone stand back," said Jim. He slapped two electric paddles on the patient's chest. The electric current ran through him, making his body jump. His heart started to beat again, strongly this time, because of the blood we had pumped in. We moved the stretcher into the hallway, I.V. bottles swinging from poles on the stretcher. We were blasted with snow and a biting wind as a drunk staggered in, holding open the outside door to the emergency room. One of the policemen grabbed my arm.

"Hey, listen—you aren't the surgeon, honey, are you?"

He was grinning as if it were all a big joke. His buddy next to him was grinning, too.

"Come on, get out of our way," I said, and to the nursing supervisor, "Please find my intern. I need him in the O.R. now. Would you ask him to call Dr. Mulveney and tell him we have a stabbing that I am taking to the O.R."

Jim and I ran down the corridor with the stretcher. I steadied the head of the stretcher as Jim, holding the foot, pulled it along. The I.V. bottles swung wildly. An ambulance driver standing by the vending machines in the hallway stared at me in disbelief, shaking his head.

I am accustomed to it but I still feel self-conscious when strangers

15

stare at me as though I am a performing mouse. They don't expect a five-foot-five long-haired girl of twenty-eight in an ugly green cotton shift to be the surgeon. They cannot believe that in a code room filled with blood and a dying stab-wound victim the other doctors are shouting for a girl.

We got our patient into the O.R. and used the blood-soaked sheets under him to pull him onto the operating table. I put on gloves and Ginny, our scrub nurse, put a scalpel in my hand. I asked Jim to stay until the intern arrived, but it was a formality. I knew he would stay to help without being asked. The anesthesiologist had attached the patient to a respirator and was straightening the I.V. lines as I made the incision down the patient's abdomen, from ribs to pubis. There was no time to waste with the ritual surgical washing of hands. Ginny splashed iodine antiseptic over the incision and my hands, as Jim tucked sterile surgical drapes around the incision. I asked the anesthesiologist to lower the operating table. It was set for a surgeon of standard height, about five-feet-nine, much too high for me. The anesthesiologist stepped on the control pedal, and the table glided down. I put my hand inside the belly, felt the intestines and pushed them aside, and groped for the aorta. This was the first step in trying to save his life. I pressed down on the aorta, stopping blood flow through it, and the massive bleeding slowed. The aorta is a huge artery that brings blood from the heart to the intestines and legs. With one hand on the aorta, I had Ginny help me to position the retractors to hold the incision open so I could operate. The blood was appalling. Then Jim was ready and held the aorta and the retractors so I could operate. I searched systematically for sites of bleeding. The liver was not injured, but the stomach was torn open, as were the small intestine, the bile duct, the portal vein to the liver, the aorta and the vena cava. The intern arrived at last. He held another retractor and yawned.

"Looks like some stabbing," he said conversationally. I was annoyed, because I was trying to concentrate. Ginny sniffed and said, "The stink is awful." I had been too busy to notice before, but the smell of half-digested sausage, sour red wine and blood filled the room. The sour wine was especially nauseating.

The blood never slowed. "It's like the Red Sea," said the intern as blood poured from the aorta and vena cava. The sutures I put in seemed to have no effect at all.

16

Suddenly Dr. Mulveney arrived. Rules of the surgery department required an attending surgeon to come to the hospital whenever an emergency operation was done. Usually the chief resident doesn't need any help and it is almost an insult for an attending to scrub in; after five years of training, we were supposed to know how to operate. But this time I was grateful. Dr. Mulveney frowned at the blood on the floor, the bloody sheets and the blood transfusion bottles that littered the room. He raised his eyebrows and resigned himself. A distinguished Bostonian and member of the Harvard Club, he was not going to enjoy this New Year's Eve.

"Elizabeth," he said, after he had put on gown and gloves, "just throw in some big silk sutures, big bites." I did, and the patient's heart stopped again. We pumped on his chest; his heart started and stopped again.

"Well, it looks like the end of him," observed Dr. Mulveney. He backed away from the table, discarded gloves and gown and walked out. He was right, but I kept trying for another hour. With the help of more blood transfusions, the heart started again. I sewed up the aorta and vena cava, again and again and again, and the bleeding slowed, but never stopped. Jim left to return to duty in the emergency room. The intern and I sewed up the abdomen incision, and brought the man, barely alive, to the surgical intensive care unit. He died forty-five minutes later when his heart stopped again.

It was a depressing and ugly way to die. According to the ambulance men, our patient and his son had been out drinking in a Danger Zone bar to celebrate New Year's Eve. His son, stabbed in the chest, was operated on at a city hospital, and lived after one lung was removed. We never learned why they were stabbed, but it was done skillfully. Probably, if we knew the inside story, our patient and his son had been victims of a gangland reprisal, but we rarely learned the real reasons for crime in the Danger Zone, not even from the victims. It was a hospital joke: "There's a guy here who says he was walking down the street at three in the morning, reading the Bible on his way to church, when a knife jumped out and stabbed him."

I left the intern in the I.C.U. filling out the death certificate.

"Happy New Year," he said sarcastically, as he wrote in "Cause of Death."

The hospital administrator notified the coroner about our stabbing victim, and to our surprise the coroner accepted the case. Coroners

17

do not have to autopsy every murder victim. When a coroner is a political appointee he may not "see the need" to bother with a medico-legal autopsy.

After changing out of our bloody scrub gowns, Dr. Mulveney and I sat in the nurses' lounge and drank coffee before he went to sleep in his office and I went in search of the nearest empty bed on the ward. We were both depressed. I wondered what I had done wrong, if I couldn't have saved my patient's life. When the aorta and vena cava are badly injured, there is an eighty-percent chance of dying. Still, I thought, if I had been faster, more organized, given more blood, done something different, I might have saved his life. It was not a good way to begin the new year. I found an empty bed in a room occupied by a woman who had had heart surgery the week before Christmas. She was almost ready to go home. I tried to sleep, but I could still smell sour red wine in my hair and on my hands, and I kept replaying everything I had done since the stat phone call.

New Year's Day was a hospital holiday, and in the morning I made sign-out rounds with Mark Lehman, the other chief resident, and Sean Stewart, an intern, who were both on call.

"Lizzie," said Mark cheerfully as we met in the I.C.U., "Jim tells me you had a horrendioma last night." After I told him about it, Mark shrugged and shook his head.

"There was no way you could have saved him. He was a bloody disaster. Chalk it up to experience. Live and learn. Go play pro-ball. Do something but don't let it get you down. Stick around if you want. Sean and I are going to shoot some basketball over at the gym in Chinatown after rounds. You can watch. That'll make you smile."

I laughed, and left them to make rounds. It was silent and snowing outside and on my way to the subway I walked past the strip joint where my patient had been fatally stabbed. There was a cold wind and soon I was too cold to be depressed, but hurried for the subway, exhausted and wishing I were already asleep in my bed.

From Harvard to Yale

My surgical career began when my mother boarded the wrong train in London during World War II. She was leaving to spend the weekend in Surrey with her parents, but the Germans bombed the train she usually took, and she wound up on the next one instead, sitting beside my father, who was in England with the OSS. He started to talk, and six weeks later they were married.

After the war they returned to the States and set up in private practice as psychologists in Virginia, near a town called Merrifield which boasted seventy-five people and a hundred and fifty cows. My two older brothers and I were born there. We attended the local school for several years, but as our grades grew progressively worse our parents grew increasingly alarmed and we all ended up in private school.

My mother and I visited several schools, and I chose Kent, which was a new Episcopal school in the Berkshire mountains. I had skipped the first and third grades in public school, so when I went to Kent I was thirteen and in the tenth grade. I was five-and-a-half feet tall, weighed 125 pounds, and looked fifteen. What I remember best about Kent was my obsession with my weight. For two years my life was a round of gluttonous schoolgirl binges and terrifyingly stringent diets. At the height of one pre-Christmas diet I was so desperate for food that I thought of the communion wafer at morning services as the first meal of the day.

I was fifteen when I graduated from Kent. My birthday is in July, so I was sixteen when I went to Harvard the following September. From the first I wanted to be a doctor, but I also wanted to be an art historian, an organic chemist, and a linguist. When I had to declare a major, I chose biology.

At that time the Harvard Biology Department was large, and divided into two camps: classical and ecologic biology, and molecular biology. Neither was enthusiastic about pre-med students, whom they regarded as interested in grades but not in learning. I chose classical biology, because its honors program allowed me to write a thesis rather than conduct a laboratory experiment, but as my last year approached the question of a thesis topic became something of a problem.

Classical biology is the study of plants and animals, which gave me an overwhelmingly large field from which to choose a topic. The faculty tried to help. Professor Welch had devoted his life to the clam, and knew more about it than anything else. Professor Weiner was studying algae. I worked briefly with a graduate student on the evolution of the skink and had a fling with South American snakes. In the end I specialized in Economic Botany, and wrote my thesis on the oat. My advisor, who was the world expert on corn, felt that corn would be better than oats, but he agreed that oats were acceptable.

Because I spent one summer taking chemistry and another writing my thesis, I had enough credits to graduate by the end of my junior year and I was ready to leave. I was bothered by Harvard's attitude toward education. Few of the faculty were interested in teaching undergraduates. The typical professor was responsible for one undergraduate course each year, but most of the lectures were given by graduate students. Their teaching salaries helped them work their way through graduate school, but it meant we learned only what they were learning for their theses. Most professors had huge government grants and spent their time in research, teaching graduate students or traveling about giving guest lectures. One biology professor, later a Nobel Prize winner, spent his time traveling and gave us one "biology" lecture: slides from a trip to Mexico. I learned about evolution and botany at Harvard, but I learned more at boarding school, even though none of the Kent teachers had won a Nobel Prize.

Although I was still a junior at Harvard, applying to medical school was now the most important thing in my life. My dean, Mrs. Dwight, encouraged me to apply to Harvard, for admission in what would have been my senior year in college. Harvard's professors all thought there was only one good university in the world. If you didn't go to Harvard Medical School you might as well not be a doctor. The only catch, of course, was that the Med School was very selective. Although I wouldn't have dreamed of not applying, I expected to be turned down for not being good enough academically. No one told me it might be hard simply because I was a girl.

I filled out Harvard Medical School's long application, asked my professors for letters of recommendation, and received in the mail instructions to arrange interviews with professors on the admissions committee. My first interview was with a physiologist, a woman. She asked me about prep school, college, being a doctor, and why I did not do well in arithmetic. I did not admit that I still counted on my fingers, but I conceded that math was difficult for me. She showed me her laboratory which had an enormous black-and-white poster mounted on one wall. She proudly explained that this poster was an enlargement of a picture of a cell, taken through her new electron microscope. She said I could expect to be accepted at Harvard Medical School. I was surprised, but very happy. The second professor who interviewed me was also encouraging.

My third interviewer was not. I set out on a rainy day for the Harvard Med School office of a doctor whose name I can't remember. He was fat, oily, gray-haired and an obstetrician. He was also chairman of the Alumni Committee of Harvard Medical School. He asked me what I was doing in his office, and laughed loudly when I said I had been asked to come for an interview for medical school.

"What are you wasting my time for? Don't be ridiculous. You'll find you are married before you leave college."

I was not sure what to say. It hadn't occurred to me that it was silly for a girl to want to be a doctor. Marriage was hardly a trap you fell into by surprise. For half an hour, Dr. X was disagreeable and rude. No matter what I said he replied, "Don't waste my time, silly girl. You're going to be married, my dear, and you will never make a doctor. How absurd can you be?" Finally he told me to leave. "You have to get out now. I have no more time to waste."

Upset and fuming, I waited in the medical school lobby for a cab. On the way back to Cambridge, the driver asked me if I was in college, and then, "What are you majoring in?"

"Biology."

"Biology? You ought to become a doctor."

"That is exactly what I want to be," I said.

He jerked his head around and glared at me. "You gotta specialize. That is what you have to do. It's not just medical school. Afterwards, you gotta specialize. We need more woman doctors."

I wanted to hug him.

After Dr. X, Harvard Medical School ignored me until Christmas vacation, when they called to say they wanted a fourth interview when I returned to Boston. The first week in January I received a postcard telling me to report for my interview at the private office of Dr. Stines, a doctor practicing in Cambridge. When I found his office, it was raining, as usual in Cambridge. The office was down a tree-lined streed in the most exclusive part of Cambridge, where some of the well-kept homes dated from the Revolution. A side door of a house had a brass plaque that read: DR. STINES OFFICE. Inside I found a wood-paneled hallway with a single wooden chair. No one was there. I panicked and thought I had come to the wrong place; now I would be late for my interview. I went outside to check the street and house numbers. They matched the interview card, so I went back inside and sat down in the wooden chair. I saw a door at the end of the hall marked PRIVATE. I was to be interviewed at eleven. At eleven-fifteen, the "Private" door opened, and a distraught woman in her early thirties rushed out the door, then down the hall and into the rain without putting on her coat. A bespectacled, stooped lady with gray hair and a tweed suit rushed out of the "Private" room after her, saw me, said "Wait there," and rushed back into the "Private" room again.

Ten minutes later the tweed lady came out of the room, shoved her face into mine, and said, in a heavy German accent, "I am Dr. Stines." She beckoned me into the "Private" room. I walked in, and the only thing I saw at first, to my horror, was a large couch. Diplomas on the wall proclaimed Dr. Stines a psychiatrist. As rain from my coat dripped onto the parquet floor, I remembered the night before at dinner when a bizarre college classmate, her long hair trailing in her soup, had warned me that Harvard Medical School never accepted girls until they had been grilled by a psychiatrist, hired to plumb the sick subconscious depths of perverted females trying to get into medical school. Last night I had not believed her, but now I was unnerved.

"The couch is not entirely necessary. Perhaps you wish a chair," said Dr. Stines, pointing to a wooden chair in a corner. I chose the chair. Dr. Stines pulled a leather armchair close to me, sat down, turned on a bright lamp beside my chair and directed the light into my face. From the shadows, she interrogated me. I answered her questions politely because I wanted to go to medical school.

Dr. Stines began by asking why I wanted to be a doctor. I said I found medicine and science interesting and I wanted to be able to help people. She brushed this aside. She wanted to know if anyone in my family was a doctor.

"No, not in my immediate family, but there is a great-aunt by marriage who was a medical missionary in India in 1920, and a cousin who is an orthopedic surgeon in England."

"So, you identify with her, a big strong masculine woman orthopedic surgeon?" asked Dr. Stines.

"No, I've only met her once, at a lunch party."

"So, who do you love best? Your mother? No? So, you love your father more, you identify with him."

"No," I explained, "I love both my parents, but I'm closer to my mother."

"You identify with your brothers, No? You want to be like them?"

"I love my brothers, but I don't identify with them."

"You really like *both* your brothers?"

"Yes, I love both my brothers."

"What about your grandparents—only your grandfather is living. You identify with him?"

"I love my grandfather very much, and he plays chess very well, but I don't want to be like him, especially."

"Tell me, when did you reach the adolescent rebellion crisis? When did you hate your parents, reject them, want to kill your family? You mean you *never* rebelled like that?"

Dr. Stines seemed dissatisfied with me. I confessed that I had not had a major identity crisis, did not have a passionate crush on male

23

or female teachers, and I did not have homosexual or sadistic fantasies. She leaned forward out of her chair.

"Of course," she said, "you have a boyfriend."

Indeed, I did. His name was Al Hume and he was on the Harvard weight-lifting team. I said so.

"You sleep with this man now? No? Why not? You don't sleep with any man?"

It was 1966, and I was seventeen. "I think I'm too young," I said. "Besides, everyone in my family marries late."

"Why don't you want to get married?"

"I do, but not now. I want to be a doctor first."

Dr. Stines seemed angry with my answers. She paused, looked at her watch, and started again.

"Tell me all about your earliest memories, your childhood."

"I grew up in Virginia, and when I was three I went to Mrs. Worley's nursery school. . . ."

"No!" she exploded. "That is not what I mean. What was the most traumatic experience in your life?"

That was easy. My most traumatic experience was failing a geometry exam in school. I had studied very hard, but the questions had been all about sides of triangles, and left me bewildered. I was thirteen, and I felt like a worthless failure who had let down her parents and her school. I was in tears when I left math class, and unable to speak during lunch. Neither my parents, whom I called that night, nor the math teacher could make me feel better. Mr. Wallace, the headmaster, made it worse by peering at me over his glasses and saying, "Have to pull up your socks and work on your math, Morgan." I felt I would never succeed. When Dr. Stines asked me about childhood traumas, I told her reluctantly about this episode.

"No, no," she said impatiently, "I mean something earlier, something important. When you were a child. Do you remember being molested by a nurse? Assaulted by an uncle?" She looked at me hopefully. I was shocked. No one had molested me. I thought of Girl Scouts, and grade school, and it was all normal until I remembered the time I murdered Percy, my parakeet. I was seven and I had read in a bird book that parakeets like to play in dirt. I filled a cigar box with dirt, as the book suggested, and put a plastic yellow Ferris wheel in it. Percy played happily in the dirt and died twelve hours later.

There was no doubt at all that I had killed him. No other pet parakeet was ever like Percy. He had escaped from his cage to make a dive-bomb landing on my head when I was in bed with the flu. Percy would land on a hamburger just as you opened your mouth to eat it. I was in despair when he died. I confessed to Dr. Stines that my childhood's most traumatic experience was when my parakeet died. She glared at me but said nothing. With an acid smile, she ushered me to the door.

Two weeks later Harvard wrote to tell me that I had been accepted to Harvard Medical School, but my Dean, Mrs. Dwight, had asked them that I not be admitted until the following year. I was eligible to graduate from Harvard, but I had not applied for advanced standing when I was a freshmen. So, sticking to the college rules, she refused to graduate me. I found this hard to believe. She had encouraged me to apply to medical school and yet must have planned all along not to recommend me for that year. Perhaps she thought I would not be accepted. When I went to her office, she told me I was too young to graduate, and needed the year to grow up. I was furious. I planned an outraged letter to the college president, and then I would withdraw from college.

When I called home, my mother listened sympathetically while I cursed Dean Dwight, then she said, "It's very upsetting for you dear, and Dean Dwight has behaved badly, deliberately misleading you, but I'm glad."

"Mother! *Why!*"

"You're two years ahead of your age already and to leave college at eighteen and enter medical school wouldn't be good for you. You need time to grow up, time for just meeting people, having fun and not feeling under pressure to work so hard all the time. You have to learn how to enjoy life."

My father agreed with my mother. I admitted I had terrible bouts of depression in college, but I blamed Harvard, not myself. Often I did feel self-conscious and awkward with men, and left out of dormitory social events, but the reason was that I didn't like beer and wasn't having a love affair, not that I wasn't grown up.

My parents listened patiently, and I finally agreed to stay in college till I graduated. My mother suggested that she could arrange, through friends, to let me spend the time in between doing research at Oxford. In the end, Dean Dwight agreed to let me graduate in

January 1967, and I spent the remaining six months of my senior year at Oxford.

Before I left for Oxford, I applied again to medical school. My father encouraged me to apply to Yale, where he had received his Ph.D., because Harvard was too stuffy. I went to Yale for three interviews. No one was rude to me. I was not grilled by mad psychiatrists and offensive obstetricians. No one thought that it was diseased for a woman to apply to medical school. The only problem came when I told Dr. Smithwick, the Dean of Admissions, that I wanted to be a surgeon. His face fell.

"Every applicant to medical school wants to be a surgeon or a psychiatrist."

When Yale offered me a place three months after I was interviewed, I accepted. I sent Harvard a telegram withdrawing my application. I knew two other girls in my class at Harvard who went to medical school—but none of us went to Harvard's.

Eleven years later, after my surgical training was done, Professor Sutherland, one of Harvard's most distinguished professors, asked me why I had gone to Yale Medical School. I told him about my interviews with Dr. X, the obstetrician, and Dr. Stines. He shook his head sadly and remarked, "I knew another girl from Harvard from about the same time who withdrew her application and went to Columbia. The admissions procedure has been changed in the ten years since you applied."

In the 1960s medical schools—Harvard especially—were swamped with applications, many from men who preferred medical school to being drafted to fight in Vietnam. Harvard came up with the "Stress Test Interview," designed to weed out "weak" applicants who weren't tough enough to be Harvard doctors. One man I knew was interviewed by a male Harvard psychiatrist who ordered him to open a window that was nailed shut. The same psychiatrist took out a pair of scissors and cut another male applicant's tie off, to see what he would do "under stress." But at least male applicants were considered normal. Female applicants were regarded as either abnormal or silly.

The system started to change in 1970 when medical schools everywhere were under pressure from militant women's groups and larger numbers of women applicants. Changes came from outside medicine—from federal laws and civil-liberties law suits—and from within, from sympathetic doctors. In 1967, medical school students were at least 90 percent male. In 1979, 20 to 50 percent of each entering class is female. Once in medical school, almost no one—male or female—drops out.

Starting Medical School

There were only seven women among ninety men in my medical school class, and on the first day we all went to a room in the old administration building and lined up to register. I was too self-conscious to put on my glasses, and all I could see along the line was a sea of men. I knew there were two women ahead of me in line—we had to be in alphabetical order—but I didn't know where they were.

Many of the men around me had been Yale undergraduates and already knew one another. They were joking and laughing casually and I felt out of place and terribly shy. A tall thin boy with a sharp face passed me as he walked away from the registration desk, and suddenly stopped and turned back to look at me.

"You must be Elizabeth," he said triumphantly. "I saw your photograph on the registration desk. I'm Frank. When were you born?"

The other men in line turned around to stare at me. "What I mean is," he went on, "you don't know me, but I'm nineteen and you're nineteen. I made a bet with this character"—he pointed to a man standing near me—"when we graduated last June that I would be the youngest student in the first-year class. What month were you born? There's a lot of money on this bet," he added, looking at me wistfully.

"You win," I said, "I had my twentieth birthday in July."

With a pleased smile, Frank went over to his friend to collect on the bet. After that the men in line around me included me in the general conversation. I was no longer a complete outsider. Medical school had begun.

I was shocked that I was not the youngest, especially when I learned there were four other classmates as young as I. But I liked it. It made me feel abnormal always to be the youngest, to have people always surprised when they heard my age.

Of the seven women in my class, none of us was married. Almost everyone lived in Harkness, a nine-story brick dormitory with a wing for married students. The single women lived on the ninth floor and the single men occupied the seven floors below us. On the first floor was the dining room, a mezzanine meeting room used by the student council, and a cathedral-ceilinged living room with a Steinway grand piano. Dr. and Mrs. Tunian, the dormitory supervisors, lived in an apartment on the first floor. By college dormitory standards, Harkness was luxurious, particularly the living room. It was beautifully appointed with windows from floor to ceiling that looked out on a green lawn where we played football. It had a fireplace, a dark red carpet and black and red armchairs. There was a smaller, casual lounge next to the cafeteria, decorated to survive years of medical student abuse with a square black carpet and six black plastic armchairs. The school had installed a telephone in each bedroom, connected to the dormitory switchboard. The telephones were a necessity for the last two years of medical school, when we would be on call in the hospital. For the first two years, they were for fun. Because of the phones, the switchboard operators knew everything that went on in Harkness, including who was breaking up with his girlfriend and when it was time to choose a wedding present.

I moved into Harkness dorm on registration day. I had brought everything up to my room when I found I had forgotten my ironing board. I went back to the first floor and as I tried to wrestle the board into the elevator, a confident young man, clearly an older medical student, offered to help. He gallantly delivered me and the ironing board to my ninth-floor room, and was then reluctant to leave. He invited me to dinner, but once we were outdoors he detoured onto an after-dark, two-hour, pre-dinner walking tour of all the undergraduate colleges of Yale. For some reason he made me nervous. When he asked me why I was afraid of him, I couldn't think of a good reason.

When he asked me again, I laughed nervously, and this made him ask me again why I was afraid. At nine o'clock, he took me to dinner in a dark underground German restaurant, and his conversational tactics began to remind me of Dr. Stines. After we read the menu, and both ordered roast beef sandwiches, he leaned earnestly across the table.

"You don't seem to trust me. Are you afraid of men?" Later, he went on, "You seem very nervous tonight. Do I make you nervous? Maybe men in general make you nervous. Have you had a deep sexual trauma in the past? Tell me all about it. . . ."

I ordered a Coke.

"Why don't you drink beer?"

"I don't like the taste."

"Of course you like beer. Everyone likes beer. You must be too emotionally insecure to have a drink with a man. You ought to do something about it. It's not good for you."

I was shy and insecure, but he didn't make me feel comfortable enough to admit it. As he pressed me for more personal confessions, I began to feel downright mulish. He gazed at me over his second beer and reached out to pat my hand.

"Tomorrow night we'll have dinner. But before that I'll take you to the gym and teach you how to play squash. Your body needs exercise." He grinned at me.

I was insulted. I was *not* fat.

The only answer that came to mind was "no," but I couldn't say it. It would sound rude, so I said I was too busy.

"Busy doing what?"

"I'm tired after moving."

"You could take a nap in the afternoon."

"I have to unpack."

"It can wait."

"I have to buy books and get started studying."

He found that absurd and laughed. "I can teach you things that aren't in books. So, it's settled."

"No," I said in desperation, "I won't go out with you."

We walked back to Harkness in silence.

Six weeks later, I was having dinner in the dormitory at a table with third- and fourth-year students, because all the places at the first-year tables were full. We didn't have to eat with our classmates, but we liked to. I was sitting next to Mike, a senior medical student who was telling me what to feed a hamster I had just bought, when the student who had taken me to dinner arrived and started talking about the hospital.

"I'm on Ob-Gyn now, and I'm late for dinner becaue I had to see a patient with the senior gynecology resident in the E.R. The patient was a fourteen-year-old who was pregnant *and* had gonorrhea."

He laughed as he described the pelvic examination the resident had conducted. "The girl thought a pelvic exam meant he was making love to her, and she had an orgasm right on the table."

I was disgusted. The men at the table had listened without comment, so I imagined they thought it was funny, too. I got up and left the table. While I was waiting for the elevator, Mike came up, looking embarrassed.

"Elizabeth, did I ever finish telling you what to feed your hamster? Good." He pushed the elevator button a few times, and went on. "About that guy in there. I want to apologize to you for all of us. We all know him, so nobody bothers to say anything. You can't make him stop once he starts on something."

I tried to thank him, but I was embarrassed, too, and Mike hurriedly explained how to wire the cage so the hamster couldn't escape.

Medical school was a crash course in dating. There were no women undergraduates at Yale then, and fewer than forty women in the medical school for the four hundred men to date. I had had only two boyfriends—Al, in college, and Dante, an Argentinian economist whom I met at Oxford—but at medical school I went out with a different man every week. Women medical students were considered fair game by some of the married faculty, but most of the men at the medical school were looking for wives. I knew I wanted a husband and children, but not right then. There was too much going on—a lot of studying and a lot of growing up. At twenty, I still developed a crush on almost every tall, handsome man who smiled at me, and I hated going into crowded rooms alone. I knew I was not ready to marry and felt too vulnerable to get deeply involved with one man.

For the time being, I was happy to spend time with a lot of men— friends as well as dates. When we'd take a night off to have dinner

31

assistance to adapt. In time, he assured us, we would harden ourselves to it. When he left, Dr. Linacre, the professor in charge of our anatomy course, took the podium. He called himself "Uncle Ted," and it was rumored he had been a New Jersey sports announcer and a truck driver before he did his Ph.D. work in anatomy. His speech was quite short.

"Ladies and gentlemen," he said, "anatomy is a science, and essential to medicine. You don't take anatomy to harden yourself. I don't want a hardened doctor treating me. Your problem ought to be struggling not to care too much about your patients. That's the hard part—not giving up when a patient dies; going ahead and doing your job as a doctor. That is what the Hippocratic Oath is about. In anatomy, you dissect a dead body because medicine is the study of disease, and disease makes a dead body. If plastic models were as good, we would use plastic models, but they are not. The human body is too complicated. I know that sick medical students have been known to cut off bits of a cadaver and send them in the mail to friends. Anyone who abuses a cadaver in my anatomy course automatically fails. If I had my way, they'd be kicked out of medical school, too. You want to be good doctors. People with faith in medicine and in Yale bequeath their bodies so you can become good doctors. If you can't treat a dead body with respect, you can't treat a living one with respect, and you should go home now. The rest of you can go upstairs to the dissecting rooms."

We walked to three green-tiled rooms filled with tables. On each table was an aluminum cover, like an enormous vegetable serving-dish cover. Under the aluminum were the cadavers, with two or three students assigned to each. Cathy Flynn and I agreed that if Yale had any sensitivity, it would assign us to work together on a female cadaver. I did not think I would faint but I dreaded the embarrass-ment of dissecting a male cadaver with a male partner. Yale did nothing of the sort. Names were assigned alphabetically, and assignment to a particular cadaver was at random. It turned out to be much the best way. My dissecting partner was Henry Bax, who had also graduated from college when he was nineteen. Henry is now a psychiatrist. A sign on our aluminum cover showed our cadaver was male. Next to us were Roy MacGregor, Lenny Turner and Art Lipschitz. Their cadaver was a female.

"Okay, you jokers, you can take off the aluminum covers," said Dr. Linacre.

We did, braced for the worst. The cadavers were wrapped in heavy plastic sheets and under that was oiled cheesecloth. I saw only a vague, mummylike form. This preserved the cadavers from drying. We had been told to prepare for a dissection of the abdomen, so Henry and I took off the cheesecloth and plastic sheet over the abdomen.

"It's terrible," said Roy, turning to me after a glance at his female cadaver. "It's embarrassing. My mother follows me everywhere."

No one in the class fainted. No one screamed. It seemed scientific and matter-of-fact, now that we had begun. The cadaver skin was dry, brown and leathery, but the smell was overpoweringly like beef soup and oil-of-wintergreen, a strong preservative that kept the cadavers from decaying. Each cadaver required years of treatment, soaking in a vat, before it could be used. The smell got into our hair and our clothes, and at the end of three hours of dissection our hands were partly pickled by it. We had been issued gray wraparound lab coats to wear over our clothes to protect them, but the oil-of-wintergreen penetrated instantly. After the first dissection, we all bought special clothes for anatomy class. I spent five dollars on a lavender and pink striped dress at Macy's, the cheapest they had, and a pair of hard-soled ballet shoes. Henry wore a T-shirt and bleached blue jeans that he had worn in his college chemistry class. They were full of holes, from the sulfuric acid he had spilled on them. We dissected three mornings a week, and even after we had showered and changed the older medical students complained loudly about the smell when we came into the dining room for lunch. When the course was over, we had a party and burned our anatomy clothes.

Cadaver dissection is not easy, because all the tissues are weakened by the preservatives and tear and fall apart if you are not careful. Besides, anatomy is extraordinarily complex. One classmate, Robert Thomas, knew he wanted to be a surgeon. His father was a surgeon, and Robert came to class with surgical gloves and instruments. We laughed at him at first, until we looked at his dissections. He did beautiful work. Every tiny nerve and artery could be seen, and nothing was torn or ragged. He was so good that the professors tried to convince him to become an anatomist.

Art Lipschitz did not enjoy dissection and was quite firm, saying that it would not help at all in his psychiatry training. He offered to supervise Roy and Lenny while they did the dissection, but they threatened him with a scalpel and he joined the work.

Roy and Lenny would try to see how far they could joke in anatomy class before Art or I protested. One day they supplied my cadaver with a cigar and a bow tie, but their favorite joke was to ask me how the dissection was going. They would say theirs was going unusually well, and would I like to take a look? I would turn around, and Roy would say, pointing to an artery, "Elizabeth, what we really need is some mustard. Can you give us some onions? What, no onions? O.K., Lenny, just send it over as it is to the dining room, it's part of the new austerity program." I was outraged when they used a hot dog to construct a penis on their female cadaver and invited me to view the sex change.

When there was too much joking, Dr. Linacre, Dr. Smithwick or Dr. Carter would walk over and ask to see our dissection. If it was poor, Dr. Linacre told us we were no-good lazy bums and had better work harder. Dr. Smithwick would look sad and disapproving and show us where we had gone wrong. Once I thought I was doing a beautiful dissection of a nerve, but when Dr. Smithwick came by it turned out to be an insignificant piece of connective tissue. I was crushed. Frank Troy, the nineteen-year-old boy-wonder, often did not study and tried to fake it. One morning, Dr. Smithwick walked by and frowned.

"Interesting dissection you have, Frank. What is this organ you are working on?"

Frank thought for a long time. "Kidney," he said.

"Kidney?" asked Dr. Smithwick, raising an eyebrow. "I would have called it the liver, which is coincidentally, the largest organ in the body."

The most frightening anatomy professor was Dr. Carter. He would stand next to you and silently watch you dissect for five minutes. Suddenly he would say, "What is that?" pointing to a nerve you had not noticed, and could not identify. He would add, "Sympathetic nervous chain. Very important. You had better study."

I worked on the sacral nerve plexus until I thought I knew it well enough to ask Dr. Carter to examine me on it, but I could only answer his first few questions. I was amazed by how much I did not know, as he pointed with his instrument to nerves and blood vessels disappearing into muscles in the lower back.

"Not bad," he said afterwards, emphasizing "bad." "Anatomy is, uh, difficult."

There is too little anatomy taught in medical school today. We had two and a half mornings a week, and should have had twice as much. The present medical curriculum has reduced that to, at most, a morning of anatomy a week for half a year. There are many areas to cover in medical school but to neglect anatomy can have unfortunate consequences. When I was a surgery resident a pediatrics resident once asked my opinion on one of his patients; the boy's liver was greatly enlarged and the pediatrics resident was concerned. He and I were both embarrassed when I had to explain that it was the spleen, not the left lobe of the liver that he was feeling. He was a conscientious doctor, and his ignorance showed how little anatomy is taught today in medical school.

Ward Rounds with Doctor Vincenzo

Besides anatomy, our courses the first year were biochemistry, embryology and physiology. The students the year before had complained to the Dean that the courses were too theoretical, and had asked for more "clinical" teaching. This was part of the '60s move toward "relevance."

In 1967, many medical students disapproved of the Vietnam war and the social injustice that they believed it created. As a woman, I was not subject to the draft, although there were rumors then, as now, of drafting women doctors. I could not in any sense be described as an activist. The TV and newspaper accounts of the war horrified me so I tried to avoid them. I thought the war was a mistake but thought the S.D.S. and Minutemen anti-war protestors too extreme until 1971 when one of my brothers was drafted and sent overseas. By that time, I was an intern and had no time to do anything more than worry about him.

The leaders of the anti-war group at Yale were Peter and Ruth who saw themselves as leaders of a radical new breed of doctors who would "liberate" medicine. Besides campaigning against the Vietnam war, Peter campaigned for legalized marijuana, long hair, blue jeans and the downfall of "rich Americans." He petitioned the Dean repeatedly for more patient contact and less "irrelevant book learning" in medical school. The result was that the faculty arranged optional rounds for us with the clinical faculty. Peter was one of the few radicals who did not waver from his ideals after medical school. He and Ruth got married and became doctors for the Public Health Service in an impoverished part of Appalachia. Most of us were alternately amused and irritated by Peter and his radicals but we all enjoyed the clinical teaching that he had made available. Optional "ward rounds" took place every week. We were assigned in groups of five to meet a faculty physician who would discuss disease with us and take us on rounds to see his patients.

My group included my anatomy neighbors, Lenny and Art. We had signed up together for the same group. Then there were Cathy Flynn and Sam Freeman. Sam, who came from an immensely rich Texas oil and cattle family, always seemed politely curious about the financial worries that bothered the rest of us.

We were assigned to meet our faculty professor, Dr. Vincenzo, at 5:30 every Tuesday evening in his office. It was November by the time ward rounds started, and it was dark when we left the dormitory to walk across the street to the hospital to meet "Enzo," as Lenny called him behind his back. The hardest decision I had to make was whether to eat dinner before or after rounds with Dr. Vincenzo. The cafeteria served dinner from five o'clock until seven except Friday and Saturday when dinner was served until nine. I hated missing dinner because that meant either stale candy from a vending machine or a five-block walk to Gino's, the nearest soda fountain-coffee shop. Gino's was nice, but the after-dark five-block walk was not. Cathy had gone for a short walk around the hospital one night for exercise and had been chased back to the dormitory by a gang of eight boys who pushed her around and tried to grab her purse.

The first time we had ward rounds I decided to gamble on getting back in time for dinner in the dormitory. Besides, Lenny appeared shocked by the idea of hastily eating dinner at five, and then going back to work. "Elizabeth," he said sorrowfully, shaking his head and lighting his pipe, "it is uncivilized to eat in a rush. You will ruin your digestion. You won't be able to chew your food. And my mother wouldn't approve," he added.

Instead we had coffee from the vending machine in the basement of the medical school and walked through the warm underground tunnels into the hospital basement, past the hospital vending machines, the medical and dermatology clinics, past the lead doors marked DANGER that indicated the entrance to the radiation-therapy machines, then up the stairs to the first floor and Dr. Vincenzo's office.

It was not like any doctor's office I had ever seen. To the left was a cramped space for his secretary. Straight ahead was his office, a small room that could hold only his desk, a black plastic sofa and a wooden chair. To the right was a huge laboratory with workbenches, scientific apparatus, shining glass culture dishes and a pretty laboratory technician in a white coat mixing a culture broth and asking Dr. Vincenzo about plans for the next day's research. Dr. Vincenzo was an incredibly handsome Italian with seductive brown eyes and a charming smile.

He set down the culture dish he had been examining and waved us into his office. There was the background hum of the agitator, shaking bacteria to make them grow, the clatter of plastic culture plates, and the radio playing rock-and-roll. Art, Lenny and I squashed together into the plastic sofa, and Sam sat on the chair. Cathy insisted on perching precariously on an arm of the sofa. My knees nearly touched the wooden desk and Lenny, who was tall, had to sit sideways to fit. Dr. Vincenzo pulled out a pack of Marlboros and asked us to introduce ourselves. There were four ashtrays within his reach, all full of cigarette butts. Smoking had not yet been publicly recognized as a cause of lung cancer and we had even had a lecture by a doctor, a smoker, who declared that there was no statistically significant evidence that cigarettes were harmful. Nevertheless, Dr. Vincenzo apologized for smoking and looked much happier when Lenny lit his pipe. Through a haze of smoke Dr. Vincenzo squinted at us, and said he didn't quite know what to do with five first-year medical students. I felt disappointed, as though we had failed to interest him.

"Would you like to see some patients?" he asked tentatively. We were like visitors in a zoo, being offered the giant pandas. Lenny said firmly that, yes, we did want to see patients. Dr. Vincenzo lit another cigarette, and said patients would have to wait for another week.

"This week we will talk about some common infections: pneumococcal pneumonia, gonorrhea, strep throat. I'd like to introduce you to my patients. I could take Cathy." He then waved at me with his cigarette, "You should be wearing a white coat, young lady. As

40

for you men, I can't take you three anywhere. There is a very nice lady upstairs that I'm treating. She has brucellosis, probably. She's a respectable wife with four children. Maybe she is conventional but she likes a doctor to look like a doctor. She will be very upset if I bring you in and introduce you as young doctors—and I would agree with her."

Lenny wiggled his left foot angrily, and knocked his pipe ash into an ashtray. "What you mean is that you prefer that your patients see you as an intimidating, superior father-figure or priest, not someone they can empathize with. A white coat won't make me a good doctor, will it? Shaving my mustache won't make me a good doctor, will it? I think your patients probably find you frightening or intimidating."

Dr. Vincenzo leaned back and lit another cigarette. "Lenny, you are very smart and I'm sure you will be a good doctor. However, your mustache has not been trimmed for weeks and you didn't shave this morning. You're not wearing a tie or socks. Your blue jeans are dirty and so is your shirt. Would you go to your grandmother dressed like that? No. My patients deserve at least the same respect as your grandmother. Right?"

"Okay, you're right," said Lenny. "But I don't think this is fair. My grandmother never told me she knew you."

The next week I wore my white coat and Lenny, Art and Sam wore ties, clean shirts and white coats. Lenny intentionally wore a red-plaid tie, a pink shirt and a tweed coat, "just to protest the establishment."

"Your grandmother must be color blind," said Dr. Vincenzo.

I enjoyed the second week of ward rounds more than the first, when Dr. Vincenzo had asked us a lot of questions about infection. I couldn't answer his questions and felt very stupid. His specialty was infectious disease, which in 1967 was a small field. Antibiotics had supposedly "cured" infections, and Lenny had even wondered, after our first rounds, why a man as smart as "Enzo" was spending his life in a dead field. Today, bacteria are resistant to many antibiotics, and infections continue to be the most fatal surgical complication. Every new antibiotic has dangerous side effects that limit its use, and Dr. Vincenzo is an eminent man.

I was prepared to pay attention to rounds the second week because I had had dinner at five o'clock. We squeezed into Dr. Vincenzo's office, and he told us we were going to see two patients with rheumatic fever. Both were women. The first was a school girl of seventeen who possibly had juvenile rheumatic fever, which is usually crippling within a few years. Adult rheumatic fever is much less severe, but no one could tell what kind she had. Her painful swollen joints were getting better, but she and her parents wanted to know what to expect, and Dr. Vincenzo couldn't tell them. He suspected that she had juvenile arthritis and within a year would need intensive physical therapy for stiffened, deformed joints. The second patient was a woman of twenty-one who had been married three weeks before. She had no health insurance and had developed rheumatic fever a week after her wedding. After spending two weeks in hospital with a severe heart murmur and heart failure, she was ready to go home, $10,000 in debt from the hospital bill. Her husband earned $10,000 a year. The heart damage was so great that pregnancy would endanger her life. It sounded too catastrophic to be true.

Dr. Vincenzo took us up to the private wards to introduce us to his first patient, the cheerful, fat girl from boarding school. She was lying in bed, eating candy and watching TV, and she was delighted to meet Lenny, Art and Sam. Dr. Vincenzo asked her to describe her illness.

"This winter everyone had flu at school, and after the flu, I got pain in my knees and they swelled up and I had a fever. So they sent me here, and now I'm all better." Her eyes drifted back to the television. We thanked her and filed out.

"I don't know what you will decide when you're doctors," Dr. Vincenzo said in the hallway, quietly so she couldn't hear, "but I couldn't tell her now that she probably has developed an illness that may cripple her, damage her heart and kidneys and make her die young. I don't think her parents would believe me. I will see her regularly every few months. She will probably be back in hospital within a year. Eventually she and her parents will be ready to listen to me. Now, they are happy that she was not 'really sick.'"

We left the private wing and took the corridor that led to the "ward" patients. The corridors were confusing and I whispered to Sam to tell me where we were. The ward had been renovated, and there were private and semiprivate rooms, just like the private wing, only the rooms were smaller. The ward secretary asked Dr. Vincenzo if we were new residents of his. He smiled and said we were joining him for rounds, which made us feel like real doctors until a resident looked up and said, "That means they're first-year medical students."

Dr. Vincenzo took us first to meet Mrs. Larelli. She was in a blue negligee, talking with her husband. She didn't look ill, but the room was dark because there was only one lamp. She told us that after the wedding she had had a fever, and felt tired to the point that she couldn't walk upstairs. She came to the emergency room and had been admitted to the intensive care unit. She knew she had a heart murmur and some heart failure but pressed Dr. Vincenzo to tell her when she could go home.

"He's such a darling," she said to us, as he stood by embarrassed. "Isn't he gorgeous? Even if he tells me I have two years to live he'd make it sound like good news, but I wish he would tell me more about what's wrong with me."

Dr. Vincenzo patted her hand and said he would return to talk to her and her husband, and we maneuvered with difficulty around each other out of the small room and into the corridor. Sam asked Dr. Vincenzo why he hadn't told her more.

"You would tell a male patient the details," Sam said challengingly.

"I have," Dr. Vincenzo replied, "I told her and her husband two days ago that her heart is permanently damaged and she shouldn't have children, because her heart could not pump blood to both her and the child. If she gets pregnant, she'll either abort the baby or die herself. They don't believe in contraceptives, they want a family, and they trust in God. When I go back to talk with them, I will say again what I said two days ago. She will be just the way she is now. She can't face not having children, so she forgets what I tell her."

"She would be crazy to get pregnant," said Art. I said nothing but I disagreed. If I wanted a baby and felt healthy I would take the risk. Doctors weren't always right.

Dr. Vincenzo smiled. "To her, I'm the one that's crazy. She feels fine and she thinks that with digitalis and a water pill she is cured. Most patients won't listen to you once they get better."

"You know," said Lenny afterwards as we walked back through the melting snow to the dormitory, "he really makes you think. I never expected medicine to be like this. I expected sick people to be sick, and either get well or die. I didn't know people my age could get diseases like this that could ruin their lives without killing them." We all agreed.

The next week when Dr. Vincenzo finished his cigarette he took us to the new surgical intensive care unit. To enter, you put a sterile floor length gown over your clothes.

"This will not prevent infection," muttered Dr. Vincenzo, putting on his gown, "Typical simplistic surgical thinking."

A button on the wall made the I.C.U. doors swing open so fast that Sam was almost knocked down. They shut automatically after us. It was like entering Ali Baba's cave. Dr. Vincenzo explained that the patient we would see was the nineteen-year-old son of a local Mafioso.

"The boy is married to a girl who his father thought would be good for him. He started taking heroin and cocaine and anything else he could buy when he was fourteen. Here a street bag of good dope costs about fifteen dollars. It costs more in New York. This boy has a ten-bag-a-day habit and has been arrested for stealing, but his father got him off. Most dope addicts don't have fathers like that. Street dope has other things mixed in with it besides the heroin. The peddlers throw in talcum powder, sand, flour, animal dung. Addicts try to buy from a 'good' dealer—someone who will sell them dope without too much junk in it. This boy, Hugo, tried to save money and bought cheap dope in New York. Whatever bacteria were in the dope infected the aortic valve in his heart. The infection destroyed the valve, and his heart couldn't pump blood out—the blood just sloshed back into the heart. He was dying and one of the heart surgeons saved his life by replacing the destroyed valve with a plastic one. The trouble is that if infection settles around the new valve it will come loose and he'll die. The infected valve had been shedding clumps of bacteria into his blood for weeks before we saw him but we hope the antibiotics we're giving him will protect the valve. A few years ago he would be dead already because this kind of heart surgery had not been developed. You are seeing something dramatic."

He led us to bed number six where the boy was being fed Jell-O by a pale teenage girl, who looked at him adoringly. "He looks wonderful," she said with enthusiasm. "You'd never know Hugo had heart surgery a month ago."

I saw a tall, gaunt boy, too long for the hospital bed, his feet sticking out at the end. His huge black eyes had circles under them, and he was so thin his ribs jutted out like ridges. He looked at us by his bedside and whispered hoarsely, "You'd never know I was on the high-school football team last year, would you, Doc? I like the Jell-O, but the soup stinks."

We could hear a faint continuous clicking, and it took a moment before I realized it was his heart, the plastic valve bouncing with every beat inside the steel shell that kept it in place. He let us listen to his heart and afterwards Dr. Vincenzo asked if we noticed his arms.

"Every vein in his arm is a scar from his injections for dope. His feet and his legs are the same. The scars are called needle tracks. When you are interns you can always recognize an addict by the scars and because they won't let you put in an intravenous needle— they want to keep their veins for dope. When all the veins are scarred an addict will try injecting into his neck or his heart. I hear a very faint murmur around Hugo's valve, and I don't think he will survive."

We continued our Tuesday rounds with Dr. Vincenzo for the next six months. He gave a lot of his time to teaching us. Later on I learned how rare that was. On our last Tuesday round with Dr. Vincenzo, I asked him if Hugo was still in hospital.

"That's a grim way to finish our six months together," he said. "Hugo is back in the intensive care unit. Before I take you to see him, let me finish this cigarette and tell you what happened. He went home a month after his first surgery. He lived with his father and got strong enough to mow the grass in the front yard. He told me he was not taking dope, but he could've been lying. His wife said he was still shooting up. Two high-school friends who were pushers came to see him regularly but I think he was doomed to die even before he left hospital. Remember I heard a murmur around the valve? Hugo lived a hundred miles away and insisted his local doctor see him instead of us. I don't know when the murmur began to get louder because his local doctor doesn't seem to have listened carefully and can't tell me. Last month his father called me to say Hugo was very tired, but the boy refused to come to see us. Last Monday he arrived in an ambulance. He had a murmur so loud I could hear it without a stethoscope, and he had bacteria in his blood. The infection had come back and was destroying the heart muscle around the plastic valve. The heart surgeon operated on Hugo that day and replaced

45

the valve. Because of the infection there was almost nothing he could sew to. Most of the stitches pulled out during the surgery. Hugo is in I.C.U. now, and he is dying. He has infection in his brain and his lungs, as well as around the valve. There's nothing we can do."

Then we went to see Hugo. We opened the I.C.U. "automatic" doors, which no longer opened automatically, and the head nurse led us back to a room reserved for infected patients. We didn't go in, but looked through a glass partition. Hugo's name was on a card by the door. I would never have recognized him. He was still too tall for the hospital bed and his feet stuck out at the end. He had a tube in his lungs and a respirator was breathing for him. The heart monitor over his bed showed that his pulse was twice the normal rate. Urine dripped from a tube in his bladder into a plastic bag by the bed. His heart could not pump enough blood to make urine and the bag was almost empty. A tangled mass of intravenous tubes led into veins and arteries in his wrist, groin and neck. His body jerked spasmodically. An arm, then both legs, then his head would twitch violently. The movement made it impossible to keep a sheet on him, so he was naked, except for a towel across his groin.

Dr. Vincenzo opened the door to Hugo's room and said angrily to the nurse, "Can't you see the boy is having continuous seizures? You can't let him die like that."

She put her hands on her hips. "Doctor, I have been a nurse for thirty-one years. I know a seizure when I see one. He's been given barbiturates, Valium, morphine and Demerol. His seizures have not stopped. When the pharmacy delivers the drugs we asked for thirty minutes ago, I shall administer them. Until then, perhaps you have a suggestion?"

"I'm sorry," said Dr. Vincenzo. "It's hard to see a patient die like this."

"It certainly is," she said, and shut the door.

"This is medicine," said Dr. Vincenzo as we left the unit. "Fortunately, it's not all like this."

We walked back to the dormitory in silence. Then Lenny remarked that "Enzo" was a good man, but he, Lenny, was now definitely going to go into psychiatry. Lenny puzzled me. I couldn't see how anyone could want to be anything but a surgeon. No matter how much of a crush I had on "Enzo," surgery fascinated me. I was not sure where the idea had come from but after seeing the surgical intensive care unit, the mystery of surgery appealed to me more than ever.

There were no women surgical residents or faculty at Yale, and no women surgeons in private practice in New Haven. Except for two women plastic surgeons considerably older than myself, the only women surgeons I know trained in surgery at the same time as I did. Of the six women in my class at Yale, three of us became surgeons. Obviously women no longer were simply fascinated by surgery; they believed they could become surgeons. It was a new era.

Welcome to Surgery

Yale Me al School gave no exams. A decision had been made in the 193 that medical students at Yale should spend their time work; on a thesis rather than being harassed by frequent exams. The tradition of the thesis is now so well-entrenched that taking exams is regarded as absurd. I would have studied more regularly if we had had exams, but it was a relief then not to spend every week cramming for exams that obliged you to learn things by heart but left no time to think.

Yale did require its students to take National Board Exams. These are multiple-choice tests given nationally twice a year and have largely replaced state medical exams. National Boards Part I is given after the first two years of medical school and tests basic science knowledge. Everyone studies hard to pass. Part II is given at the end of the second two years, and almost no one studies, because they are busy worrying about internship. Part III is given during the internship. After you pass the National Boards, you can get a license to practice medicine in almost any state. (In some states, you can still practice without an internship or National Boards if your medical school was in that state.)

I took National Boards at home in Washington at the end of my second year at Yale. Along with most people in my class, I stayed in

New Haven to study and the level of panic was so high that no one was sane. Cathy Flynn wandered around the dorm muttering biochemical reactions, and came to my room one night to ask me if the dalmatian dog excreted uric acid or urea in its urine. Lenny asked me at dinner if *Pseudomonas* was a lactose-fermenting bacillus. Roy pounced on me in the library and demanded that I recite the eight main branches of the external carotid artery. I couldn't, and Roy said, "Aha!" and rushed away. I had studied by reading Beeson and McDermott's *Textbook of Medicine*, which is two thousand pages long. The day I finished Lenny told me that none of the information in it would be included in Part I of the Board exam, which would be basic science, not clinical medicine.

"Liz, you've been studying all the wrong stuff. How can you possibly hope to pass?" asked Lenny.

The limousine left for La Guardia Airport two hours later, and I was in it. I took Part I in D.C., surrounded by male medical students from George Washington University, none of whom I knew. They were all too worried to pay me any attention. The test was multiple-choice and lasted eight hours. Multiple choice is difficult for me because I am distracted by unlikely answers, the ones that might be true, depending on how you interpret the question. There were questions about the dalmatian dog's urine and the branches of the external carotid artery. Beeson and McDermott had not been irrelevant, but it did help me more when I took Part II.

I did not have a summer vacation, but flew back to New Haven after Part I to start my first clinical rotation. This was ten weeks of surgery. Most of my classmates took the summer off. I was simply starting my third year three months in advance. I was still interested in being a surgeon, but I had been warned that surgeons did not want women in the field and that physically, women did not have the stamina needed for surgery. The third-year students warned us that surgery was the roughest rotation, especially emergency surgery in the New Haven Unit where I would be working.

"They'll really work you over because you're a girl," warned a senior medical student. If I couldn't take it, I wanted to find out now.

If I could survive ten weeks of surgery in the summer, I could arrange nine months of free time—two summer vacations back-to-back, plus the free time allowed for the thesis—and go to Oxford to research my thesis. Dr. Hunter, an Oxford professor who was former chief of medicine at Yale, had agreed to take me on in his laboratory, but he asked that I have at least nine months free to do adequate research.

My first day on surgery started when I arrived on the ward, Larkins-5, at eight in the morning. The surgery department secretary had told me to report there, but no doctors were around. There was a confusing number of patients, nurses, orderlies, social workers, breakfast trays and dietary workers, but no doctors. It was a hot, humid day and steam poured from the kitchen carts from which the dietary workers served hot coffee, oatmeal and scrambled eggs. My dress and white coat were already limp from the heat. Timidly I waited by the ward desk at the end of the corridor. The walls were gray, the linoleum tiles were gray, and the lights were dim. There were twenty patients' rooms built along the corridor. It was discouraging. Five nurses sat around a table giving morning reports.

"The new patient in room 609 was admitted last night with rectal bleeding. There is no diagnosis yet. His signs are stable. Dick wants him to get a unit of blood." The head nurse looked over at me. "You're the new medical student?" she asked in surprise. "I didn't know it was a girl. You're much too well dressed to work on L-5. It's a zoo up here. All the doctors are in the operating room, except Dick. You might find him in the cafeteria. They usually start rounds up here at 6:30." She went back to morning report.

Dick turned out to be the intern. He called to me as I wandered vaguely around the cafeteria which had more steaming oatmeal and eggs. I didn't have my glasses with me and looked myopically about the nearly empty cafeteria, but I couldn't see anything that might be a surgeon. I turned to walk out, feeling conspicuous and out of place. Some self-assured student practical nurses in blue uniforms breezed past me with empty breakfast trays. At least they knew where they were supposed to go. Suddenly I wished I were a nurse.

Then a midwestern voice called out, "Are you the new medical student? Come over here. I was told to look for a lost female medical student. Sit down. I'm the intern."

I saw a pale, thin man with a tight mouth. He did not smile. He said his name was Dick Callahan. (Seven years later, I saw Dick smile briefly at a surgical convention in Miami.) I sat down obediently, intimidated partly because he was a man and I thought he was angry with me, partly because to any medical student the

50

intern was a person of the greatest importance. Interns were doctors, and the only thing better than an intern was a resident. Interns gave orders, operated and knew how to handle emergencies. It seemed almost impossible to know as much as an intern. I had met a number of medical professors, some of whom I respected very much. Others I did not respect: the ones who got drunk at Happy Hour, or who gave medical lectures full of dirty jokes. Over ninety percent of the medical students were men and the professors, all of whom were men, knew they could get away with a bad lecture if they threw in slides of Playboy bunnies. But it was the interns and residents who worked harder than anyone else and were too preoccupied with important work to speak to a second-year medical student. They were the ones who ran down the corridors to answer a "Code 5"—cardiac arrest. Many professors did so much research and teaching that they were not as good at cardiac resuscitation as the residents. Two years later, as an intern, I realized that I was ignorant and so was every other intern. It did not seem that way when I met Dick.

"Why are you two and a half hours late? Work rounds started at 6:30 A.M., and blood drawing rounds began at 5:30," he said irritably.

Dick was referring to the fact that every blood sample in the hospital had to be drawn by a doctor. I did not want to believe it then, but I soon learned that all the interns, residents, and medical students were, and still are, used by hospitals as cheap labor. This remains the flaw in medical and surgical training—that we did not exist to be taught but to do mindless work for little or no pay. "Patient care comes first. You learn on the job," was the excuse given by the salaried professors who gladly canceled lectures they had not prepared for because all the residents were busy drawing blood samples, putting in bladder catheters, starting I.V.s and filling out forms for x-ray and laboratory tests.

In private hospitals, private physicians' time is too valuable for such work and the hospitals hire nurses, technicians and secretaries to do these routine jobs, and they do the job better than doctors, because they do the same job all the time. Likewise, students, interns and junior and senior residents also spend hours in the operating room holding retractors while chief residents and professors operate. Whenever I held a retractor, I was always craning my neck to see the operation, and had to be told to stand back because I was blocking

51

the light. Again, private hospitals pay operating room technicians to hold retractors. The technicians are strong, rested, and are not trying to learn surgical anatomy at the same time.

This enormous load of scut work also interfered with studying. Surgeons have a well-earned reputation for being ignorant of other fields of medicine, part of which is due to their having little time left over for studying textbooks and reading journals. Some of my professors got lazy because no one had time to attend the lectures. If a resident complained he had no time left to study, the professor would be indignant. "You just make time to study. Your trouble is you're not tough enough to hack the pressure of surgery."

The best surgical teaching conferences at Yale were organized and given by the private surgeons, not the salaried professors who, with some exceptions, were too busy to teach. Their time was spent on "important" jobs like getting money for federal grants, flying around the country to meetings and sitting on committees. This was true of the majority of surgical teaching programs in the country. To most of the faculty, students, interns and residents came next to last. Last came the patients.

Dick told me I had better expect to work while I was on surgery. "It won't be easy just because you're a girl." He added almost in desperation that he needed my help. He had been an intern for ten days and he had had no sleep for two nights. He told me I would spend all day and every other night working in the hospital. In my spare time, I could read Schwartz's surgical textbook. All the lectures were cancelled for the summer. I decided to spend most of my time in the O.R. and leave studying for later. I knew I could read a textbook. I was not sure I could take care of patients or be a surgeon. In the long run studying Schwartz's textbook would have been a better idea, as I soon realized that I loved the excitement of surgery. (I also found surgeons more attractive as men than most other doctors—more dominant, more decisive and more masculine.) However, recommendations for a surgical internship depended on the opinion of the residents as well as the professors. Good recommendations are given to students who work hard and help the residents. Students who disappear to the library to study are fit to be fleas (internists) or shrinks, but not surgeons.

After breakfast, Dick told me to go to the operating room. I wondered if blood would make me faint, but if I had survived anatomy I imagined I could survive surgery. The O.R. area was tiled in green and air-conditioned to an icy chill. A grim-faced disapproving nursing supervisor showed me where to change into "O.R. clothes"—a baggy, gray cotton shift and white cap. She told me not to wear a nylon slip under the scrub gown because it might set up electric charges, cause an explosion of the anesthetic gases, and damage the operating room. She didn't care if it damaged me. She clearly disapproved of female medical students. She then led me down a green-tiled corridor to a small room next to Operating Room 5 which contained four steel sinks, a steel autoclave and steel storage cabinets. The supervisor said the circulator would take care of me and left. The circulator turned out to be the nurse in charge of the operating room. Even hidden behind a mask, she looked young, pretty and friendly. Her eyes were expressive and heavily made up. In the O.R. the face is hidden and eyes are the only means of expression. Most O.R. nurses wear eye makeup. She asked if I was the new medical student, told me to ignore the supervisor because she was an old prune, and taught me how to do a surgical scrub. She kept me from feeling that because I was a woman, I didn't belong.

The idea behind the surgical scrub is that by scrubbing your hands with a sterile brush and sterile soap, you can make your hands sterile. The fact is, you can't because the water is not sterile, and the bacteria that live in your hair follicles are irritated by the scrub and come to the top of the skin, but the ritual persists. The nurse showed me how to scrub my nails first, then the fingers, then the back of the hand, all in a specific order, up to and including the elbows, keeping my hands up in the air so "dirty" water from the elbow would not drip over "clean" hands. I had to scrub for ten minutes and at the end my hands hurt. Then I had to back into the O.R., my hands over my head. I felt ridiculous, but this was approved technique. Three masked men wrapped in green cotton floor-length gowns were bending over a form covered by a green cotton sheet on a table. When I backed into the operating room, one of the masked men turned around.

"I'm Dr. Chase," he called out. "You must be the medical student and I am very happy to see you." He winked at me above his mask. "Come and join the fun," he continued. "We've just got into the belly. I'm trying to teach Mat how to operate and break the bad habits the other surgeons around here have been teaching him. Mat

The Same Day

Once the difficult part of the surgery was over, Dr. Chase left the operating room and I assisted in an operation for the first time. As Gene and Mat sewed up the abdomen they showed me how to hold the suture scissors with my thumb and ring finger so I could cut the sutures after they were tied. If I cut the suture short, they said it was "too short," and if I cut it long, it was "too long." This was discouraging until Gene told me that medical students always cut sutures too long or too short, and I shouldn't let it bother me. "Actually," he said, "women have better hands for surgery than men, more delicate, but don't tell anyone I said so."

I helped him wheel Mr. Homer into the recovery room after the surgery. Gene wrote the postoperative orders, and showed me the O.R. kitchenette, where coffee, tea, orange juice and grape juice were stocked for the O.R. staff.

"There are also graham crackers and peanut butter and jelly, but they don't arrive until later. You'll learn to appreciate peanut butter and jelly when you've been in the operating room all day without lunch," Gene told me. "You should plan to scrub in on the next case we are doing."

This was a gastrectomy, done on a frail, seventy-year-old Italian man who had an enormous cancer of the stomach. The operation was not being done to cure him but to make it possible for him to eat until he died. The cancer was blocking his stomach completely and no food would stay down. I watched in wonder as the resident cut through the skin with one stroke of the scalpel, cut through the deep tissues, ignoring the bleeding which Dr. Chase sponged away and pulled up a hard mass of pink tissue. He felt it carefully.

"It's all cancer," he said. "It's filled up the stomach completely."

The stomach was removed, but the cancer had already spread into the liver and the lymph nodes next to the stomach. Dr. Kaliphides was the chief resident doing the operation. Dr. Chase and another surgery professor scrubbed with him on the case, for "old times' sake," because Dr. Kaliphides was going to Chicago to be a professor of surgery. He had just finished his chief residency the day before, but had stayed to do this operation because he was fond of the patient. I realized that Mat must have been a chief resident for only one day, if last year's residents were just leaving. Dr. Kaliphides was a rich, aristocratic Greek and Dr. Chase teased him about being the best man at the wedding of the King of Greece. They ignored me completely.

The gastrectomy did not seem to take long and Gene was called upon again toward the end to sew up the abdomen while Dr. Chase and Dr. Kaliphides went to lunch in the hospital cafeteria. I realized then the first rule of surgery: scut work is always done by the person at the bottom. Gene had been left with the boring part, but it wasn't at all boring to me. Gene told me that as many as five layers of sutures could be used: peritoneum, fascia, retention, fat and skin sutures. We used retention sutures, supporting sutures that are put through the whole thickness of the abdominal wall. They are used in people who have cancer or who are alcoholics, because their healing is delayed. Gene put in five layers of sutures and I cut all the sutures too long or too short. As we wheeled our patient into the recovery room, we found Dr. Chase and Dr. Kaliphides still there, standing around Mr. Homer's bed, talking with Mat, the chief resident, Dick, the intern, and an anesthesiologist. A nurse in the recovery room was bustling around Mr. Homer and the doctors were clearly in her way.

"Could you men go talk somewhere else?" she exploded suddenly. "I'm trying to take care of a patient."

No one paid her any attention. "Dumb bitch," said another senior resident, casually. Then he saw me. "You must be the new female.

They didn't tell me you were so good looking." He put his arm around my shoulder. "Don't ever let those nurses boss you around. By the way, the problem is that Mr. Homer seems to be bleeding to death. Dr. Chase is trying to decide if we should reoperate, and we need blood for him. Do you know where the blood bank is?" he demanded.

"No, but I'll show her," Dick said. "Come with me," he ordered.

He ran out and I followed him down the corridor, up two flights of stairs, down another gray-walled corridor and into a brightly lit laboratory.

"We need three units of blood for Homer," announced Dick, "He had surgery this morning. Have we used up all the blood typed on him?"

The laboratory technician said there were some left and turned to a refrigerator with steel and glass doors, but Dick leaped ahead of him.

"I know how," he said to me, "and I'll do it faster."

The blood was kept in plastic bags. Each bag had a tag with the patient's blood type, name, and hospital number. The name and number of the blood bag had to match a card Dick brought stamped with Mr. Homer's name and number. It was absolutely necessary to match number as well as name. A father and son with the same name had recently been in the hospital and received each other's blood, because only the names and not the numbers were checked. They both had massive blood reactions with severe, but temporary, kidney failure. Dick took three units of blood for Mr. Homer out of the refrigerator and showed me where to sign them out in a blood bank record book.

"We need at least eight units," he called to the laboratory technician. "Do you still have a blood sample for him?"

"Yes, I can have them ready for you in twenty minutes. I'm not busy," said the technician, "but you know you aren't allowed to take three units out of here at one time. One person, one unit. You could be grabbing someone else's blood by mistake. We have to protect the patient from your mistakes."

"I don't make mistakes," said Dick, shoving him aside. "Bye."

He rushed back to the O.R. and I followed behind. I could not keep up with him. On his way down the stairs he called over his shoulder, "You have to be strict with those lab guys. You can't run up and down stairs all the time when your patient is bleeding to death. You're a woman and they'll just push you around if you don't get tough."

We ran into the recovery room. The nurse plugged two of the blood units into intravenous tubes in Mr. Homer's arms and Dick put the other unit on the stretcher. I gathered Mr. Homer was bleeding so much that he would need all three units in quick succession. Dr. Chase and Mat had disappeared, but I could see they had decided to reoperate because the anesthesiologist and the nurse were getting Mr. Homer ready to move back into the O.R. "He would be ready a lot sooner," complained the nurse, "if some of these surgeons did a little work instead of playing God all the time." Dr. Kaliphides had either gone to lunch or to Chicago. Even under the sheets Mr. Homer's abdomen looked to me more protuberant than it had when we finished the operation in the morning.

"It's all the blood collecting inside," explained Dick. "See this tape measure under him? One way to see if a patient is bleeding is to measure his abdominal girth. If it gets bigger and bigger, you know he is. Of course, Mr. Homer is bleeding so fast that we don't need to measure but the nurse did it anyhow because Gene had written it in the postoperative orders. Unless you cancel an order, the nurses will go on doing something forever."

I helped Dick and the anesthesiologist wheel Mr. Homer into the long green-tiled corridor, past other stretchers in the hallway and back to the same O.R. we had been in that morning. The nurse went back to the recovery room. The men lifted him onto the operating table and told me I was not strong enough to help. After that I stood in the corner, trying not to get in the way, and just watched. There was blood oozing slightly from between the stitches in the incision in the abdomen. The anesthesiologist, who was called Vincent, seemed very relaxed and talked to Mr. Homer who was awake and frightened, and told him that everything would be fine. The circulating nurse was hurriedly opening sterile sponges and instruments for the scrub nurse, who was scrubbing her hands furiously by the sink in the anteroom. The intercom that connected the O.R. to the front desk buzzed and a voice announced that eight units of blood were ready in the blood bank.

"I am ready to pass gas any time you guys are ready to cut," said the anesthesiologist cheerfully. "Why don't you send for the blood, Gene?"

"Get the blood, Dick," said Gene.

"Get the blood, Elizabeth," said Dick.

"She doesn't know how to get blood, does she?" asked Gene.

"Yes, I just showed her. Good-bye, Elizabeth," said Dick firmly. "Get it fast."

I went off to get the blood. I didn't like the way Dick ordered me around but I was happy to be useful. It took me several minutes to sign the blood out. I did not remember exactly how, so the lab technician took pity on me and showed me again. It helped being a girl. He gave me a cardboard box to carry the eight units. Lab rules allowed more than one unit to be released when the patient was having surgery, so he didn't object to giving me all eight units. It seemed like a lot of blood, but Dick had not told me how many to bring. I was afraid he would be angry if I brought too little. When I returned, Mr. Homer was asleep. Dick, Gene, Dr. Chase and the other surgical professor had their hands in his belly and there was blood all over the floor. I felt disappointed because I had missed what was going on. I was greeted with a cheer from Vincent and Gene when I said I had brought all eight pints of blood. Mr. Homer was bleeding massively. His blood pressure was low, his pulse rate 200, and he needed blood quickly to live. Vincent told me to throw all the blood on the floor behind him because he would need it. The blood was in pint-sized plastic bags and I lined them up on the floor where Vince could reach them from his stool. Then I asked Dick quietly if I could scrub in.

"No," said Dick. "There's no room."

"There's always room for a medical student," said Dr. Chase, who had overheard us. "What's the matter, Dick, don't you like girls?" He was one of the rare professors who believed in teaching students.

I went off to scrub, feeling triumphant. I didn't wash the full ten minutes, because my hands still hurt from the morning. I dawdled with the soap for seven minutes and scrubbed with a bristle brush for three. A research article this year said that a thirty-second scrub is as effective as a ten-minute scrub. I didn't know that then, and I felt guilty. When I finished, and was gowned, gloved and standing by Dr. Chase, there was blood over everyone but they still had not found out where Mr. Homer was bleeding. Blood poured out of his belly onto the sheets, the floor and me. I felt it seep through my scrub gown.

"Light!" shouted Dr. Chase. "Fix the light! We can't see a thing."

The circulator quickly swung around the heavy overhead operating light, too quickly. It bumped Mat in the back of the head. "Jesus!" he said laughing as he ducked. "You women are aggressive."

Mat and Dr. Chase were tying off every bleeding blood vessel they found, but Mr. Homer's intestines—around the sutures in the colon, around the place where the spleen had been and everywhere else—oozed blood rapidly. Dr. Chase explained that this was the result of liver damage from alcohol. Mat made a sudden dive deep into the belly shouting that he saw the "bleeder," but it was a blood vessel they had cauterized before that had started to bleed again. Mat asked the circulator to call a hematology consultant and over the intercom they talked with a hematology resident. He told us to give Mr. Homer more fresh-frozen plasma, more calcium, and to send out more blood samples so he could check the lab bleeding tests. He added he would call his attending to discuss the problem. There was so much blood that Dr. Chase held one suction tube and gave me a second, simply to suction away the blood as it rose to the top of the abdomen. I stood on tiptoe to try to see into the belly. Vince, the anesthesiologist noticed, and announced, "The new female medical student that no one has introduced me to needs a stool to stand on."

"Don't flirt now," pleaded Mat. "This is serious. Someone get the kid a standing stool."

Vince shook his head sadly, pumped in another unit of blood, then leaned over to whisper to me, "Mat has no poise. A typical surgeon. Now anesthesiologists are good lovers. If he calls you a kid again, slap his face." I giggled, and Dick glared at me.

The fresh-frozen plasma appeared to work. It has blood factors that are not in regular blood. The bleeding slowly subsided. We started to sew up Mr. Homer's abdomen. The intercom crackled again and the nursing supervisor asked how long we would be, because the other surgery chief resident had a patient with a ruptured spleen and needed the operating room. Mat and Dr. Chase hurriedly closed with just one layer, the retention sutures. Fine sutures would not hold because the incision was swollen after two operations. Dick cut the sutures, the scrub nurse started to clear the instrument table, all as fast as possible. The circulator was pulling wrapped bundles of instruments out of the cabinets for the next case. Gene had scrubbed out to write the postoperative orders. The other surgery professor asked Dick if Mr. Homer's family knew about his emergency reoperation.

Dick said, "His family isn't interested. His parents are dead. He has one brother but doesn't know where he lives. He has a female cousin who lives twenty miles away. I spoke with her when he was admitted, and she hadn't even known he was still alive. He disappeared from her life when he took up heavy drinking."

"Excuses," said the professor. "You mean you didn't tell the patient's only living relative that he was about to have emergency surgery because he was bleeding to death? Would you care to tell that to the hospital lawyers?"

No one spoke and I felt embarrassed.

"Do you think you'll have time to talk to the patient's cousin after the surgery?" asked the professor sarcastically.

"Yes, sir," said Dick.

Just then there was a crash as the circulating nurse brought a full-size hospital bed into the O.R. Patients who are very sick go directly to the I.C.U. instead of Recovery, as it's better to move them only once. Dr. Chase and the other professor left the room and the rest of us lifted Mr. Homer onto the bed, after arranging all the tubes attached to him so that none were yanked out when he was lifted. This time no one told me I wasn't strong enough to help.

When Mr. Homer had been settled into the I.C.U., Gene and Mat disappeared and Dick told me to come with him to the conference room at the back of the I.C.U.

"Write the orders," said Dick. "I'm calling his cousin." Gene had shown me how to write postoperative orders that morning, so I took out the notes he had made for me: 1. blood pressure 2. pulse 3. feeding 4. urine output 5. medicines, etc. It seemed very complicated. I did not know how often Mr. Homer's blood pressure and pulse should be checked, or whether he could eat. I struggled for a while, but Dick was still on the phone. There were coffee and peanut butter and graham crackers on a side table, and I noticed that according to the conference-room clock it was now six in the evening. Gene had been right when he said I would appreciate peanut butter.

After Dick hung up the phone, he drank two cups of coffee and ate peanut butter, grape jelly and graham crackers for fifteen minutes before he looked at my postoperative orders. They were all wrong and he made me rewrite them, telling me line by line what to put down. I resented him. He was condescending and bossy, but he took the time to teach me more than anyone else that summer.

Gene and Mat came in a few minutes later, dressed in regular clothes. We were still in our scrub suits, olive green cotton limp with blood.

"You look disgusting," said Gene cheerfully. "How do you like surgery, Elizabeth? What do you want to be, a pediatrician?" I said I thought I wanted to be a surgeon. When Gene realized I was serious, he slapped me on the back and said I was crazy.

"Enough socializing," announced Mat. "It's time for evening rounds. You can't see patients in scrub clothes. Dr. Chase will have a fit. We will meet you on Larkins-5 at exactly six-fifteen."

When I changed out of my scrub dress I found my stockings, bra and pants were also soaked in blood. It was disgusting but there was nothing I could do.

Rounds lasted until eight. We spoke to every patient, examined every wound, decided on new diagnostic tests. All the routine scut work was to be done by Dick and me and the list of things to do grew very long. At eight Mat went home. Gene was on call, but Dick, being the intern, had to finish the scut work before going home. Dick had been in the O.R. or the I.C.U. all day and none of the scut had been done. We started I.V.s, hung blood transfusions, cleaned out infected wounds and wrote orders. Two new patients had been admitted to the service while Dick was in the operating room. He sent me to examine one patient and he examined the other. When I was done, he examined my patient, too. I had not done a rectal examination on my patient, who was a man, because I was embarrassed, and Dick sent me back to do it. At 11:30 Dick went home, after telling me to meet him on the ward at 5:30 the next morning to help him draw blood samples. He would teach me how.

"Shit rolls down hill," said Dick. "Scut work is shit and we get it all. Good night."

Almost as soon as he left, the ward secretary said that Gene was on the phone, looking for me. He had just seen a patient in the E.R. who needed an operation now. His girl friend had stabbed him.

"What do you think of that?" asked Gene. "That's real women's lib." He told me to join him in the operating room.

"Did you get any dinner?" he asked. When I said no, he said he hadn't eaten either. He had been seeing patients in the E.R. since rounds finished.

"Stop by Recovery. You have time for more peanut butter and graham crackers before the case starts. It will take the intern fifteen minutes at least to get the patient ready. We can't work you too hard the first night. You'll change your mind about surgery."

That was Friday night. I was awake until Monday night, when I went home to sleep for the first time in sixty hours. For some reason, although I felt ignorant and did things wrong, I was having a wonderful time.

Heart Surgery Heroes

Those were the first three days of my ten-week surgery rotation. I slept on alternate nights when I was not on call, and I was usually in the O.R. with Gene or Mat all night when I was on call, which was every other night. There was no formal teaching but Dick announced he would be at D&C from four to five o'clock each Tuesday.

"What's D&C?" I asked.

"Death and Complications conference. All the surgical complications—bleeding, infection, wrong diagnosis, et cetera—are discussed by the attending surgeons and the chief residents."

"That should be interesting," I said, making a note of the time.

"You aren't invited," said Dick. "You'd be thrown out if you tried to come. This is a no-holds-barred conference. They really attack each other for mistakes."

"What's wrong with students being there?" I asked.

"You don't think a surgeon's ego would tolerate his being ripped apart in front of a student? Especially a woman! Anyhow, if students come, then the nurses will want to come, and pretty soon everyone. This is a private conference. Surgeons only and you're not a surgeon."

There was hardly anyone else to help me complain, because I was one of the few medical students who took a summer rotation. Cathy

Flynn was doing an anesthesiology rotation in the Memorial Unit and Frank Troy, the youngest member of the class, was also doing surgery but he worked with the other surgical team. On weekends when I was not on call, Cathy and I would go to dinner together. The dormitory cafeteria closed for the summer and there was a limit to how much hospital cafeteria food we could eat. I became very tired of O.R. peanut butter, but the hospital's stewed prunes and peppers stuffed with rice were not a thrilling change. Cathy and I usually went to Gino's and I always had a bacon, lettuce and tomato sandwich and a hot-fudge sundae. It put the furthest possible distance between me and hospital food.

Cathy and I were good friends, but she often seemed to be thinking about something else. Once she said she was not sure she could ever be a good doctor. Another time, she said she was too tired to go to church the next day. She was Roman Catholic, and I asked her if it was still Roman Catholic teaching that if you missed church you would go to Hell. The Kent school chaplain had told me that, and I always wondered if he had been right. It seemed too extreme to be true.

"Yes, it is true," said Cathy abruptly, "and that's why I ought to go to church. I'm afraid of burning in Hell." I never talked to her about religion again.

After six weeks of working with Dr. Chase, Mat Manning, Gene Verdi and Dick Callahan on the general surgery service, I was assigned to a two-week rotation on cardiac surgery. I was reluctant to leave general surgery. I had become part of the team and I enjoyed working with them. It was like being part of the crew on a small boat in rough water. We never knew what dreadful emergency would develop. Besides, I was something of a general surgery mascot, being the only woman medical student in years with an interest in surgery. There was nothing I could do to stay, though, and I felt more resigned after I learned that Dick rotated off to work on the other surgical team the same day I left, and Gene would go to the Veterans Hospital in another month. Friendship and a good team in surgery are transitory, because residents as well as students leave for a new rotation every six to twelve weeks.

Cardiac surgery was not a favorite medical student rotation. Older students told me to expect thankless hard work and professors who were unpleasant. The chief cardiac surgeon was Dr. Coe, a very eminent man. The other was Dr. Bryant, who looked like a brown bear. Dr. Coe had invented several heart operations but Dr. Bryant was the better surgeon. Vincent Romano, the anesthesiologist, told me Dr. Coe operated so slowly that the operating room had invented a new measure of time, the Coe-Unit. One Coe-Unit was the time it took Dr. Coe to finish a minor operation, roughly twelve hours.

Dr. Coe told me on my first day that women should not try to become doctors, but he seemed perfectly content to have me work on his service. This was partly because I said I might want to be a heart surgeon—it did have some appeal to me at the time—and it appealed to Dr. Coe to train the first woman heart surgeon. I changed my mind the next year, and he was annoyed, complaining, "You're too indecisive, just like a woman. You have to learn to make up your mind." By that time I had decided to be an orthopedic surgeon. The chairman of orthopedics was very kind when I later decided not to be an orthopod because I wasn't strong enough to set bones.

I was an intern then, and had been called to the emergency room to reduce a fractured wrist. The bone was angled up thirty degrees at the fracture site. The patient was a 55-year-old woman with weak muscles who had broken her wrist in a fall at home. I numbed the wrist as I had been taught, gave her intravenous Valium to relax her muscles, and tried to straighten the bone. Nothing happened. I pulled harder. Nothing. I changed my angle of pull—the orthopedic resident had told me it was all a matter of direction of pull. Nothing happened.

"Is it fixed?" the patient asked me hopefully.

"Not quite," I said, and I tried again. I thought I had succeeded that time but an x-ray showed I was wrong. I called the orthopedic resident, a short, thickset man.

"Easy, hon," he said. "It's all a matter of pulleys. Like so." He showed me the right direction. I pulled with all my might. Nothing. He looked at me, disappointed.

"It's easy. A baby could set the wrist. You don't have to be strong. Like this." He pulled just as I had been pulling but his greater strength pulled the bone straight. I thanked him, put on the cast and the next day told the chairman that bone surgery was not my field.

He laughed when I said I wasn't strong enough but I knew better. He had been an All-American college football player, and most orthopods, even if they weren't All-American, were still far stronger than I. I didn't like to admit my relative weakness, but I wasn't going to choose a field where being a woman put me at a clear disadvantage.

During my rotation in cardiac surgery, Dr. Coe was nice to me and even invited me to dinner at his house. He took me on rounds with him to see his private patients and introduced me to his devoted research assistant, who had been with him for thirty years. Together they developed new electronic gadgets for the heart. Dr. Coe was not fond of Dr. Bryant and would try to call me out of the operating room when I was scrubbed on Dr. Bryant's cases. He told me his favorite medical student story to show me how important I could be.

"It doesn't matter to a patient, Elizabeth, that I am a famous heart surgeon. The patient does not know who I am, or what research I have done in heart surgery. Once I was asked by the medical service to see a lady with rheumatic heart disease. I examined her, and she needed me to operate on her to replace her mitral heart valve. I talked to her about the surgery I had to do. She was upset and could not make up her mind to have the surgery. Finally, she said she wouldn't let me operate unless the doctor in the hospital looking after her agreed that it was the right thing to do. She said his name was Reynolds. I knew all the professors and had never heard of Reynolds, so I asked the nurse. Reynolds turned out to be a third-year medical student. He was assigned to this patient and she looked on him as her doctor. I had to wait for him to approve before the patient agreed. It was outrageous that I, an eminent surgeon, had to waste my time, to await the approval of a medical student. Sometimes I don't know what is happening to medicine. Where will we be in ten years?"

Unlike Dr. Coe, Dr. Bryant did little talking. He saw a lot of patients and kept the residents busy. Sometimes more than half the beds in the intensive care unit were filled with Dr. Bryant's patients recovering from heart surgery. Most of the surgery was done by the cardiac surgery chief resident, assisted by one of the two interns. The resident and the two interns were the cardiac "team."

Heart surgery was exciting. There was a definite routine, which has not greatly changed since then. Morning rounds began at 5:30 A.M. in the I.C.U. with the two interns, the medical student—myself—and the chief resident, who had done five years of general surgery and was starting his second year of cardiac surgery. He was thirty-five years old, board-certified in general surgery and tired of being called "boy" by Dr. Bryant.

By the end of the first week I knew the heart surgery routine. At 7:30, we went to the O.R., leaving one intern to look after the patients on the ward and in the unit. The patient would be on a stretcher in the corridor outside the "heart" room, which was larger than the other operating rooms and equipped with heart monitors hanging from the ceiling, special overhead lights and steel storage cabinets around the walls. As soon as the chief resident arrived, the circulating nurse and anesthesiologist wheeled the patient through the double doors. The chief resident put x-rays up on the lighted view-boxes on the wall and studied them. The patient climbed from the stretcher onto the operating table and I wheeled the stretcher out while the nurse buckled a strap across the patient's knees to keep him from falling off the table. The anesthesiologist put an intravenous needle in one arm. The intern put a central vein line in the other arm—this was a long thin plastic tube that went almost to the heart and was used for monitoring the pressure in the veins, which could indicate early heart failure. Then the anesthesiologist injected Pentothal, gave the patient oxygen through a mask, put the laryngoscope in the mouth, held up the jaw and pushed down a tube into the windpipe that was attached to a respirator.

"We're ready to roll," said the anesthesiologist.

The intern would put in a bladder catheter to measure urine output during the case. Heart monitors were taped to the skin of the back and chest and the patient's heartbeat flickered silently overhead on the monitor screen. Then we scrubbed, washed the patient with iodine soap from neck to toes, draped towels and cotton sheets around him.

"Okay," said the cardiac chief resident, "we're ready to cut. Is Dr. Bryant in the hospital?"

"Yes," said the nurse.

"Scalpel," said the chief resident.

The scrub nurse assisted me as I operated on the leg, removing a leg vein if the operation was a vein bypass to repair blocked arteries in the heart. For heart-valve operations, no vein was used. The intern dissected out the femoral artery in the groin so that the patient could be put on the heart pump. The cardiac chief resident got even less sleep than the intern and even in the morning, before surgery began, would often sway with fatigue.

Unless we asked for help in removing a vein, the chief resident operated on the chest and ignored us. First with the scalpel he cut the skin of the middle of the chest from neck to belly. Next he dissected away the tissues beneath the bone, and with a vibrating saw he cut through the bone.

"Once I saw the bone cutter angled wrong. The heart was cut wide open," said the chief resident as he started the saw.

"Did the patient live?" I asked innocently.

"Are you kidding me?"

The chest bone was now split. A special retractor was put in and a handle cranked around. The bones were split apart.

"Call Bryant and tell him we're in the chest," said the chief resident.

With forceps and scissors he carefully cut away the membranes around the heart. There was the heart going *thump-thump-thump*. If there was an arrhythmia, it went *thump-quiver-thump*. That was all there was between being alive and being dead.

The chief resident put his hand in the chest and felt around the heart. "Arteries are hard as rock. Amazing he's alive." With scissors and forceps he dissected out the diseased arteries, which lie on the surface of the heart. "Okay. How are you guys in the groin? Let me see the vein you've got, Liz. It'll do." Then to the intern, "Are you ready for the pump?" He checked the artery and vein in the groin. "Call in the pump team."

"We're right behind you," said the pump technicians who were checking the machine they had rolled in on a trolley. Tubes and wiring were strung around bubbling chambers.

"Tell Bryant I'm going on the pump."

Clamps were placed on the artery and vein in the groin, and tubes shoved in and tied in place.

"Don't touch this. If this tube comes out he bleeds to death."

It was now eleven o'clock. A clamp was placed around the aorta, the main artery out of the heart.

"Are you going on pump without Bryant here?" asked the anesthesiologist.

"He'll be here. He always times it perfectly."

Just as the aorta clamp was in position and ready to be clamped down, Bryant came in.

"How is it, boy?"

"Hard as a rock, all three arteries."

"Do you have enough vein?"

"Yes."

"So what the hell are you waiting for? Want me to scrub in and hold your hand?"

The chief resident closed the clamp around the aorta. Potassium was given to stop the heart. The intern stood on the other side of the table to assist the resident.

Clamp-clamp-clamp, and the blood flow from the heart stopped.

"Vein open. Artery open. We're on the pump."

The pump technician repeated that, to signal that the inflow and outflow to the pump was working.

"Veins up." The nurse handed over the veins I had dissected from the leg and the chief resident cut them to size, cut a hole in the aorta to sew in the vein, and another in the artery beyond the obstruction.

"Don't sew like that, boy, be delicate," drawled Bryant. "You're a heart surgeon. Don't let your hand shake." That made the chief resident nervous and his hand shook more.

Dr. Bryant looked at me. "Sweetheart, you don't think his hand shakes because I make him nervous, do you?" He laughed. "You're doing fine, boy. Call me when you're ready to come off the pump."

Then the tedium began. The chief resident carefully sewed in the veins. The pump bubbled and whirled and I watched as the technician checked the blood to be sure there was enough oxygen in it. There was nothing else to watch. The longer the time on pump the more damage to the heart muscle, which was not getting oxygen. For three veins, it took two hours or more. I yawned, felt hungry, leaned forward.

"Get off his leg," snapped the chief resident who saw me out of the corner of his eye. "He's not an armchair." I straightened hastily.

"Watch the lines," screamed the pump technician. I had inadvertently jerked a pump line.

At last the resident was finished.

"Call Bryant. We're coming off the pump." This was the moment of greatest tension. Would the heart start beating again? The anesthesiologist started sodium bicarbonate in the I.V. line to counteract the acid that had built up in the heart muscle while oxygen to the heart was stopped.

"Through, boy? How is it?"

"Good."

Bryant looked over the drapes at the veins sewn in place. "C-plus. Maybe a B-minus. Get off the pump. What are you waiting for? I hate a slow surgeon."

"Artery off. Vein off. Aorta off."

The pump technicians repeated the words after him.

The heart quivered, then nothing.

"Get ready to go back on pump," ordered Bryant. The heart jumped suddenly into life, an erratic abnormal rhythm.

"Lidocaine in and running," said the anesthesiologist. The heart abruptly fell into a normal *thump-thump-thump*. The resident sighed in relief.

"Close up, boy. Call if you need me." The chief resident started to close. The cardiac chief resident would sew up the hole in the artery, and I would sew up the skin. In cardiac surgery I learned to use forceps and a needle holder easily, and could do simple suturing. The chief resident cauterized bleeding vessels in the chest. Then steel wires were run through the chest bones and then tied down to bring the bone together. Tubes were placed around the lungs to drain blood.

"Liz, scrub out and write orders."

It was four o'clock. We were running behind schedule. There was a second bypass-graft to be done. That operation went till ten o'clock, then eleven, then midnight, as they tried without success to get the patient off the pump. His heart simply would not start pumping again.

Later, as a surgical resident in Boston, I saw the other extreme of heart surgery. The heart surgeon there, Dr. Anjou, ran the cardiac service like the armed forces, and he was commander in chief. He was present at every case from the beginning, along with two other heart surgery professors. One professor supervised the running of the heart pump, one operated on the patient, and one prepared the vein and groin. Dr. Anjou also had a cardiac chief resident, a general surgery resident and an intern in the O.R. to assist, and a cardiac surgery professor, a surgical resident, an intern and two physician's assistants looking after his patients on the ward. His patients recovered faster.

I enjoyed the heart operations, but it was hard to see much of the surgery. I was not tall enough, except when I stood on a stool high enough for me to see the heart deep in the chest. One day I could not see anything because Dr. Bryant scrubbed in and blocked my view. It was equally boring for the scrub nurse. Heart operations were routine for her. She only did heart cases. Her eyes were amazing. She wore heavy black eyeliner and blue shadow, and could say anything with her eyes. While Dr. Bryant was trying to decide how best to place the valve, and to be sure the heart pump was working, the nurse told me in a whisper the names of the various surgical instruments and we played tic-tac-toe on the sheets with a surgical marking pen. As the valve was being sewn in, I tried to peer over Dr. Bryant's shoulder and his elbow hit me in the eye.

"Get out of my way," he snarled.

"Don't be a sourpuss," said the nurse. "She can't see a thing."

"Honey, why the hell should she see anything?" said Dr. Bryant. "She ain't never going to do this operation."

The nurse was almost as tall as Dr. Bryant and could see what he was doing, but it was a long reach and she had trouble getting instruments into his hand. She handed me the long steel clamps and forceps he needed and gestured to me to duck under his elbow and slap the instrument into his right hand. I was doing it quite well and feeling pleased with myself when the intercom crackled, "Dr. Morgan is to join Dr. Coe in clinic to see his patients." My heart sank. Clinic was boring. Dr. Bryant snorted in disgust. He glared down at me over his mask.

"This is more exciting than Coe's clinic, isn't it, sweetheart?" and he snapped at the intercom, "Dr. Morgan can't leave. I need her. Good looking women always help me operate. Stitch!" And he turned back to sewing the valve into the heart.

Messages came over the intercom for the next two hours, as Dr. Coe ordered me down to the clinic and Dr. Bryant ordered me not to leave. When the operation was over I went reluctantly to clinic. Dr. Coe was still talking to the first of his three patients, but he was angry with Dr. Bryant, and told me how wrong it was of me to have stayed in the operating room. "I shall have to speak to Dr. Bryant," he announced angrily, but I knew it was empty boasting. Dr. Coe was smaller than I was and Dr. Bryant was the size of a grizzly bear, which was one reason he could behave so outrageously.

When my two weeks of cardiac surgery were over, I felt I had had enough.

Booze and Dope:
Introduction to Internal Medicine

My surgery clerkship ended in late August. I spent a week at home, catching up on sleep, telling my family about the summer, getting my hair cut and buying new clothes for the fall. Cathy decided to stay in New Haven until the academic year began again and I wondered how she managed without her family. My conversations with my mother were a favorite pastime.

Before leaving New Haven, I had learned that my plan for the coming year had been approved. I would spend twelve weeks doing an internal medicine rotation, then a three-week pediatrics rotation and another three weeks on psychiatry. That would be the first semester. With my ten weeks' credit from surgery and nine weeks of thesis elective time and summer I was free from mid-January until the following September to work in Oxford. Professor Hunter had written to say he was expecting me to arrive in mid-to-late January, and enclosed a list of seventy papers which he said I should read to understand the research projects in his laboratory. I was very happy. Two years before I had spent six delightful months in Oxford going to parties and meeting men after graduating from Harvard and I had been hoping to return ever since.

My medical rotation was spent on Kinmuth-1, and Claire Christiansen, Cathy and Sam were assigned there also. I was the only one of us who had worked on the wards, and after ten weeks on surgery I was a blood-drawing expert. This made it easier for me the first two weeks, but after that Claire became the best of the four of us.

Medical students were unpaid blood-drawing technicians for the hospital. For a busy medical service with fifty beds, it took an hour or more for the four of us and the intern to draw, label and record the blood samples, and at the end I always had blood on my dress or stockings. Most hospitals now hire laboratory technicians to go from ward to ward each morning to draw blood at a salary of five dollars or more an hour. They still leave the difficult patients, on whom blood-drawing is not easy, to the intern, but it gives the medical student more time to study.

Sometimes a patient needed six or more tubes of blood taken for different laboratory tests. One patient complained that all this blood testing would "thin his blood." He was in the hospital for three months and developed an unexplained anemia. We attributed it to his chronic abdominal infection until we calculated that three months of daily blood samples, each small in itself, had caused his anemia. When we stopped taking blood samples, his anemia improved.

It is easy to draw blood from the normal person with large healthy veins. Most of our Kinmuth-1 patients were elderly, chronically ill, and had had many intravenous needles in their veins that had scarred the veins closed. A patient with bad veins can mean an hour of needle-sticks, looking for a vein. This was a nightmare for the patient, and an ordeal for me, caught between the patient asking for "that man, the real doctor," and the intern who sent me in with the command, "Don't come back without that blood."

On our first day the medical resident told us the apocryphal story about the medical student who never came back without the blood sample. He closed the door to the patient's room, and emerged within a few minutes with every tube filled with blood. He was a model medical student until it was discovered that his infallible method involved plunging a four-inch "spinal" needle through the patient's ribs into the heart. The student was dismissed from medical school. We believed the story then, but later Claire told me she heard the same tale at Stanford, and I know doctors from Harvard, Tufts, Boston University and Tulane who claim it for their schools.

Many of our patients were drug addicts with hepatitis. It was very hard to find a good vein in a drug addict's arm, and even harder to persuade them to let us use it for drawing blood. Our intern on medicine did not mind the addicts but he detested the ones who were drug pushers as well. One patient was a fifteen-year-old boy in hospital for hepatitis. He boasted that he earned $30,000 a year, tax free, from pushing drugs, and that his business had not fallen off since he came into hospital. His supplier brought the drugs to him in hospital and he sold them there. He kept a suitcase full of heroin under his hospital bed. He allowed no one to come near it, and he never left the room unless his girl friend was there to guard it for him. Visiting hours started at noon, and he had a steady stream of teenage visitors in groups of three or more, and a deluge of visitors after 3:30 when school was over. The security guards told the intern that there was nothing they could do unless they caught the boy in the act of selling drugs, but whenever anyone approached his room—a private one because he had infectious hepatitis—he flung his arms around his girl friend and began to kiss her passionately, so we were embarrassed to intrude.

Claire worked harder than I did. She was thinking of specializing in internal medicine, and it was important for her to get good recommendations. I did the necessary work and went to the lectures, but nothing extra. For one thing, the intern and the two medical residents were not as much fun as the surgeons had been. They seemed scornful of me, which I attributed to the fact that I had said I wanted to be a surgeon.

Also I was still tired after my surgical rotation, and although internal medicine was fascinating I became a little restless. I missed the action of surgery. The internal medicine working day began at seven, which seemed a late start after surgery. At eight o'clock we made rounds with the intern and junior resident, standing silently until they spoke to us. They were not nearly as important as the medical chief resident, with whom we made rounds on the patients at nine o'clock. (In surgery, every general surgery resident ends up as chief resident, and there may be four or more chiefs, one for each service. In medicine, being a chief resident is a special honor, and is an extra year of residency.) At ten o'clock we sat down and talked about the patients with the attending professor assigned to supervise the ward. At eleven o'clock we either went to Medical Grand Rounds, which is a lecture given once a week in the amphitheater, or stayed with the attending until twelve. We had lunch at twelve and then returned to the ward to do work-ups and scut work such as electrocardiograms and blood cultures. We had lectures from two-thirty to four-thirty, and then returned to the ward to examine new patients.

Patients were assigned to us in order, so each of us examined one of every four patients. Often only one or two patients were admitted each day, and if it was not my turn for a new patient, I was free after 4:30. If the weather was fine, I joined the touch football game in front of the dormitory, where I didn't really play but helped to distract the opposite side. If it rained, I read the magazines in the lobby and hoped that a senior medical student, whom I had a crush on, would walk by and say hello. I spent only every fourth night on call in the hospital to see emergency admissions, and even then I could go home after ten. Claire and Sam stayed to work late almost every night, but Cathy and I did not. Cathy was talking about a career in anesthesia. She seemed even more abstracted than during the summer.

"Patient care is frightening," she announced once as we were walking to the dormitory for lunch.

"It is," I agreed. "The responsibility is overwhelming."

"More than that, I wonder if I can be a doctor. I really have my doubts."

"Cathy, you'd be a wonderful doctor," I said, amazed. "You're very conscientious and very smart."

"You don't know," said Cathy. "Let's talk about something else."

The medicine rotation was much easier than surgery, partly because I did not choose to work as hard as I did on surgery, and partly because there were four of us to share the work. I learned a lot about alcoholism and a lot about heroin addiction.

One of my first patients was a friendly eighty-year-old Italian gentleman. He came into the hospital because he had some mild bleeding from an ulcer. His doctor wanted to be certain that he did not have a stomach cancer causing the bleeding. I asked him all the routine questions. He said he did not smoke cigarettes, but he did take drugs. I asked him what kind, because most ulcer patients take antacids.

"Sodium bicarbonate and heroin."

"I beg your pardon? Sodium bicarbonate, but what was the other medicine?"

"Heroin."

"Heroin? For how long?"

"Since I was eighteen."

He spoke with a heavy Italian accent and interrupted his own answers by patting my hand and saying, "Nice girl, very nice girl." I decided I must have misunderstood him. I asked the intern if someone could take heroin for sixty-two years. He thought it was unlikely, but changed his mind when he examined my patient's arms. The veins were completely scarred. My patient was amused, and slapped his wrist and legs to point out possible veins in case we had to put in an intravenous needle.

A psychiatry professor had given us a lecture once, saying he would rather be a drug addict than an alcoholic. I had thought it a foolish remark at the time, but I changed my mind when I compared my eighty-year-old heroin addict to my next patient, a woman alcoholic. She had been a whiskey drinker for years, but on a flight from California to New Haven had developed a case of D.T.s. She was hallucinating when the plane landed, and the airline sent her to the hospital in an ambulance. The intern had examined her in the E.R. before I saw her. It was nine o'clock in the evening, my night to be in the hospital. The intern said I would find her interesting.

When I came in, she was wriggling in bed. I asked her what the matter was, and she said she was trying to escape the ants and insects that were crawling under the sheets. D.T. hallucinations can be horrible, but fortunately she did not seem disturbed by them. She may have been used to them. She remarked that she was not frightened but the ants were tickling her. I asked how long she had been in New Haven and she asked what made me think I was in New Haven. I did a physical examination of her, but she wouldn't take deep breaths so I couldn't hear her lungs, and when I tried to listen to her heart she wiggled under the stethoscope and I heard nothing clearly. I had to leave most of the "history" section blank, with a note that the patient was unreliable.

The next morning on rounds my patient was angry with me. "Who let them in here last night?" she demanded. "Who let those Indians in here? They came in through my window. They were wearing brown, and had on feather headdresses. They tried to set my bed on fire. Look, I fought them off!" She pointed to her water pitcher which was lying on the floor.

The resident told the nurse to increase my patient's sedative dose and to give her a sedative injection immediately. At ten o'clock I was asked to "present" her to our medical attending—the professor supervising the work of the residents. A presentation is a recital of the pertinent medical facts in a prescribed order: "This was the first admission here for this 56-year-old white female, admitted from the emergency room to which she had been brought by ambulance after her arrival in New Haven," etc.

After my presentation, which was short, we all walked into her room, and I introduced her to the attending, a formal and pompous man, who had explained condescendingly that there were "lots and lots of secretive housewife alcoholics who start drinking as soon as the children leave for school."

"Darling," shouted my patient, when I had introduced them, "where have you been? We had such a good time together at the Forty-ninth Street Bar last night. Why did you leave so early?"

The attending froze in horror for a moment, and then suddenly relaxed and pointed at me. "Do you know her?" he asked my patient. "Do you know this nice young lady?"

She looked at me anxiously and then smiled. "Of course, why, we were together just last night at the Forty-ninth Street Bar. We had a lovely time."

"Do you know Korsakoff?" the attending asked her.

"We drink there all the time. A good bar, a nice man," she answered.

We left her room and in the hallway the attending told us that Korsakoff was the nineteenth-century physician who first wrote about my patient's problem: confabulation and hallucinations from alcohol.

Alcoholism was common in our patients. Claire looked after a girl of twenty-one with alcohol liver failure. Her skin was a bright yellow from liver-failure jaundice. She had started to drink when she was fourteen and drank at least a quart of whiskey every day. She was also a heroin addict and had supported her habits by working as a prostitute. She had a four-year-old child. This twenty-one-year-old girl died in a coma two weeks later in the I.C.U. Every possible treatment had failed. It was especially upsetting to Claire and me to see a girl, younger than us, die so horribly.

My favorite patient, of whom I grew very fond, was a sweet lady, Mrs. Jones. She lived alone in an old apartment building and had been sent to the hospital by ambulance when a neighbor had found her asleep in a pool of filth and whiskey with her pet dog, a mongrel, whimpering beside her. Her liver was badly damaged by years of alcohol drinking and as a result her blood did not clot quickly. She was still in a coma when I saw her, and the intern told me to get some blood samples from her. The veins in her arms were terrible, and I finally had to take the samples from the femoral vein, a large vein in the groin. I held pressure over the needle puncture for twenty minutes to make the oozing stop. Normally you only need to hold pressure for a few minutes. The next day she was black-and-blue from her knees to her chest.

Mrs. Jones woke up from her coma after being in hospital for a day. Our goal was to get her liver function to improve before she was discharged. It improved rapidly with a good diet and Mrs. Jones enjoyed hospital life, except that she worried about what had happened to her dog, Spot. She began to hallucinate and claimed that she had seen Spot trotting down the hospital corridor looking for her. The intern wrote in her hospital chart that she had "Korsakoff's," but had to cross it out when the security police came looking for a mongrel dog that had gotten into the hospital and had last been seen by the ward secretary running along the Kinmuth-1 corridor.

Mrs. Jones's neighbor fed Spot, but Mrs. Jones did not live to go home. She developed pneumonia just as her liver function tests began to improve. It had been my night to stay in hospital until ten, and I was getting my coat to leave. I said good night to the senior resident whom I admired becuase he seemed especially competent but whom I found intimidating as well because he was critical. Suddenly a nurse shouted down the corridor, "CODE FIVE!" The senior resident was the only one on the ward with me. We rushed to the room and found Mrs. Jones limp, her skin a mottled-blue, covered only by her hospital cotton shift. The nurse had pulled the sheets off to check her pulses when she first found her. The resident told me to start an intravenous line while the nurse gave her mouth-to-mouth breathing and the resident pumped her chest to try to get her heart started. Her hand felt cold but I had found a vein and was trying to get the needle in—my hand was shaking—when a group of medical interns and residents arrived to help. The secretary had called in a stat page and "Code 5-Kinmuth-1" had been announced over the hospital speaker system. A woman intern slapped me on the shoulder and told me to get out of the way.

"They shouldn't let medical students clutter up a code," she said to no one in particular.

I stood with my back against the wall, watching, and ran to the desk with test tubes filled with blood when the head nurse handed them to me. Mrs. Jones was pronounced dead after half an hour of unsuccessful attempts to start her heart pumping again. She must have regurgitated some of her dinner after she fell asleep and the food had blocked her windpipe. Before the woman intern left she turned to me, looking severe.

"You should never answer a code unless you know enough to help. A well-meaning incompetent can cause enough delay to kill someone."

She walked out. The senior resident went back to finish his work. The Kinmuth-1 intern started to fill out the death certificate and there was nothing for me to do except go back to the dorm. I was crushed. I had seen people die on the surgical service but I had never before been blamed, even indirectly, for their deaths. It made it even worse that I had been accused by another woman. There were very few women doctors at Yale, or anywhere, and they were intelligent, efficient and severe in looks and manner. My dream then was to become as sharp, cool and commanding as they were. It took me many years to learn that their manner—and their overly critical attitude toward women medical students—reflected their insecurity and jealous protection of their own uncertain position in a man's world.

The next day, the senior resident said on rounds, "It was a shame we lost Mrs. Jones, but she was cold when the nurse found her. She must have been dead for fifteen minutes already."

I felt suddenly relieved. It hadn't been all my fault after all.

The chief resident then told us that attending rounds this morning were to be with a visiting Boston cardiologist whom we would all find "terribly impressive." In the past I had found this meant "boring and egotistical." The visiting professor turned out to be a short man with bright, watchful eyes, a dark blue, pin-stripe, three-piece suit and a hearing aid on his right ear. Whenever anyone spoke, he tilted his head slightly to the right and looked at the speaker attentively, like a robin.

He met with the four of us—Sam, Claire, Cathy and me—in the conference room at the back of the ward, next to the I.C.U. I presented a patient of mine called Joe. He was a gray-haired black man, a retired short-order cook with high blood pressure and repeated bouts of heart failure. Joe had had three doctors in five years who told him to lose weight and take his heart pills. Each of his three doctors had died of a heart attack. Joe's weight had stayed the same and he now refused to take the pills, saying it was bad luck.

"Are you going to tell Joe to take his heart pills and lose weight?" the visiting cardiologist asked me.

Caught off guard, I stammered, "I know it's the accepted medical therapy, but I don't think he would follow my advice."

"That is true," said the visiting professor, "and from a statistical point of view, perhaps not for you, at your age, but certainly for me, such advice to Joe would appear to increase his doctor's attack-risk considerably. I'd let Joe do what he pleases. He's the one who's still alive." He smiled, and we went on to the next presentation, a patient of Sam's with a heart murmur. It was a good presentation, and the cardiologist told him so.

"However, you told me what the murmur sounded like." He tapped his hearing aid. "I have never heard a heart murmur. It is too soft for me to hear, and I was born slightly deaf. If you would take me to see your patient, I would like to feel the murmur."

We thought he was joking. You cannot feel a heart murmur. The four of us accompanied him to the bedside of Sam's patient, a lady with rheumatic fever and a birth defect of the heart. The nurse offered him her stethoscope but he politely waved it away and asked the patient to sit up. He put his hand on her chest, sides and back, still holding his head tilted slightly to the right.

"There is a definite grade four out of six harsh systolic murmur here," and he put Sam's hand on the patient's upper chest. "A diastolic rumble here, at the side, and you can feel them both at the back, but it is faint." He made us feel the chest and to my astonishment I felt the rumble caused by the murmur we had only heard before by stethoscope. Sam's patient was equally impressed.

Back in the conference room, the visiting cardiologist told us that he made his own residents leave their stethoscopes at home when they worked with him. If they insisted on wearing stethoscopes on his service, he would clamp the tubing so no sounds traveled through it. He said that with a week's practice, his residents could tell more about a murmur by touch than they could before with a stethoscope.

He spent an hour with us, teaching us about heart murmurs and the diagnosis of heart disease. He spoke quietly, and several times told us we must not believe something just because he said so—to learn we ought to know at least three different opinions on a subject. We were sorry when rounds were over, and two medical professors and the medical chief resident came to take him to lunch. In medicine as in every field there are a few naturally gifted teachers and he was one of them.

Love Story Leukemia

After six weeks on Kinmuth, I had an elective medical rotation which I spent on the hematology service. I had to know some hematology to work with Professor Hunter in Oxford. The hematology service saw many patients in consultation, often for a suspected leukemia, or for anemia. Hematology had relatively few patients under its direct care, and usually advised other doctors. There was no scut work, and the teaching was excellent. I spent two to four hours a day being taught by an attending physician.

As the medical student, I was sent to see a consultation patient first, and then I brought the hematology resident and professor to examine the patient with me. I had to write my opinion of the problem in the patient's chart before the resident and professor saw the patient. This would take me a long time, often an hour, because I had to include the patient's history and physical exam which I had done, as well as my own inexpert evaluation, diagnosis and recommendations.

One morning we had a consult from the private surgery service, signed by Dick Callahan, my intern from Larkins-5. Dick had just started to work on the private general surgery service the day before. He found one of his new patients had a very abnormal white blood cell count after surgery. Normal is about ten thousand white blood cells per cubic centimeter of blood. An infection might raise the count to twenty thousand, because white blood cells fight infection, but this patient had a count of a hundred thousand! It might be a "leukemoid reaction"—a temporary rise in white blood cells seen sometimes after stress such as surgery—or it might be leukemia. Dick's consult read "Possible leukemoid reaction. Would appreciate evaluation."

I went over to the private surgery ward and examined the patient, a frail, blue-eyed, white-haired man, who thought it entertaining to be examined by a "lady doctor." He was seventy-eight and rather confused by his surgery, and could not tell me much about his past illnesses. He just smiled. I found nothing wrong with him other than the surgery wound, so I sat down at the nurses' desk to read his hospital chart. Surgery charts tend to be brief, but the intern before Dick had written less than usual, a few scribbled sentences the night before surgery. The physical exam was incomplete, and the intern had ordered no laboratory data before the surgery, just two white counts after surgery with readings over a hundred thousand. I knew from my surgeon's training in the summer that this was poor care. Dick had made a page-and-a-half "on-service" note, and had done his own brief but complete physical exam. His maniacal compulsiveness had irritated me when I worked with him, but it included self-criticism, and helped keep his patients out of trouble.

I turned to the patient's old records—the folder with notes from past hospital admissions. The man had been in hospital ten times, and there were three fat folders to read. I read them all. Admissions one through eight, and ten, all for stomach ulcers, were irrelevant, but his ninth admission four years before explained his white blood count. He had developed leukemia four years ago, a kind called C.L.L. or chronic lymphatic leukemia that has a very slow course. People can live with it for twenty years without needing any treatment. With this leukemia, it was natural that his white blood cell count was over a hundred thousand.

"Don't tell me that they send a medical student when I need a hematology consult," said a voice behind me in disparaging tones. It was Dick. He was wearng a green surgical scrub suit and it occurred to me, as it often did, how plain and fat the shapeless green cotton outfits must make me look, if they made the men look so bad. Dick looked as pale as ever. "I don't want to dump on you," he said, without sounding apologetic, "but when I ask for a consult I want an expert. I know more than you about hematology. You're just a beginning third-year student."

"Actually, he has leukemia," I said, feeling intimidated, yet triumphant.

"How do you know?"

I pointed to the old records. "I read it in the chart. He has had leukemia for four years."

Dick read the old chart, scowling. Then he said, "Good girl. I'm really embarrassed that a female medical student had to teach me to read the medical chart. I'm proud of you. It makes me feel I taught you something this summer."

He almost smiled at me, looked at the clock over the desk, and hurried off to the O.R. I finished my note and went to fetch the rest of the hematology team. They were amused that a surgical consult had been solved by my reading the old hospital record. They were also appalled that a patient with leukemia, or any patient, could have major surgery without any laboratory tests being done. The chief hematology resident, a graying man in his mid-forties who had completed cardiology, infectious disease and several other residencies and still could not decide in what field he wanted to specialize, wanted to write a rude note in the chart, but Dick had already written "Thank you for this very valuable consult," so he instead simply countersigned my three-page note. When a surgeon had been properly grateful after an obvious error, it was considered poor etiquette to rub it in.

We all went off to lunch in the hospital coffee shop. "Elizabeth, if you have a coffee ice-cream soda every day you'll get fat," said Dr. Cox, the chief of hematology. "Meet me at three o'clock to see two of my private patients." After lunch, suppressing an urge to rush back to the dorm and weigh myself, I sat in the laboratory with the residents and studied blood cells under the microscope.

"Here's your man from the surgical service," said the chief resident, and under the microscope I saw a slide of blood in which thousands of small white cells were crowded together. It seemed odd that this was leukemia. The tiny cells looked harmless. Under the microscope white cells look blue, because they are stained with a blue dye that makes them visible and deceptively pretty. After looking at slides, we did "bone marrows." Many blood diseases can be diagnosed from bone marrow samples because blood cells are made in the bone marrow. For instance, a virus infection can sometimes make the blood cells in arteries and veins become abnormal and look like leukemia, but examining the bone marrow under the microscope will show that leukemia cells are not being made.

The junior resident took me to watch as he did a bone marrow. I had not seen one, and thought of it as a minor procedure, similar to drawing blood from a vein. We went to the patient's room. A technician stood by ready to take the specimen to the lab. The resident told the patient to turn on her stomach. She had been sedated so the bone marrow sampling would not be too painful, but she became wide awake once the resident walked in, despite his reassurances. She turned on her stomach, and the resident injected Novocaine where the bone marrow sample would be taken—the posterior iliac crest, a wide flat bone with a lot of marrow, off to either side in the lower back. The patient was nervous, and grabbed my hand when I sat down next to her bed. The resident picked up a scalpel from the sterile tray open at her bedside and cut through the skin. Then, with a sharp cutting instrument like a miniature trowel, he cut down to the bone. This did not hurt because of the Novocaine. He stood up and pressed on the instrument, turning it clockwise, to cut through the bone. The woman said, "It's a funny feeling, but not painful." The resident warned her, "You'll feel a brief sharp pain— and that will be all." He plugged a syringe into the end of the instrument and pulled out the barrel of the syringe suddenly, creating a vacuum, drawing a few drops of a dark blue material into the syringe. The woman screamed, turned white, and squeezed my hand until it hurt. The technician squirted the bone marrow into a sterile dish.

"It's a good sample," the resident said happily. "Quite a few bone spicules. You were very good, dear. Did it hurt a lot?"

"I'm sorry I was such a baby, but I had to scream. The pain is unbelievable. It goes right into your chest."

The resident patted her hand. "You did fine. The results will be ready in the morning." We left the room, while a nurses' aide came in to straighten her bed. It had taken less than fifteen minutes, but the patient looked exhausted and was sweating. After that, I thought of her each time I looked at a bone marrow slide under the microscope.

I joined Dr. Cox at three o'clock, and he took me to see two patients of his who had been admitted to hospital. One was a lady of fifty, who told me she was a housewife and was in hospital because she began to develop bruises. She noticed them first while gardening, two weeks before. She felt tired, but otherwise quite normal. She showed me huge purple bruises that covered her stomach, her legs and her arms. "They appeared out of nowhere," she said.

Dr. Cox explained to me later that according to the bone marrow done the day before, she had acute leukemia and would be dead in a month. It gave me a strange feeling of being in the present and the future at the same time, to see her alive, and imagine her dead so soon.

The second patient of Dr. Cox's was a teenage girl who had leukemia. She was in hospital for drug treatments, but she would probably be dead in a year. As we walked down the hall to her room, a nurse stopped us, and pleaded in a whisper with Dr. Cox to try to cheer the girl up if he knew how.

"She's just been reading the book *Love Story*—you know, the one about the girl who gets married to her boyfriend and then dies of leukemia. They shouldn't allow that book in hospital, Dr. Cox. I told her not to read it but she did, and now she's been crying all afternoon. She knows she's going to die; I know she's going to die; but it doesn't make it any easier. I could kill the wimp that wrote that tear-jerker. He's a professor at Yale, did you know that, but he doesn't care. He's made his million. I hope he can't sleep at night." She walked away shaking her head.

The girl was fifteen and very pretty. Her room was filled with flowers, get-well cards, and stuffed animals from friends. In her left arm was the intravenous needle that was giving her the anti-leukemia drugs; in her right arm was a stuffed teddy bear. She was crying, her face turned away from the door. School books and her weekly assignments from her teacher were on the nightstand next to her, with *Love Story* on top of them. Dr. Cox sat on her bed and held her hand as she sobbed that she did not want to die. It was four o'clock and the sun was setting on her hospital-room window that looked out on the Yale undergraduate campus and its Gothic spires, where the author of *Love Story* had his office.

Saber-toothed Tigers

My last rotation before setting out for Oxford was psychiatry. Surgery had been exhausting, medicine had been hard work, and I was looking forward to psychiatry as six weeks of rest and relaxation. All I would have to do was to sit down and either talk or listen and I was prepared to enjoy it. My psychiatry rotation would be on the Alpha psychiatry ward, and joining me were Claire and Sam. Alpha was a ward designed for "salvageable" patients who needed sudden, brief care. The ward was run by a psychiatrist who despised Freud and psychotherapy and believed that most mentally ill patients would either get better quickly with a little help or need long-range custodial care. Many of the patients were well-off. They had to be—it cost $1,000 a week to stay on Alpha. The ward's success was that the patients, when faced with the choice of going to a long-term mental hospital, often improved rapidly and went home. No one pretended the patients were cured but Alpha aimed at training them to behave "normally," even if their thoughts were "crazy." This way they could be sent home to torment their families rather than their psychiatrists, who were much more expensive.

Claire Christiansen and I first met with the psychiatry chief resident, who was a woman. She told me that being women in medicine was hard because we had no role models.

On psychiatry I sat in on a group therapy session and then attended a staff meeting to discuss the group therapy session. Then I had lunch. In the afternoon, I sat in on a nurse–social-worker–patient conference and then a meeting run by the patients. Doctors, nurses and students could attend this meeting but, by Alpha rules, could not say anything. During this conference patients voted on each other—how much each was improving, how each should try to improve, and if anyone needed to be punished for breaking Alpha rules. The rules were written by the patients but the psychiatrists and nurses had absolute power of veto. The Alpha goal was to introduce "reality" by way of the patient vote, so that the patients could "learn" how to be normal. It was very real because, as in any public vote, powers behind the scenes—in this case, the psychiatrists—really made the decisions, and would "suggest" to patients in group therapy what topics to discuss and how to vote. The assistant professor who supervised Claire, Sam and me told us to regard ourselves as "intimately involved with the decision-making process and the ongoing reality-testing of the group," which meant we attended assigned conferences. We were assigned to "develop rapport in an in-depth ongoing therapeutic endeavor," which meant we each had to study one patient. At the end of six weeks we had to hand in an "in-depth analysis of experiential insights" on the patient—in other words, a long paper.

One patient was a Chinese lady who spoke little English. It is difficult to analyze someone's emotions if they speak a different language, but we understood the Chinese lady to say that there were people who surrounded her house at night, climbed over the roof and watched her. The psychiatrist called these "paranoid ideations." Her husband was also Chinese and had arranged her commitment to Alpha. My psychiatry group leader said that Orientals are more paranoid because they keep their emotions inside. He had treated only two Orientals, neither of them Chinese, but he said it was obvious from the psychodynamics.

Another patient was a thirteen-year-old girl with anorexia nervosa. She wouldn't eat, presumably for psychological reasons. Some psychiatrists treat such patients with psychotherapy and hope they will begin to eat. On Alpha the psychiatrists force-fed anorexics, on the grounds that a dead analyzed patient is not a therapeutic triumph and that severe starvation by itself will make most people mentally abnormal. So the thirteen-year-old girl was put in a strait jacket three times a day at breakfast, lunch and dinner. Three nurses held her down. An orderly dashed cold water on her if she had hysterics, and a doctor placed a tube down her nose into her stomach and poured in blended food. This treatment had started before I came to Alpha and was still going on when I left. The girl did not contribute a great deal to her therapy discussion groups.

The patient I chose for my in-depth analysis was Sara, aged twenty-four, plump and attractive. She had worked as a secretary and lived with her parents in a New York suburb. Her parents were very rich or at least her stepfather was. Her mother had been divorced three times, had a hard face, dressed in expensive pants suits and occasionally came to see her daughter. Sara was always upset after her mother came.

I spent four hours talking with Sara the day she was admitted to Alpha, trying to find out why she wanted to commit herself to a psychiatric hospital. First she said that she had had no problems until a boyfriend took her to a party two months before. After an all-night binge of wine and marijuana, she woke up crazy.

"I had a revelation that I was doomed. I would always be incredibly bored."

She added that she had tried three or four times in the past to kill herself by slashing her wrists. She had also taken a bottle of her mother's tranquilizers a year ago. She had her first love affair at fifteen.

"That was when I started analysis for two years."

"You were in analysis for two years?" I asked.

"No, my mother was in analysis."

"Oh, your mother was in analysis."

"No, neither of us have ever been in analysis."

"Oh," I said.

Sara went on to tell me that she had had an abortion at fifteen, been supported by an allowance from her parents, slept with many men who were "just friends" and that her mother had never forgiven her for the time she tore up the sofa. She went through a buying phase, a motorcycle phase, and an older-man love affair. This ended with a fight during which she threw milk in his face at breakfast and cut all the telephone wires. She then went to live at home again. She fought with her stepfather almost daily and after a fight she would cry in her room or fire a shotgun out of the window, and once she tried to strangle her mother. After the marijuana party, she had more vivid dreams than before. Her dreams were about evolution.

"In the dream," Sara explained, "I evolve through the centuries, through millions of years of incredible bloodshed. I am a cat, a rabbit, a bird. I torture and kill people. Sometimes I am a saber-toothed tiger, dripping blood from my mouth."

I asked her if she thought she was a saber-toothed tiger while I was speaking with her. She said that she thought she was, but that because of the lipstick she wore I could not see that her teeth were bloodied.

Sara was one of the more normal patients on Alpha. She became an active member of the patients' meeting and proposed motions about who should have open-door privileges. Alpha kept its doors unlocked. Patients could wander off the ward with permission when there were not scheduled activities. This privilege was denied if a patient went AWOL, e.g., went shopping all day in New Haven, missing group therapy or the scheduled noontime basketball game.

Sara dressed in a strange way. When she had a good day—if the people in group therapy encouraged her and her mother didn't visit—she wore pants. When she had a bad day, she wore a short red skirt that came just below her hips, and nothing underneath. Once in group therapy a male patient, Teddy, said he wanted to discuss Sara's skirt. He thought such an all-revealing skirt was a body signal that Sara was upset and wanted to upset others, including her psychiatrist.

Sara replied, "I don't think the way I am dressed is upsetting. I think it's normal. Are you upset, Teddy?"

"No," said Teddy, "I'm not upset, but your shrink is. Look at him, the way he's sitting. You're embarrassing him."

"Are you embarrassed?" Sara asked the psychiatrist. He kept on smoking his pipe. He looked from Sara to Teddy and back, but he never spoke. Psychiatrists never answered direct questions in group therapy. After this encounter I thought it was a wise practice.

Group therapy was upsetting because everyone criticized everyone else, but family sessions were worse. Here five or six patients and their parents, brothers and sisters sat in a crowded room with psychiatrists, nurses and medical students and everyone made "helpful suggestions" to each other. Each parent tried to prove that his or her child or spouse was not as crazy as someone else's. Teddy never spoke at group or family sessions. In fact, his remark about Sara's skirt was the first I had heard. He was called a catatonic schizophrenic, and had come to Alpha thinking he was Christ. He stood in the hallway with his arms stretched out. When group therapy met, he would be led into the room and would stand there with his arms outstretched while the group discussed whether his presence was upsetting. After a few weeks he put his arms down and walked around, but he did not speak. His parents were meek and quiet and just sat next to him during family sessions. Suddenly one night, in the middle of a particularly disagreeable family therapy session, Teddy began to talk, looking around rather wildly.

"There I was at home and it was no good, so I hitchhiked out, and I was on drugs and dope and I got to L.A. and I was high on STP and LSD and speed and I was far out and I got to Washington and the same thing, and the same thing, and then I hitchhiked some more and here I am." He stopped talking.

The family therapy session then discussed Teddy and decided it was good for him to talk, and that he had been punishing his parents by not talking. Everyone congratulated him. After that Teddy talked to his psychiatrist about being Christ, killing people, flying through the air and disintegrating. "Crazy talk" like this was discouraged on Alpha. The theory was that no one cared if you hallucinated if you didn't talk about it, so the nurses had to retrain Teddy.

"That is crazy talk, Teddy," a nurse would say, if he talked about being Christ.

When I left Alpha, Teddy knew when he was talking about hallucinations and he would suddenly say, "No, Teddy, that is crazy talk," and stop talking.

I spent an extra hour a day with a psychiatry resident who would analyze group therapy sessions to show me what had happened.

"It was a very interesting session," he would say.

"Yes, it was," I would agree, "a lot happened."

"Yes," he would say, "I thought Teddy was expressing inner anger."

93

"Yes," I would add, "and Sara was expressing *her* inner anger."

"That is not anger. If you analyze it, she is expressing hurt, isn't she? The way she spoke about her parents, the way she used her body?"

"Oh yes, it was more like inner hurt."

After a few weeks, I could discuss group therapy without attending it.

Alpha must have helped most of the patients because at least half went home, but one girl bothered me terribly. She was an ugly fourteen-year-old daughter of a millionaire. At home she had violent rages and broke the furniture, so she was sent to psychiatric hospitals. She seemed to try to do or say the right thing, but never could. She was upset if a nurse or patient said she ought to try harder. One day I read her chart. The child had been born with half a brain. Literally, one side of her brain was absent and she was retarded. I could not understand why a brain-damaged child was on a mental ward instead of in a special school. She seemed to be doing as well as she could with the brain she had. Perhaps her parents preferred to have a "disturbed" daughter rather than a retarded one.

Just before I started on Alpha, Cathy Flynn, who was on another rotation, had begun to worry me. She spoke very little to anyone and seemed far away. One morning the telephone operator at the dormitory switchboard asked me to check if Cathy was all right. She had sounded "funny" on the phone when she asked the operator what time it was. Cathy opened her door only a crack at first but then let me in. She had been crying. She was in her bathrobe and nightgown. They were clean, but rumpled and torn. Books and clothes were strewn about her room. The bedclothes were thrown off on the floor. We talked for fifteen minutes but she said nothing was wrong, she was perfectly all right. She decided to get dressed and go to breakfast. On the way down in the elevator she said casually that she had taken a sleeping pill in the middle of the night and that always made her look awful. I went off to work, worried about her but not knowing what, if anything, I should do. Cathy looked fine after that, and made a point of talking cheerfully with me after dinner in the dormitory.

Three weeks later, when I was assigned to Alpha, I was called one morning by the telephone operator again. She said an ambulance had come to take Cathy to the E.R. after a sleeping pill overdose. Would I go over in the ambulance with her? I reached Cathy's room just as two ambulance attendants wheeled her out. Wrapped in a sheet, strapped to a reclining wheelchair, she was tossing her head restlessly but she couldn't speak above a mumble. We arrived in the E.R., which was around the block. In a cubicle, two residents started to pump out her stomach and put in an intravenous. They asked me what happened, but I didn't know, except that she took an overdose. There was nothing else I could do. I left after they wheeled her to her hospital room on the private ward, accompanied by a medical intern, a resident and a psychiatry resident. She kept mumbling but no one could understand her.

Two days later she was allowed to have visitors. An older brother had paid her a brief visit and had gone home. Claire Christiansen and I went to visit her. Cathy looked horribly pale, with red-rimmed eyes, but her face was blank and obstinate. She said everyone was making a fuss about nothing. All she wanted to do was get back to medical school. I came out of her room certain, for some reason, that unless someone miraculously could help her change her mind, she was determined to kill herself. Her psychiatrist at first wanted to let her go back to the dorm, have a daily session with a psychiatrist and keep on going to medical school. He agreed with her that she had had a mild acute depression over a boyfriend and would soon recover. He changed his mind when, after reviewing the pharmacy records, he discovered that she had been collecting barbiturates and other sedatives, through forged prescriptions, for over a year. This gave him second thoughts, although he was not surprised to see a woman medical student behaving this way.

"Cathy and I have been close friends," said Claire one afternoon, "and I don't know what is going on with her. She talks about guilt a lot but she has nothing to feel guilty about."

"She told me she was depressed about her boyfriend but they broke up months ago. It doesn't make sense," I said.

"That's too superficial anyhow," said Claire. "I hope these shrinks stop talking about a woman medical-student adjustment reaction and get real with her. The male ego is unbelievable. I wouldn't kill myself over a guy, and you wouldn't either, but these guys are willing to believe anything. We have to convince them she's in deep trouble."

At Claire's suggestion, we went together to talk with a psychiatry attending. The professor we talked to said you could only help a person to a limited extent. If a person wanted to die, they would eventually kill themselves. I learned from Claire that Cathy had already been admitted once for an overdose, earlier in the month.

Cathy was a patient on Alpha while Claire and I were there on our rotation. We thought it would be embarrassing for all of us, but it was not. Cathy did everything she was supposed to. She looked quite normal, and attended the group therapy sessions I was assigned to. Her psychiatrist took Claire and me aside to reassure us. He was sure Cathy would be all right. He said that medical school was stressful, especially for women, and that a suicide "gesture" was statistically common in women her age and was rarely followed by successful suicide. In group therapy, when a nurse asked Cathy how she was doing, she said, "Very well, thank you." When asked why she had taken an overdose she said, "I was upset." She said the same thing to her psychiatrist. In morning report, in which psychiatrists reported to each other their progress with patients, her psychiatrist said she was well on the road to recovery. Cathy was discharged from Alpha and returned to the wards as a medical student, though she was to meet every week with her psychiatrist. She looked better, but still far away.

Psychiatry rotation ended when I submitted my in-depth analysis paper on Sara. I discussed Sara's past life and her probable future, but it seemed too factual to be submitted for psychiatry, so I softened it by inserting here and there on every page the words "deep," "meaningful" and "significant." Another problem was that I had consulted no sources, so the paper had no references. This problem was solved over the telephone one night, when my mother said I should quote Freud, whom I had indeed read one summer. I went to the library and took down Freud's *Complete Works* in twelve volumes from the reference shelves. I opened each volume at random and selected the first sentence of the first paragraph of the page at which the book happened to open. I inserted the quotations, one every three pages, and one on each of the last four pages of my psychiatry paper. The psychiatrist assigned to teach me had previously noted that I did not seem enthusiastic about psychiatry. My paper completely changed his opinion.

He and a professor had to read and grade my paper. They both cited in their notes the unusually pertinent, insightful quotations from Freud which added greatly to the understanding of Sara. The paper was given an A. My grade for the rotation was B+. I celebrated the end of psychiatry and the beginning of Oxford with Roy, Art and Lenny at dinner in the cafeteria. Lenny diverted the dietician's attention, Art kept a look-out, and Roy and I poured a fifth of whiskey into the coffee urn.

Rats, Mice and Oxford

The night before I left New Haven for Washington—I was leaving for Oxford from Dulles Airport—I had the same dream I had dreamed at Harvard exactly three years before, just before I took my last exam and left for Oxford for the first time. In the dream I was taking a Latin course but I went to the wrong course all semester, failed the exam and could not graduate. The dream was just as convincing the second time and I woke up thinking I was back in college.

I arrived in London at 7:00 A.M., after an all-night flight in an almost empty plane. No one visits London in January. I had a hotel room—I was staying one night in London before going on to Oxford—but the room would not be ready until two in the afternoon. It was exciting to be in London, but the fatigue impaired my judgment. I was looking for an umbrella because it was raining, and I almost bought the first one I saw—a frilly French parasol, in a Bond Street shop—priced at $120. The weather was cold and gray and I was freezing. It was 1970, the year of the miniskirt, and my coat ended just above my knees. I returned to the hotel and slept in the lobby until my room was ready. The next morning I took the first train from Paddington Station "up" to Oxford. Every train leaving London goes "down" except the one that goes "up" to Oxford.

Somerville College had allowed me to become a member of its Middle Common Room, which is the graduate student body, and I had a room in the new graduate building, with a picture window that looked directly into the second floor of a Chinese restaurant. The street was narrow and medieval, and I loved it.

There was an electric heater vending machine in the room. It heated the room for fifteen minutes if you put a half a crown (about a quarter) into a coin box. There was no other heating in the building, and the day I arrived I bought warm underwear. The college supplied a "scout," or maid, called Trudy who cleaned my room, made the bed and drank my sherry, filling the bottle with tap water so the sherry level would not look lower. She suggested once that I ought to buy a bottle of gin to see if I liked the taste.

At the end of the corridor was the bathroom, with a tub so deep you could bathe submerged with your nose poking out of the top of the water like a hippopotamus. Three other graduate students lived on the same floor: Laura, a Canadian scientist; Ann, a Welsh social worker; and Katherine, an Irish girl doing her graduate thesis on medieval German and Italian painting. They invited me to tea the next day, and we became good friends.

Besides being a member of the Somerville M.C.R., I was allowed to rejoin Queen Elizabeth House where I had lived the first time I went to Oxford. Q.E.H. was a club dining room and living quarters for Oxford students who came from British Commonwealth countries. Americans were allowed because America was an ex-colony. Q.E.H. was a former private home behind high iron gates with a stone wall around it and a large well-kept croquet lawn, frequently used for parties. The food was good, except for the Brussels sprouts and prunes, and the other members were delightful.

My first time in Oxford my Q.E.H. friends had included two American Rhodes Scholars, a Jamaican diplomat, a Vietnamese agricultural economist, a former chief of police of Madras, India, and a Pakistani princess with bodyguards and a staggering collection of emerald and diamond jewelry which she wore every day. By Moslem tradition she was a direct descendant of God via Mahomet, and considered herself above mere mortals such as myself. My best friend had been Antonia Miles, a lawyer from South Africa doing graduate work in economics. Antonia was still in Oxford, working for a D.Phil. degree, living half a block from Somerville in a basement flat with a herb garden. She was still a member of Q.E.H., and we met there for lunch. The Q.E.H. dining room was intimidating because I did not know anyone, but after lunch Antonia took me to the Common Room, where coffee was served.

I met "George," H.R.H. Toupouto'a, Crown Prince of Tonga. George's distant ancestors had been Mongolian invaders, coming to the Tonga Islands from the Chinese mainland. George still looked like a Mongolian warlord, and was in anguish that day because he could not grow a good mustache, just Fu-Manchu wisps, after six months of trying.

"Jackson," or Epele Nailatikau, was George's cousin and a member of the Fiji royalty. He had been sent to Oxford to keep George out of trouble. Jackson was a tall, strong army officer who grew a beautiful mustache. They were both studying economics, and could both drink alcohol in enormous amounts without any apparent ill effect. One evening I talked with them in the Common Room as they each drank a sociable quart of Chivas Regal and discussed Third World politics.

Also at Q.E.H. were Ahmed, member of the royal family of Afghanistan and grandson of the King of Afghanistan who beat the British at the Khyber Pass; H.R.H. Dlamini, Crown Prince of Swaziland; and a former member of the Tanzania parliament. Ahmed was dark-eyed and handsome, and although I had never met a prince before, I adore dark, handsome men. Ahmed spoke excellent English but he said little and just watched me intently while I talked with George and the others. As Antonia and I left Q.E.H. that afternoon she remarked casually, "You know, Elizabeth, you have to be wary of these Moslem men. They are *all* married. Some have several wives."

I arrived in Oxford on a Friday. On Monday morning at eight o'clock I was in the Oxford teaching hospital, called the Radcliffe Infirmary, looking for Professor Hunter, but all I found was a charlady who was startled to see me. She explained that "nobody" came until nine in the morning. Professor Hunter was the first person to arrive, at 8:30, long before his secretary. He was very nice to me, and sat down to talk with me about my research. He was well-built, handsome, had silver-gray hair and looked the part of Eminent Professor, which he was. He was pleased that I had done all the reading he had recommended and reassured me that I would soon learn how to do research quite handily but it would take time to get my project started. His laboratory was doing research on the eosinophil, a kind of white blood cell that fights off parasite infections. His plan was that I would show whether a combined infection of parasites and bacteria would increase or decrease eosinophils in mice and rats. I took notes as Professor Hunter outlined my work for the next nine months. It seemed simple. I would infect rats and mice with *Trichinella*, a parasite which causes trichinosis. *Trichinella* increases the eosinophils in the blood. Then I would infect some rats and mice with bacteria, so they would get pneumonia as well as trichinosis. I would kill the rats, examine the blood and bone marrow to see whether eosinophils were being increased only in the marrow or were being released into the blood. Pneumonia might prevent eosinophil release from the bone marrow.

Professor Hunter observed that the first problem was "getting the techniques down," and assigned one of his three graduate students to help me. John Miller, a doctor from Rhodesia, was the one chosen to teach me because he was using the *Trichinella*, too. With great solemnity John showed me the ether jar where we anesthetized the rats. To infect them with *Trichinella* we threaded a tube into the stomach. To inject the bacteria, we inserted a hypodermic needle into a large tail vein. Then John explained how to prepare the *Trichinella* parasites for injection. Special rats were grown as *Trichinella* parasite carriers. Whenever we needed *Trichinella*, we killed a special rat by chopping off its head.

"It is a bit messy," said John, "but you'll get the hang of it. Do wear a white lab coat over your dress." We skinned the special rat, discarded the skin and put the skinned carcass through a standard meat grinder. "Sounds a bit macabre, but it's not so bad," said John. He told me I could kill mice by chopping their heads off or holding them by the tail and whacking them hard against the edge of the counter. I could kill the rats the same way, but the rats we used were so inbred their tails tended to come off before you could crack the head against the tabletop. Then the rat would fall on the floor and you had to chase it about the lab. It was easier to give the rats ether instead.

I spent that day learning how to grind rat carcasses in meat grinders. Everyone met for tea at eleven o'clock and four o'clock, and after the afternoon tea I went to meet my own rats and mice. There were eight plastic cages set aside for me, with two to three rats or ten to twenty mice per cage. The cages were stacked one on top of another in wire slots, twelve cages across, and six high. The rooms were installed with specially controlled heating and lighting, because variations in heat or light could upset the eosinophils. I was fascinated by the mice. One of my mice had just had babies and they crawled all over her, squeaking. In another cage, three acrobatic mice crawled upside down along the underside of the wire cage top. When they lost their footing and fell into the cedar chips on the cage bottom, they squeaked happily and started all over again. I took a mouse out and let it climb up my arm, under my already grubby lab coat. It walked hesitantly up the arm, across the back of my neck and appeared down my other arm, peering up out of the lab coatsleeve. When I tried to pick it up, it backed up my arm again. I finally had to take off my coat and shake the mouse gently back into the cage. The mice were sweet. The rats looked horrid. They had dirty-white, short stiff hair, pink eyes and long faces with sharp teeth. I was startled to find that I had spent an hour playing with the mice. They reminded me of my brother's pet hamster, Snuffy, and I didn't like the idea of skinning an animal that looked like Snuffy and then putting it through a meat grinder. I also was not attracted by the idea of infecting the mice with *Trichinella*. John Miller's *Trichinella*-infected mice looked dispirited, lying with their heads on their paws, panting. However, to be a successful university doctor you have to do research, and if I was going to stop my research because the mice reminded me of Snuffy, I would get nowhere. I started on my project the next day. I wrote down outlines for various experiments and made charts of how many rats would be assigned to each experimental group, and it was a very tidy chart. I labeled my research notebook, and wrote a paragraph on the design and goal of each experiment. Then it was one o'clock and I went to Queen Elizabeth House for lunch. Antonia was not there and Ahmed sat next to me. When I returned at two, it was clear that I had dawdled long enough on paperwork. It was time to get down to work, and John suggested I infect some test rats for a dry run.

I gathered up ten rats in a basket. They were ugly rodents, and I didn't think it would bother me at all to kill them. I brought in my special parasite rat and killed him with ether. I watched as the rat ran around the glass ether jar, first angrily, then frantically, and then very, very slowly, until it lay down. After a few more minutes, it stopped breathing and died. It was still warm when I took it out and cut through the skin. Skin and fur hang loosely on a rat, and can be peeled off like a coat. Then I chopped up the carcass, which smelled rather awful, and pushed it through the meat grinder. Finally I had a cup of ground rat, and I shook it up with culture medium to get the *Trichinella* parasites in the liquid. It was now time to feed the parasite solution to the ten experimental rats, but I wasn't sure I could do it. I thought of putting it off until the next day, but if I did, I would have to grind up another special rat. I had to be tougher. One after another I put the ten rats into the ether jar. The first flopped over, anesthetized. I pulled him out, pushed a second into the ether jar, shoved a tube into the mouth of the first rat, pushed the tube down to his stomach, and injected the parasite solution. Then I remembered I had not brought a cage for the parasite-injected rats. The first was still asleep. I set him down on the counter, and hastily pulled number two from the ether jar, almost dead. Number three went into the ether, and I injected parasites into number two. I pulled out number three, pushed number four into the ether, and injected number three with parasites. Then rat number two took a deep breath and died. Rat number one woke up, walked to the edge of the counter, and fell off. I picked him up, but had no cage to put him in. I rushed out of the room closing the door behind me and went to find another cage. I found one. When I returned, rat number four had died because I left him in the ether jar. Rat number three had also woken up and walked off the edge of the counter. He was now under the sink, trying to crawl into an empty laboratory flask. This was too much. I chased him furiously around the flask and caught him by the tail. He gave a jerk and I was left with just the tail. The rat was as surprised as I was, and came back to look for his tail. I caught him by the scruff of the neck and put him in the cage, along with rat number one. I threw the tail into the trash with the two dead rats. It was now five o'clock. As the sun set over the ancient city of Oxford, I watched white rats flop over in an ether jar and I injected them with parasites. I finished at about seven, and took the rats back to their special heat- and light-controlled rat room. I took off my lab coat and washed my hands several times but they still felt dirty. I rushed to my room at Somerville, changed, and sprayed on too much perfume. I felt as though I smelled of rats. At dinner I had little appetite. A sympathetic Persian remarked flirtatiously that if the charming American lady did not eat more than those tiny bites, she would become too thin and loose all her beauty. Mr. Ali, the man from Somalia, said no one could eat the awful English food, which had no taste. He offered me his special imported very hot pepper pickle and promised it would help. Later that evening I made coffee for myself in the Somerville Common Room and sat thinking about research. I decided perhaps mice were better than rats.

For the next several months, I tried both mice and rats. I wondered if there was a sex difference when it came to animal research. The men didn't mind but I hated killing the animals, or watching them sicken with *Trichinella*. I especially hated the meat grinder. Finally I decided to do one big experiment, so big that if I made enough slides, I could spend a long, long time studying those slides. I did, and it worked.

The results of my experiments interested Professor Hunter, but I think he realized early that I did not have a talent for laboratory research. It puzzled him, because he was very gifted himself. When he learned that I hoped to be a surgeon, a look of enlightenment came over his face. He was an internal medicine-hematology-infectious disease specialist. He did not expect surgeons to be able to think or to have a flair for research. Nevertheless, he spent a lot of time advising me on the project and insisted that we publish my results. I felt famous when the short article, "Post-infectious Eosinopenia," by Morgan et al., was published in a British medical journal.

It took me a long time to resign myself to the fact that I did not like research and was not good at it. In American medicine, research had become so fashionable that people said you could not be a good doctor unless you did lab research. Fortunately for me, Nixon cut back research grants, and by the time I returned to America, most chiefs of surgery did not insist on experimental animal research during residency.

Oxford was lovely when I was not doing research, and I had a wonderful time, although later I regretted not taking time off to travel for a few weeks around Europe. I was too much in awe of Professor Hunter to ask for a vacation and the idea of anyone wanting to take time away from the laboratory did not occur to him. Life was not bleak though. Oxford inspires people to give parties. Antonia Miles, Katherine Walsh and I gave dinner parties at Somerville, and I gave a surprisingly successful "American cocktail party" for fifty guests. It lasted all night. I had not been sure that the English would like cocktails but we went through dozens of bottles of gin, Scotch and bourbon. George, the Prince of Tonga, took the all-night survivors on to his suite for a champagne and caviar breakfast "to help us recover."

I went to Paris with Antonia one spring weekend, and stayed with Christian and Gigi, friends of ours from my first Oxford stay. Antonia traveled back to England in a first-class boat train with Prince Toupouto'a of Tonga and his cousin-bodyguard. I went back by plane, because I wanted to be in the laboratory on Monday, and because I missed Ahmed. Yes, he was married, and yes, I knew I was foolish and would regret it, but I had never been deeply in love before.

In June, term ended and the tourists began to arrive. Two weeks after the end of term, Ahmed had to return to Afghanistan. The night before he left I started to cry.

"Don't cry," he said angrily, "I can't stand it. In Afghanistan a man can never go away for one night without the women weeping and wailing. I hate it."

I stopped. The next morning I drove him to the train and said good-bye. At the end of the day I called my mother transatlantic and cried for an hour. I was saved from complete loneliness by my younger brother, Rob, who came to England and spent several weeks touring with me in the ancient car I had bought for $50. Just before I left Oxford, Rob sold it for me to a junk and scrap-metal dealer for five dollars. Then Rob and I met my mother in Paris and we traveled to Geneva, Rome and Venice. My only regret was not having had the courage to ask for more time off, but I had had a wonderful nine months.

Cathy

When I arrived at medical school after nine months away, the rest of my class had not yet recovered from Cathy Flynn's suicide. In June, when I was in Oxford and the academic year was about to end, Cathy disappeared. A few days earlier her psychiatrist had gone on vacation, leaving her in the care of a colleague. Everyone thought she had gone home. She had taken no more overdoses since the episode that landed her on Alpha, and she had seemed happy. A week after she disappeared another woman student noticed a bad smell coming from Cathy's room. The security officer broke down the door, and found she had shot herself through the head with a shotgun. No one knew where she got it.

When we met at meals in the cafeteria all that year, men in my class would ask me, "Why did Cathy do it? She never acted as though anything was wrong. What's wrong with medical school that a woman has to kill herself?"

I certainly didn't know. Each medical school class usually had one person commit suicide, or try to. In my four years two women tried and two men tried, and one woman and one man succeeded—but only eight percent of the school were women. Perhaps that made it easier for Cathy to feel lonely and isolated. The men relaxed with rowdy parties, drinking and sex, but the women in the dorm couldn't have a boyfriend to dinner without having it noticed and commented on. We were always on display.

"Who cares?" exploded Claire one day when she was asked at lunch if another woman student was sleeping with one of the men. Claire moved out of the dormitory, but I couldn't afford an apartment in a safe neighborhood, and besides, I liked the sociability of the dorm.

I never knew the reason Cathy killed herself. She insisted up to the end that nothing was wrong, but she was determined to die. I had often felt oppressed by the pressure of medical school and isolated as a woman but Cathy's suicide was too much for me to understand. And medical school was three-quarters over when she died.

During my first rotation that year, which was pediatrics, I began to worry about where I would do my internship. Our class was divided into the East Coasters and the West Coasters. The West Coasters included Claire, who had gone to Stanford and longed to go back to California where she could play tennis all year round. The East Coasters included me, Leslie Andrews and Maureen Corcoran. For some reason none of us understood, we all three wanted to become surgeons. Maureen was interested in a New York internship, Leslie in New England, and I in the South or New England. I applied to six university teaching hospitals in the North and South.

The attraction of applying for internship was that each hospital required a personal interview, which meant we had to take a week or more off to travel around the country. The drawback was that we spent a small fortune on plane fares.

The first hospital I visited was in the mountains of North Carolina. The buildings were beautiful, the teaching was good, but there were few patients.

Next I visited a major training hospital in the South. I was interviewed at nine o'clock in the morning along with a man who was also applying for a surgical internship. The surgeon interviewing us started by saying, in a deep Southern accent, "Let me give you an idea of the kind of doctor we're looking for here." He smiled at me and said, "Young lady, you're from Yale, aren't you? Yes. Well, look at the pictures of this year's interns. You'll notice we don't have any Indians in our internship. We don't need to take them. We always fill up with superior candidates. We don't have no blacks, either. Young lady, I just want you to see that we don't need no furriners in our program here. We're a strong program. We've never taken a female. We don't need furriners in our internship." The male applicant looked at me sideways, embarrassed but complacent. He knew I wouldn't be competing with him for a place.

"We have a lot of violence in this city," the surgeon went on. "Now, in the hospital itself a few people have been shot, but only two people killed. One patient was gunned down standing right by the front elevator. We have not lost a doctor yet." Security officers with guns stood at every hospital entrance. The violence didn't appeal to me, and I wasn't wanted. I refused an invitation to stay for lunch and left.

Though the violence surprised me then, a resident from a hospital in a bad Chicago area told me that the residents carried guns in shoulder holsters under their white coats, and one day in an argument over a girl two residents had a gun fight in the hospital cafeteria.

I arrived at my third hospital after dark. The cab drove through miles of square two-story houses and rows of concrete and wooden buildings. It was warm, but there was no one on the streets. The next day I was interviewed, and a surgeon warned me that the residents did so much emergency surgery that they could never attend the teaching conferences.

"You certainly learn how to operate," one surgeon said, "but you may not know what operation you ought to be doing. Our boys—we don't have any women—spend too much time cutting to have time to think."

On our tour of the E.R. he said, "We see mostly shotgun blasts and they can blow you away. People don't kid around here." The E.R. had a "shotgun room," with intravenous solutions hanging from the ceiling, blood in the refrigerator, an x-ray machine focused on a fully equipped operating table. According to my calculations, one percent of the population was shot every year. On the way to the airport, my cabdriver told me what he did after his son was beaten up by a boy at school. "I took my shotgun and went around to speak to the boy's father. I fired at his house, and said if it happened again, I'd shoot at him instead of his porch. My son was never beat up again."

That didn't sound good to me. I had thought I wanted a hospital with a lot of trauma but I hadn't realized that a lot of trauma meant a lot of violent crime. It was bad enough at Yale where you had to be careful after dark, but in these places, a woman couldn't walk on the street safely in daylight. I had to think again, and spent a long time studying the A.M.A. green manual which listed all the teaching programs in the country.

My surgical faculty adviser had given me no help. Back at Yale we talked constantly about what to look for—was it high salary, good teaching, a prestige name, lots of cutting? Many classmates were headed for the West Coast. I agonized, tore my hair, wondered if surgery was the right field for me, and finally sent my list into the computer where all the nations' senior medical students are matched with the hospital that wants them for an internship. I had decided to stay in New England.

In my spare time in my senior year I would go to the E.R. to see if there was any sewing for me to do. I had learned on surgery how to put in stitches but that had been almost a year ago. The residents in the E.R. were glad to have senior medical students help out, and I was glad of the chance to practice. I could hold surgical instruments properly, with my thumb and ring finger, for more control and power, but I was clumsy and slow. One day Dr. Mendelssohn, the chief private plastic surgeon, walked through a cubicle where I was working. I was hunched over the cut arm, tense, concentrating on putting the stitch in right.

"Relax, relax," said Dr. Mendelssohn, patting my shoulder. "It can't be as hard as it looks."

I looked up. It was my chance to meet an important surgeon. "Dr. Mendelssohn, I don't think you know me. I'm Elizabeth Morgan, a senior medical student going into surgery."

"Oh, I know you. Women are easy to remember. It's all the men who are hard to keep straight. I want you to think about specializing in plastic surgery, but first I want to see you put in that stitch properly. Sit up, get your head out of the light. Now pronate your hand so the needle goes through the skin at a right angle. Pronate more. More. Good, now bring the needle up through the skin of the other side. Now tie it down. Only three knots with silk suture. Good girl. Now do them all like that." He smiled and left.

Starting Over
Internship

Internship Begins

My first choice for internship was an Ivy League teaching hospital in New England. A nationwide computer system matched student choices against hospital choices, and those results were mailed to the Dean of each medical school, who handed them out on a Wednesday afternoon in April. I was accepted by my first choice, and everyone in the class "matched," even if not with their first choice. Claire was accepted by Stanford, and it turned out that Mark Lehman, Leslie Andrews, Eric Nieman and I would be interns together at the same teaching hospital. We all congratulated one another, a keg of beer arrived, compliments of the Dean, and we all said the four years had gone quickly.

"Even for me," said Mary, Mark Lehman's wife.

Maureen Corcoran, Claire Christiansen, Leslie Andrews and I all had our first choices.

"All right, kids," said Claire to Maureen, Leslie and me, "now you can tell me why you all want to be surgeons. You have at least five years of being on call every other night, and professors who will drive you extra hard because you're women. Why?"

We had a lot of reasons. Surgery was interesting, challenging, and. . . .

"Beats me," said Leslie. "We like it, we can do it, and why not?"

We didn't know it, but we were part of the new wave of women in surgery which started with women like us in the class of '71.

I began to worry about my internship the next day. My last rotation at medical school was dermatology. There was no weekend or night call, which left plenty of time for further agony. I started to study surgery and found I was ignorant. The more I read, the more certain I became that I would never remember enough. I knew I could never manage a surgical emergency alone.

We graduated in June and it felt strange to be an M.D. so suddenly. I spent the three weeks before my internship started sitting on the living room rug at home in Washington, remarking at invervals that I would never survive a week as a surgical intern and would be sent home disgraced. To take my mind off the future I tried out recipes in a cookbook my mother gave me, but I was too preoccupied. Instead of grinding up peppercorns, I pounded them into the steak. No one would eat more than a bite except my father, who courageously chewed and swallowed the whole peppercorns embedded in the meat. It was a relief to the family when my internship finally began.

It started at 7:00 A.M. on June 23, 1971. The temperature was already in the 90s as eighteen new surgical interns gathered in the hospital auditorium. The men were issued white pants and jackets. Leslie and I were given white skirts instead of pants. The skirts were too wide at the waist, too narrow in the hips, and ended three inches above the ankle. This was the small size.

A senior surgical resident gave us an orientation lecture. He said, "I know all of you are scared of going into the wards as surgeons when you were just medical students yesterday. I was scared, too. You guys assigned to the private wing had better go over there now and find out what's happening. You've inherited some sick patients to look after."

"You guys" meant Mark Lehman, Eric Nieman, me, and an intern I did not know. The private unit was a five-hundred-bed hospital annex, reserved for the patients of doctors in private practice. There were four surgical wards, each with forty patients. One intern was assigned to each ward. There was an eight-bed I.C.U. supervised by a first-year resident. Mark Lehman introduced the other intern, Zach Bernard, who came from Texas and later went back to Baylor to do heart surgery with DeBakey. Zach was last heard of, single again after his divorce, successful in a heart surgery practice, scooting around Houston in a Maserati sports coupe. From the first day I met him he knew he wanted to be a heart surgeon. Mark was cheerful and confident. He slapped me on the shoulder, called me Lizzie, and asked me how it felt to be facing slow death by torture on private surgery.

"This is supposed to be the most horrible way to begin, kid," he said happily.

I was too nervous to say anything, but my face had a grimly determined look which amused Mark. "Cool it," he said, "the surgeons won't ride you just because you're a girl."

The four of us walked over to the private ward and were greeted by the senior resident in charge.

"If you can survive this place in summer, you can survive anything in your internship or in Vietnam. The service is very busy. Everyone schedules their elective surgery in the summer. The emergency admissions from car accidents come in all the time. There is no air conditioning. Even at slow times, do not expect to sleep your nights on call. You'll get used to it. Two of you are on call every night in the hospital. Elizabeth, you have Monday, Monday night, Tuesday, then Wednesday, Wednesday night, Thursday and Friday. You get Thursday and Friday nights *off*—because you will be on call in the hospital this weekend from Saturday at 8:00 A.M. until Monday at 8:00 P.M. or so—whenever you get your work done. Next week, night call is reversed. You are expected to start seeing your patients by 6:00 A.M. on weekdays, because it will take you an hour and a half to see them and you have to be in the O.R. by 7:30. You will get at least five, usually ten, new patients a day to work up. History and physical exams on each of them have to be good, or you'll kill someone. On a weekend you get about twenty new patients. Tom, the intern who just finished here, claims the all-time record—thirty new patients on a Sunday afternoon. The four of you should go to your wards and start work. Check the operating schedule first to make sure you're not scheduled to assist in the O.R. this morning. Good luck, and don't worry, most of you will do fine. Elizabeth, the private surgeons really objected to the idea of working with a woman, but don't let it bother you."

The patients on my ward belonged to general surgeons, urologists, plastic surgeons, orthopedic surgeons, and neurosurgeons. The head nurse, Miss Libby, a thin, energetic woman, devoted herself to helping me, stood up for me when surgeons complained, and tried to remember what orders she should remind me to write.

No matter what I was doing I felt ridiculous and awkward in my hospital whites. They were hot, uncomfortable, and the tight hip cut made me walk like a duck. At the end of the week I hated them so much that I sent the skirts to the hospital laundry and never picked them up. I worked in my street clothes and carried the offensive white jacket. The nurses were upset, for my sake. They said my clothes would be ruined with blood—and other things—spilled on them, but they showed me how to remove blood with hydrogen peroxide and the rest came out with soap and water.

In the second week I lost my white coat. Several surgeons objected. "You have to wear whites," said one of them. "It's a surgery department rule. Otherwise, no one knows you're a doctor. Especially being a woman. You're a professional now, a surgeon, so dress like one."

I said I had lost the coat, and the skirt did not fit, but I was cowed and had decided to go back into whites when Dr. Wallace walked by me. "Fantastic," he said. "I like it. I like it."

"What do you mean?"

"Your clothes, your street clothes. You look like a woman again, Elizabeth. Don't let these turkeys tell you what to wear. They're not your mother."

"I don't look like a surgeon in street clothes."

"Wrong, dear, you mean you don't look like a male surgeon. There are no female surgeons. You can wear anything you damn well please."

I successfully avoided whites for four more years, until Dr. Mulveney in Boston ordered everyone on his service to wear them. I could only find a size 42 discarded coat belonging to a surgeon who was six feet tall. I wore the coat for a month, and lost it when I threw it into a wastebasket instead of the laundry basket. Dr. Mulveney did not ask me to get another coat.

On Call

On my first day as an intern I began to learn the true meaning of being a doctor. I had read some patients' charts and walked off the ward to see an x-ray, when Miss Libby ran after me asking for an order for aspirin. I could not remember each of the fifty patients so I ran back, my hair soaked from the heat, to check the chart carefully to be sure that the patient was not allergic to aspirin. In medical school we were taught all the possible drug complications. People with stomach ulcers, for example, can develop fatal bleeding if they are given aspirin, so even as simple a task as writing the order for aspirin filled me with anxiety. I saw myself wreaking havoc on people's lives, with patients collapsing everywhere from strange drug reactions, but nothing untoward happened. I lived in a state of fear for most of my internship, but after two days I had so many other things to worry about that I was less anxious about fatal aspirin reactions.

I spent the first day reading patients' charts, trying to decipher other interns' handwriting to learn what was wrong. I admitted three new patients, which included writing up a history and physical examination for each one, sending laboratory blood studies, and ordering a cardiogram and a chest x-ray. It took me over an hour for each patient. The routine lab tests are done to detect "silent" diseases that might kill a patient during surgery, e.g., a recent heart attack, pneumonia, diabetes, anemia. I ordered all the tests, but I did not have time to think clearly. One patient was admitted to have his prostate removed the next day. He had severe heart disease and frequent angina, but his cardiogram that afternoon showed no new heart damage. I was called at 3:00 A.M. because he had a bout of severe angina. The nurse wanted an order for nitroglycerin for him. At 3:00 A.M. I was still doing the "day's" work, giving blood transfusions, even waking patients to have them sign permits for their morning surgery four hours away. I ordered the nitroglycerin, checked the patient, who said he felt fine, and kept on working. I had to draw blood, examine patients with fevers, and complete paperwork for patients scheduled for surgery. I had had no lunch or dinner, but grabbed a chocolate from a box left by a grateful patient each time I passed the nurses' desk. (Internship ruined my teeth—my dentist is still working on them—and I gained ten pounds.) I would have done more good if I had junked the scut work and done a cardiogram on the patient with chest pain.

The next day in the recovery room I overheard two surgeons talking.

"He just arrested on the table. The anesthesiologist gave him Pentothal and started to put the tube in his lungs. I looked over at the cardiac monitor and suddenly a straight line, no heartbeat. We resuscitated him but look at him." He nodded toward a patient on a respirator with cardiologists around him, deciding on anti-ar-rhythmic drugs. "He'll go out of here in a casket. He had a massive heart attack last night and he complained of chest pain, but the stupid intern just ignored it."

I looked closely. It was my patient. I wanted to quit right then, but I was called to help on an operation. The senior resident took me aside later.

"Elizabeth, the man was dying from heart disease before he came into the hospital. He had almost constant angina. He didn't have long to live. As an intern you'll make lots of mistakes because you'll always be tired and overworked, but remember—the death rate for giving anesthesia to someone who's recently had a heart attack is fifty to eighty percent, and anyone who complains to you of chest pains has had a heart attack until proved otherwise."

My patient died a few days later, and I've never forgotten him.

I didn't quit either. The private surgeons' reaction would be "typical hysterical female" and I wasn't going to give them that satisfaction, or leave the rest of the interns in the lurch to do my work.

At 5:30 A.M. three days later, I had finished the previous day's work, and was half an hour away from a new day's work. I went to the on-call room, which was right on the ward, and lay down. Immediately the bedside phone rang and a nurse screamed, "Dr. Morgan, Mr. Antonelli has just arrested!"

I ran down the hall into Mr. Antonelli's room. I could not remember who he was or what operation he had had. It didn't matter. His heart had stopped and he needed to be resuscitated. Instead, I pounded his chest, which was the wrong thing to do. Pumping the heart will not keep you alive if there is no oxygen in the blood. Just behind me, fortunately, was Tom, the first-year surgical resident. He seemed so skilled at resuscitation that I felt inept. He told me to stop cardiac massage, and slipped a tube into Mr. Antonelli's lungs. Mark Lehman arrived to help. Tom told me to start cardiac massage again, and as I did so, Tom put an intravenous catheter into Mr. Antonelli's neck vein and Mark squeezed the oxygen bag to breathe for him.

"He's under control now," said Tom. "What's he in for?"

I could not remember. The nurse brought back his chart as Mark sent off emergency blood tests. "Don't worry," Tom assured me, "It's your first week." Mr. Antonelli had just had an exploratory operation which had shown incurable stomach cancer. He had a few months to live.

"Let me call his private doctor," said Tom.

When he returned a few moments later, Mr. Antonelli's heart had not responded, but Mark and I were still working to save him.

"Call it off," said Tom. "His surgeon agrees we shouldn't bring him back so he can suffer with cancer."

We stopped. The nurse pulled the tubes out from his lungs and his vein. His skin turned the color of dough. Tom told me to pronounce him dead and then call the family for an autopsy. I checked my watch for the time of death—6:03 A.M. Then I called his wife at home. She did not know me, and I had a curious feeling of detached cruelty when I introduced myself and went on to say that her husband had just died. I said I was sorry, and asked her, as we had to, if she would permit an autopsy. I remembered the cadavers we dissected in anatomy, and I imagined a pathology resident doing the autopsy in the morgue. Cadaver dissection on Mr. Antonelli seemed macabre, and I felt strange asking for his body. She refused, saying, "He has suffered so much, I don't want him to suffer any more."

Tom had been listening in astonishment, and when I hung up he said, "Elizabeth, you won't get an autopsy that way. You have to be tough. You may even have to try a few tricks—say we need it to remove valuable gold suture material or else we add the cost of the gold to the hospital bill."

I knew I had not been good at it, but gold suture tricks sounded a bad idea. At least I survived my first arrest. Mark called me from his ward to suggest we meet in the cafeteria for breakfast.

"Lizzie baby," he said, "internship is going to be hell. Have a cigarette."

He bummed two—one for me, one for him—from a lab technician at the next table. I had quit a year before, but smoked at least a pack a day for the rest of my internship. Then I stopped again—permanently.

Birthday Cake

Life is hard after two weeks of twelve-and-a-half working days, including seven days without any sleep and the other five ending at seven at night or later. I slept a total of fifty hours in those two weeks. I knew this was what surgical internship would be. The surgery was fascinating, and I learned an enormous amount about taking care of patients and diagnosing disease, but it was hard. The four of us on the private service were continually criticized by the private surgeons for being five minutes late for surgery, for forgetting to order a test, for not doing what we could not do because we spent the whole day in the operating room. Dr. Hillebrand, chief of surgery, made a point of taking us on teaching rounds every week, arranging a weekly two-hour teaching session for us, and listening to us when we felt a patient was not being treated properly or getting adequate attention from his surgeon. Several surgeons encouraged us, tried to teach us, and make life easier for us; several made a point of shouting at and complaining about interns; most of them just took us for granted. We took care of their patients, held retractors in the operation and, in exchange, had glimpses of what they were doing during surgery.

Teaching conferences were hardest. I wanted to learn but as soon as I sat down I fell asleep. So did Mark, Eric and Zach. We would listen for a few moments, at the back of the lecture hall, and then our eyelids would droop and our heads would slump forward until one of us snored and woke us all up.

"Aren't you guys interested in learning?" said Dr. Chester angrily one morning after Surgical Grand Rounds. "This is a teaching program. These conferences are for you."

"Screw you," said Mark under his breath.

I was scrubbing my hands later that morning to assist Dr. Wallace on a gallbladder.

"Jesus," he said, "are you sick?"

"No."

"You look dead white. Have you checked your hematocrit? You look anemic, but you're probably just tired, aren't you? How much cutting are you getting?"

"Not much."

"No appendix? No hernia? Okay, now you can't take my patient's gallbladder out—that's for next year—but I want you to make the incision. I bet you haven't held a scalpel yet."

I hadn't but I did that day. I stood on the right side—the operating side—and I was about to become a real surgeon.

"Scalpel," I said.

"All right!" said Dr. Wallace. "Give the lady a knife."

I took the scalpel.

"Hold it like a pen," said Dr. Wallace.

I was too nervous to remember how I held a pen and he took my hand and positioned my fingers correctly. I cut along the incision he had marked out in blue surgical ink on his patient's belly. I cut a fraction of a millimeter through the skin.

"At this rate we'll be here till midnight," said Dr. Wallace. "You have to lean on that blade to get through the skin. Don't think nice thoughts. Think mean. Tough. Cut that skin."

I leaned on the scalpel and cut through. I concentrated to keep cutting on the marked line, obscured now by blood.

"Keep the blade at ninety degrees to the skin. Don't bevel the edge or it's hard to sew closed," said Dr. Wallace.

He put a surgical sponge—like a flat towel—on either side of the cut skin to absorb the blood.

"Torpedoes ahead. I want you to cut right through the muscle. Forget the bleeding, let me take care of that." He had clamps ready, one in each hand.

I cut into the muscle, hit an artery immediately and jumped with surprise.

"Cut! Cut! A little bleeding never hurt anyone," commanded Dr. Wallace, and I kept cutting.

"Whoa. Stop. Gentle. You're about to get into the belly, and I told you you had to wait till next year. Give her an inch and she takes a mile. Typical surgeon." It was the ultimate compliment.

My birthday came on July 9, two and a half weeks after internship began. I would be 25. I love birthday cake and ice cream and having a bit of fuss made over me on my birthday. You do not have cake, ice cream and fuss when you are an intern, and I knew it. The nurses knew it was my birthday and wished me happy birthday as I walked on the ward at six in the morning. The rest of the day, from seven until four, I spent in the O.R. I had no lunch, and my legs ached. The operation I was scrubbed on was a varicose vein removal on the fat legs of a fat lady of forty. She had large varicose veins from the groin to the ankle on both legs. They did not bother her, but she wanted them removed because they were ugly. The surgeon arrived late, causing me to lament the extra hour's sleep I had lost by being on time. I had felt quite friendly toward the patient at seven that morning but we started surgery at nine, and by noon I hated her legs. I was so tired that I couldn't keep my eyes focused. The main varicose saphenous vein had been stripped out by the surgeon but the strippers were not the right size, and it had taken us three hours to do. The rest of the operation would take another three hours. The surgeon and I each bent over a leg, cutting through the skin, poking, finding each small bloated vein that had not come out with the stripper, and trying to dissect it out. Her being fat made it harder. Hold it, shake my head to wake up, pull it, blink to focus, hold it, pull it—and then the vein I was working on ripped out, because my hand jerked involuntarily from fatigue.

"You'll never be a surgeon if that's the best you can do," the surgeon snapped. "Keep working—don't stop."

I apologized and shook my head to wake myself up.

"Don't do that. You're shaking the table."

My shoulders slumped with fatigue.

"Sit up straight. Your head's blocking the light."

I gritted my teeth, leaned back to try to focus my eyes, then sighed and started again. I hated fat. My skin felt dirty. I had had no time to

123

take a shower or change my underwear in twenty-four hours. I hated varicose veins and began again to cut, poke, grasp, pull, grasp. "Fat, fat, fat," I chanted to myself angrily. I felt sadistically triumphant as I extracted a thick, blue, four-inch wormlike vein.

Behind my angry chant, I was unhappy. Surgical interns never felt sorry for themselves, but I did, and I knew it was very weak of me. It seemed hard that I should work all the time and get no appreciation on my birthday. The surgeon didn't know it was my birthday, but I was sure he wouldn't care if he did know. No one cared about me. I was surprised by how sorry I felt for myself, because I didn't think I was quite so immature, but I was still unhappy. It gave me some satisfaction to imagine how astounded the surgeon would be if I suddenly started to cry, contaminate the operation with unsterile tears, and say I wanted a birthday party, clean clothes and a bath.

We got the last vein out at 3:15, and by 4:00 I had scrawled the postoperative orders, dressed, and was dragging my way back to the ward to see what work awaited me and what disasters had taken place since seven.

A nurse greeted me, saying that the man in room 507 had suddenly gone into shock. His blood pressure had just fallen to $80/20$. "Bit of a rotten birthday, isn't it?" said Miss Libby happily as I rushed to room 507. The patient was a pink-faced Irish man chewing gum and watching TV. He was not in shock. His blood pressure was $130/70$. He watched me take his blood pressure in amazement, and asked me what was going on.

"You are absolutely fine," I said. "You are doing beautifully. Just a routine check," and I walked out of the room saying to myself, "Stupid nurse cannot even measure a blood pressure correctly."

"Dr. Morgan," called Miss Libby, "might I see you for just one moment please? In the nurses' lounge. It *must* be private."

"Now what have I done?" I asked, annoyed and depressed, as I walked toward the nurses' lounge. I got on well with the nurses. They did everything they could to help me, and most important, they were friendly. They liked me, too. I hate mess, and cleaned up blood I spilled on the floor instead of leaving it for them as a male surgeon would do. I tried not to write absurd, work-making orders like "Vital signs (blood pressure, pulse) every hour" on a perfectly healthy patient, and they tried not to call me at night. So why was Miss Libby making my life hard now?"

The lights in the lounge had been turned off, the curtains closed, and there was a table in the middle with twenty-five lighted candles on top of a large chocolate birthday cake. The nurses started to sing "Happy Birthday." I stood in front of the cake saying, "I can't believe it," until the ward secretary said, "Stop talking and blow out the candles." There was nothing I could say to tell them what a wonderful thing they had done. The nurses were happy because they thought I had guessed after seeing the patient in room 507. There was ice cream and a gallon can of apple juice from the hospital kitchen and a birthday card. We made a lot of noise and the patient next door banged on the wall and shouted that it was disgraceful, so his nurse took him some chocolate cake, and took some to the patient in room 507.

The man in 507 said, "I can see that lady doctor works very hard—she runs around all night—and when she ran into my room just now I thought she was cracking up."

A neurosurgeon stormed in abruptly asking for me. He said he did not want any cake, ate a large piece, and forgot why he wanted me. So he patted me on the head, wished me happy birthday, and went away, licking his fingers. It was a wonderful birthday.

Weekend on Call

The on-call weekends, of which I had been so afraid, were routine after five weeks. Zach made "Sign Out" rounds with me Saturday morning. We met in the cafeteria at seven so that we could finish our rounds in time to be at Surgical Grand Rounds, the main weekly teaching lecture, at nine.

Zach was wearing his O.R. greens and had not shaved. He was drinking black coffee, making notes on three-by-five cards.

I asked him how the night had been.

"Terrible. Eric had to go to the O.R., and so did the senior resident, so I covered the whole house. If you count that up, it's over a hundred and fifty patients, including the I.C.U. Some idiot on your ward kept calling me for laxative orders, and I had to start Mrs. Cullen's intravenous twice. I think she pulls them out, but I like her. Otherwise, your side was no problem."

That was a relief. Zach was thoroughly hard-working, also censorious. I was always afraid that I was leaving him something to do for my patients that I should have done before I left the hospital. He never complained but he would mention it to me the next morning, then close his mouth tightly and frown slightly. He was not like that with Mark, who would have laughed at him, but he managed to make me feel a bit second-rate. It also upset him if I had to do something for his patients that he should have done.

"You should have called me at home to come and do it," he would say, but I never did. A night off is a night off.

This morning Zach was writing down the name of each of his patients and the diagnosis on a card. When he finished, he gave them to me.

"I'll do all the blood drawing and discharges before I go. Let me show you what has to be done this weekend." He pulled out another card, filled neatly with items to be done.

"Tomorrow, send home Mr. Giamattio. You admitted him your first weekend. He had colon cancer and obstructed ureters. He has lost thirty pounds and needs to be sent home with extra urine bags. He smells of urine because the bag leaks, but otherwise he's fine." He looked at his watch. "Let me show you my patients. We have time. Mr. Benson is a problem."

Mr. Benson was thirty-two, a former truck driver who had had his right leg amputated two years before after a car accident. The stump had never healed and had been infected with bacteria. He was now in the hospital because he had broken his right hip in a fall.

"They put him in a body cast," explained Zach, "because with the infection, they couldn't put a pin in the broken hip."

We went into Mr. Benson's room and examined the leg. He was oozing pus from under the cast.

"It stinks," said Mr. Benson. Outside his room, Zach said the cast had to be removed.

"Yes, I can do it," I said.

"I will," offered Zach. "He's my patient."

"I will do it. It's my weekend on," I said, determined not to let him patronize me.

Zach paused. He was weakening.

"It will take at least an hour to clean him up," I pressed. "You won't be home before one. Let me do it. Isn't it your wife's birthday?"

It was, and Zach agreed to let me look after Mr. Benson. It was only fair. I did his work on my on-call weekends. He did mine on his.

I cut off the cast. The infection had started from his amputation stump, and Mr. Benson had yellow infected ulcers all around his right hip. When I cut off the cast, the cast cutter pressed painfully on the infected ulcers. He said nothing, but I knew it hurt because the muscles in the stump of his leg twitched repeatedly. I asked if he wanted some morphine, but he said, "I can take it. Keep cutting."

That was the start of a busy weekend. My first two weekends on the private service had been relatively quiet, but this time I admitted four patients on Saturday and nine on Sunday. Mark admitted eleven. I had become more efficient and my examinations less complete during the five weeks, and I could now do three work-ups in an hour if the patients were healthy and admitted for routine surgery. One patient arrived with three folders of old hospital records. My heart sank, because it meant over an hour's work just reading the charts. Mark and I both preferred complicated cases because we learned more, but they did take a lot of time. I no longer tried to be too thorough. For instance, in medical school we were taught to test every patient for tuberculosis. On surgery there was no time. The tuberculosis test solution was not stocked and tuberculosis was uncommon. I just could not do the test. My exams had become short. One "history of present illness" this Sunday went:

"Thirty-five-year-old white man with right flank pain beginning yesterday. Past history of kidney stones, otherwise healthy."

Mark sympathized when I said that my work was getting sloppy.

"I was sloppy by the fifth day. At least you held out a couple of weeks. If an attending complains, tell him you do a hundred-hour work week for eight thousand a year. Cheap labor does cheap work. They ought to be happy we speak English."

Covering two wards, Zach's and my own, I had a total of 80 patients, counting my new admissions. Four of them were emergencies, and by Sunday afternoon, after being up all night, I began to lose momentum. I had examined seven patients between lunch and dinner. Dr. Lindsay, an orthopedic surgeon who had taken a lot of time the night before to show me how to pin a fractured hip, asked me to do an especially thorough exam on a patient of his with Paget's disease, an uncommon bone disease. I started at six and, with all my other work, could not finish until ten.

After doing the careful exam on Dr. Lindsay's patient, I had to return to Mrs. Cullen, a patient of Dr. Rice, a general surgeon who was thorough to a fault. He wrote all his patients' routine orders, which interns were supposed to do.

"Dr. Rice, why don't you trust me to write the orders?" objected Mark.

"I know I'm compulsive, Mark, but I can't help it. I am much less compulsive than when I was an intern. Why should I trust you anyhow? You told me to bet on the Yankees, and I lost ten dollars."

Dr. Rice cared about his patients, was a good surgeon and was nice to me, but if a patient of Dr. Rice's needed two pints of blood, he gave them three. If they needed one intravenous, he ordered two.

"They need it," he insisted. "What if the needle comes out in the middle of the night and you and Mark are too busy to start a new one?"

It was not a bad philosophy, but it was compulsive. Dr. Rice never gave up on his patients. I spent Sunday night looking after Mrs. Cullen, a 72-year-old lady who weighed 64 pounds. After months of vomiting, she went to see Dr. Rice, who had operated on her on Tuesday and discovered a huge cancer of the pancreas which had spread everywhere and was blocking her stomach. Dr. Rice bypassed the block by creating a new opening between the stomach and the intestine, but it was only palliative. If the surgery was successful, Mrs. Cullen would be able to eat without vomiting and would be comfortable for the few more months she had to live.

After surgery, Mrs. Cullen had a tube down her nose into her stomach and intravenous needles in her arms. Saturday morning the tube in her stomach had been removed and Saturday night she began to vomit thick green bile. Dr. Rice ordered the nurse to feed Mrs. Cullen nothing and told me to put another needle in her arm and another tube down her nose into her stomach. Stomach tubes make you gag, hurt your nose when they are threaded into your stomach and, once in, are uncomfortable. The tube comes out the nose like a proboscis, and irritates the nose and the throat. When I walked in to put in the tube, Mrs. Cullen was in tears. "I can't take it any more," she sobbed, "I would rather die. I want to go home. I won't have a tube. I do not want to have it."

I was acting under Dr. Rice's orders and was kind but firm. I tried to put the tube in twice and got it half way down, but it hurt her nose and she pulled it out.

"Mrs. Cullen, Dr. Rice wants you to have this tube so you will not go on vomiting. I have to put it down."

"I cannot understand what you are saying. I am deaf."

"Mrs. Cullen," I shouted, "you have to have this tube."

"Please do not torture me," she whimpered, pulling the sheet up to her chin.

"I will not force it on you, Mrs. Cullen, but you must understand that Dr. Rice thinks that you need it to keep you from vomiting."

"I cannot hear you."

"The tube—Dr. Rice wants you to have it," I shouted. "Do you want me to try again or do you want to refuse to have it?"

A nurse looked in to see what the shouting was about. "She hates that tube," she said sympathetically.

"I know," I said desperately. "But she won't tell me she refuses. Dr. Rice will ask me if she actually refused. No one *wants* a stomach tube, and she has a right to refuse, but she has to say she refuses it."

"What are you saying about me?" asked Mrs. Cullen fearfully.

"Do you refuse to have the tube?" I yelled.

"I do not like to refuse," she said, "but I do not want it."

"Tell Dr. Morgan that you refuse to have it," shouted the nurse. "Then we can leave you alone."

"Will Dr. Rice be very angry?"

We both said no. The nurse held her hand encouragingly.

"I will not let you put it in my nose, if that is what you mean. If you would leave me alone in peace and quiet, and let me get a good night's sleep, I will be all right."

I went away, taking the tube with me. Monday morning she looked much better and did not vomit at all during the night. Zach asked about her when he called on Monday to check on his patients after the weekend.

"You ought to ask Rice to take that tube out of her," he said. "It makes her miserable, and she can't live much longer anyway." He was happy to know the tube was already out. She had a heart attack and died in hospital on Zach's weekend a week later. Dr. Rice had written a "No Code" order, so we did not resuscitate her.

Mission Impossible

Some patients were difficult because they were suffering. But there were those who were intentionally difficult because they did not like residents and interns. Most patients did not know that interns were M.D.s. Because of this, the hospital allowed surgical interns to be called residents, to avoid patient complaints that they were examined by "interns, not doctors." But we still had problems.

One evening Mark and I met over cold pizza and Coke in the nurses' lounge on the fifth floor. The food was left over from a birthday party that afternoon for a nursing aide.

"Liz, do me a favor. There's a patient of Dr. Solomon's over here who is so rude that I think I'll punch her in the nose if I have to speak to her again. Can I trade you a work-up? Maybe she'll like you better because you're a woman."

I agreed. Once you start to argue with a patient, it is almost impossible to do a good work-up.

"I am sorry to do this to you Lizzie," he said as we paused in the hallway. "I know you'll regret it."

The patient was a Mrs. Briggs, admitted for surgery, but she had refused to tell anyone what the operation was to be. I walked to her room, fairly sure that with a little patience I could get on with her.

She was sitting on the edge of her bed, heavily made up, in a blue satin negligee.

"Hello," I said. "I am Dr. Morgan, one of Dr. Solomon's surgical residents."

"This room does not have a private bathroom."

"I am terribly sorry for the inconvenience. Perhaps tomorrow they can arrange a better room for you. I have to talk with you about your past medical history, and do a physical examination."

"I told Dr. Solomon everything. It's in his records."

"When you are admitted to the hospital you have to have another exam, to be sure surgery will be safe for you."

"Dr. Solomon is a very good doctor. Are you suggesting that he missed something?"

"No, not at all, you are right to trust him absolutely, but I do have to do this exam. I am one of his residents. First of all, can you tell me your age?"

"What do you mean?"

"Your age—how old are you?"

"This is terrible!"

"It is embarrassing to tell your age to strangers, but every patient does it."

"I find it rudely inquisitive."

"Mrs. Briggs, why not tell me the year you were born?"

"1920. Is that all?"

"I'm sorry, I am not finished. In fact, we have only just begun."

"You're going to make me miss my favorite television show. How do I order a private television?"

"Have you been in this hospital before?"

"Often, but I have no idea when or why. It is all in Dr. Solomon's records. If the hospital has destroyed my records I will complain to the director."

"Mrs. Briggs, I still have to ask you some questions."

"Are you a medical student, practicing on me? I didn't know they let girls into medical school."

"I am a licensed doctor. I do not want anything inaccurate or misleading to be in your hospital record because this exam was not completed."

"Have you discovered that someone has gone back into my records and altered the findings?" She was shocked. Then she brought out pictures of her grandchildren, the entire album collection.

"Aren't they pretty?" she asked. "Isn't he like his grandmother? He's only four years old. I have the pictures of the wedding, too."

"Mrs. Briggs, we must leave them for now."

"I beg your pardon? Do you realize that you have a most domineering manner? If you studied Dr. Solomon's bedside manner you could learn a lot from him."

"Mrs. Briggs, may I explain? I must ask you these questions. At this rate, you might not finish in time to have dinner, and I have to go to an emergency operation at seven o'clock."

"Really? Who is he? What is wrong with him?"

"I cannot discuss other patients."

"I don't feel like a real patient."

"I still can't tell you about any of my other patients."

"Has anyone told you that you are a very rude young lady?" she asked. "You probably aren't married. Do you have any boyfriends?"

"Mrs. Briggs, tell me about your health just for a moment."

"I like your ring, is it an engagement ring?"

"Mrs. Briggs, can you tell me what brings you to the hospital."

"An ambulance. Has anyone made that joke before?"

"Yes."

"I have no idea at all why I'm here. Dr. Solomon mentioned it to me, but it's slipped my mind. Have some candy. Can I leave to get a cup of coffee?"

"Perhaps you can wait until later, Mrs. Briggs."

"Open the window, would you? It's warm in here. More. All right. No, shut it."

I did so, and asked, "If you can't remember why you have come to hospital, perhaps you can tell me if you are allergic to anything. Are there any medicines or food that break you out in a rash, or make you sick to your stomach?"

"Are you the dietician?"

"No, I am one of the surgical residents."

"You can't be. You look only eighteen. How old are you?"

"Mrs. Briggs, do you take any medicines?"

"Hundreds. Some are yellow, some are pink and some have purple stripes. The doctor just gives them to me and I go right on taking them until they run out. I like your dress. Did you make it? You ought to learn how to sew. Every girl should."

"About your medicines . . ."

"How much did your dress cost?" She reached out to feel my hair. "It looks like a wig. Now go away, whoever you are. I refuse to be cross-examined."

I left her room, beaten, and paged Mark to the phone.

"Should we throw her out the window?" he asked.

I suggested he call Dr. Solomon. Mrs. Briggs had to have an examination before surgery, and if she would not let us do it, Dr. Solomon would have to come in tonight and do it himself.

"I like Solomon," said Mark, after he thought about it. "It's too bad it's his patient. He won't mind coming in. I wish it were a turkey like Chester I had to call instead."

"Chaperone me," said Dr. Chester one morning as I walked down the hall. "I have to do a pelvic and there's no nurse around. You'll do." He grabbed my arm and propelled me into an examining room. He had left the door open and his patient, a woman of thirty, was on her back with her legs up in the stirrups. I closed the door behind me.

"Leave it open," he said. "That way I can shout to the nurses if I need something."

"I'll get you whatever you need," I said.

"I don't mind, Dr. Chester," said his patient, "if it's important to you."

"No big deal. Get ready, honey. I'm gonna begin." He put on gloves and looked up at me as he lubricated his fingers with surgical jelly. "The lady has stomach pain, either appendicitis or else her husband has been screwing around and given her V.D. Right, honey?"

"I guess," said his patient without a smile. "Whatever it is, it hurts."

A pelvic exam enables a doctor to check whether the woman's tubes and ovaries are inflamed, as is the case with gonorrhea; if not, her pain probably indicates appendicitis. Unless performed gently, a pelvic exam does hurt.

Dr. Chester pressed on her abdomen with his left hand while feeling within the vagina with his right (undignified and uncomfortable for his patient, but necessary). Her left and middle abdomen did not hurt. Her right side did. She bit her lip and grabbed my hand as he pressed down.

"Oh yeah, it feels like your appendix is red hot. Does that hurt, dear?"

"Yes."

"Yeah. I'll bet it's really sore." He reached higher into the vagina and pressed down harder.

"Right there. Oh, Doctor, that hurts."

"You'll need an operation to get that appendix out. I'll just feel again to be sure."

Till then I had had my doubts about Dr. Chester, but now I watched him carefully. He broke into a big smile and pressed unnecessarily hard and deep, even as his patient squirmed between his hands and screamed with pain.

"I think she's had enough, Dr. Chester," I said coldly.

"Sorry, dear. I didn't mean to hurt you." He looked at me. "You come over and examine her. See what a hot appendix feels like. You have to learn."

"No thank you. She's had enough."

"She can take it. She's tough, right, honey?"

"If it's necessary, Dr. Chester. I'll trust your judgment."

"It's not necessary," I said.

"Sweetheart, you'll never be a good surgeon with that attitude. You have to keep learning." He shrugged. The lady was helped onto a stretcher by an orderly waiting in the hall and Dr. Chester whispered to me, "You gotta learn. These dames overreact. It's not painful."

Fortunately, he was a general surgeon, not a gynecologist, and didn't have much occasion for pelvic exams. He was a well-trained, though impatient, surgeon, tolerated though not greatly respected by his colleagues. No one who had never watched him conduct a pelvic exam would be aware of his tinge of contempt and sadism toward women. I avoided him.

The "Q" Sign

Dr. Linacre had told us in anatomy that we should not allow cadaver dissection to harden us. It did not, but between too much to do, too little sleep, and criticism from nurses, consultants, senior residents, patients' families and attending surgeons, I tended to become short with patients and ignore most criticism. If everything I did was wrong, there was no reason to try. Then something would happen and I would feel very guilty and try to improve.

Mr. Ramal made me feel especially bad. He was operated on for cancer of the prostate when he was seventy-two and seemed to be cured, but five years later the cancer spread to his spinal cord and was pressing on the nerves to his legs. Anxious and worried the night he came into the hospital, he tried to seem playful by refusing to answer my questions and making silly jokes. I was tired. It was only 7:00 P.M., but I had been awake for sixty hours and I wanted to go home and to sleep. Curtly I told him to at least try to answer my questions. He timidly answered each question after that, looking frightened. He had large bleary brown eyes like a spaniel and his thin face was white and wrinkled, covered with moles. When I went home I felt so guilty for being unkind that I couldn't sleep, and I planned in the morning to be especially nice to him. It was too late. During the night he had emergency surgery to try to save his spinal cord so the tumor would not paralyze him. He had a heart attack and a stroke during the operation and was now in the I.C.U. I went to see him. He could raise his left arm, but apart from that he could not speak, move, or understand what was going on about him. He gurgled with each breath, from secretions he could not cough up, and every hour one of us had to shove a tube through his nose into his lungs to suction out the secretions. He hated the tube, and shook his head to try to avoid it.

He was not better after a week, and because he was dying he was returned to my floor, so the I.C.U. bed would be free for someone who might survive. When he arrived his nose and mouth were crusted with blood where the suction tube had scraped the skin, and when I suctioned his lungs with a tube, lumps of phlegm and blood came out. Mr. Ramal opened his eyes and shook his head to try to remove the tube and tugged feebly at my hand. I felt guiltier than ever that I had been unpleasant to him the first night. One night the senior resident came to the ward and looked into Mr. Ramal's room, then sat down at the nurses' desk to smoke a cigarette and slapped me on the back.

"The gork in that room has the 'O' sign, did you notice?"

I didn't know what he meant.

"The 'O' sign means you lie with your mouth open so wide that a fly can buzz in and out and never get wet. After the 'O' sign comes the 'Q' sign." The resident sprawled back in the chair, his mouth sagged open and he stuck his tongue limply out at the side. "That's the 'Q,'" he said, sitting up. "Your patient isn't far from it. Don't keep him alive too long. Hospitals are expensive."

No one came to visit Mr. Ramal. Whenever I heard his lungs gurgling I felt I was neglecting him, and I suctioned him regularly. He still tugged feebly at my arm and shook his head against the tube, but he breathed more comfortably afterward. It was a waste of time. I knew he was dying, but I had to do something. One morning I decided it was cruel to continue. I went to see him on my morning rounds, drew the curtains around his bed, held his hand and said, "Good-bye, Mr. Ramal. I am leaving you in peace for a change. You will feel better soon."

He died two hours later. I called the senior resident. He had met the family and said it would be nicer for them if he was the one to tell them their father was dead.

137

"Good work, Liz," he said over the phone. "Did you notice the 'Q' sign?"

"I didn't look for it. I liked Mr. Ramal."

"Liz, he was too old for you. But seriously, go back and check him. The 'Q' sign is an infallible sign of death." He laughed and hung up.

"Who was that?" asked Dr. Hillebrand, the chief of surgery. He was reading a patient's chart at the desk next to me.

"Alf, the senior resident. He was telling me about the 'Q' sign."

"Which sign?" Dr. Hillebrand put the chart down and looked at me attentively.

"It's just something that happens when a patient dies."

"Tell me about it, Doctor Morgan. I always like to learn more about surgery."

"The 'Q' sign?" I lowered my voice. "He said that when a patient dies, the mouth falls open and the tongue lolls out the side." My voice trailed off.

"I see. Alf seems very ebullient; orthopedic surgery will suit him. You're thinking of being an orthopod, aren't you?"

"No, no. I had thought of it, but I changed my mind. I hope to stay in general surgery."

Dr. Solomon walked onto the ward and looked over his bifocals for a nurse to help him change a patient's dressing. Like Dr. Hillebrand, he was a superb surgeon, about sixty years old, quiet, intelligent and good to his patients. The rest of the general surgery staff asked him or Dr. Hillebrand, or both, for advice on how to treat their difficult patients.

Dr. Hillebrand turned to Dr. Solomon. "Karl, do you know about the 'Q' sign?"

Dr. Solomon raised his eyebrows, and his bifocals slipped down his nose. "Should I?"

"No." Dr. Hillebrand turned to me. "Dr. Morgan, may I suggest that you will learn a great deal more about good surgery by joining Dr. Solomon and learning from him."

He smiled and went back to his chart.

Dr. Solomon and Dr. Hillebrand were legends in the hospital. Dr. Hillebrand, trained at Harvard, was the hospital's full-time chief of private surgery. He had control over all the private surgeons and all the students and residents on the private service. He never criticized anyone in public and, if he criticized at all, did so politely. He knew all the private surgical patients in the hospital. If he thought that a patient had been misdiagnosed or the wrong operation was planned, he would wander around the wards until he found the patient's surgeon, as if by accident.

"Mr. Smith has a most difficult problem," he would say casually as he read the bulletin board. "You know a lot more about him than I do. What do you think the chance is that the mass is an abscess, not just an inflamed gallbladder?"

"Oh, I don't think it's an abscess."

"No, it is unlikely," Dr. Hillebrand would say and wander away, while the other surgeon rushed to reexamine his patient. He kept an especially close watch over Dr. Chester.

Dr. Hillebrand tended to be right. He was one of the famous names in surgery for esophageal varices, but he was hated by many of the full-time university teaching surgeons.

Political power in a surgical department depends on money. A surgeon who brings in large grants or does a lot of surgery is powerful. The money he makes for the department, in fees, and for the hospital through hospital bills pays for equipment, office space, and the salaries of nurses, residents and secretaries. Dr. Hillebrand did not bring in big grants or lots of patients. He had a moderate practice and spent the rest of his time teaching residents and keeping the standards of private surgery very high. He thought that the full-time university faculty spent too little time teaching students and residents. Although he made the private surgeons teach, he pointed out that the full-time faculty, who were supposed to do most of the teaching, canceled their lectures to medical students, told the residents to "learn on the job," did research of poor quality and spent their time fighting for more secretaries and bigger offices. Dr. Hillebrand said that any qualified surgeon should be given hospital privileges because more good surgeons meant more competition and better patient care. He was indignant when the university chief of neurosurgery refused to allow his chief resident hospital privileges when he finished his training. But the chief held fast, saying, "There are already enough neurosurgeons in town." He didn't want to lose patients, and the money and power to be derived from them.

139

"Then why did you allow him to be trained?" asked Hillebrand. "When you refuse a good surgeon hospital privileges, it sounds as though you might be afraid he's too good."

A year later, as punishment for his campaign to improve training, the university surgical faculty voted to demote Dr. Hillebrand to the position of a primary care physician in the geriatric service at an affiliated veterans' hospital. The private surgeons protested, but they could not vote at the faculty meeting. Dr. Hillebrand was still so well known that even from the V.A. hospital he could find a resident a job anywhere in the country. Everyone was shocked, but that was power politics.

Dr. Karl Solomon had also fought with the medical school faculty, thirty years before. Legend claimed that he was born in Russia and escaped the Bolsheviks by swimming across the Volga by moonlight in winter. This may not be true. Dr. Hillebrand, who knew him best, told Mark and me, "The only river I know of that Karl Solomon has swum across is the East River. He told me he grew up in New York."

Regardless, Dr. Solomon did swim a mile a day at the medical school gym. He had trained at the medical school and had been a member of the full-time faculty after World War II. He had considered himself much the best surgeon on the faculty, but he was not appointed chairman of the department of surgery four years later, when the former chairman retired. He thought this was because he was Jewish. Upset that the surgeons had chosen someone less qualified than he was, and that the local Jewish community had not supported him against the University faculty surgeons, he resigned from the surgical faculty and went into private practice, and also left the Jewish faith and became a Unitarian. An anesthesiologist who had known Dr. Solomon for years told me the rest.

"You would not think Karl would be vindictive, but he won the battle in the long run. For the past thirty years every Jew who moves to the city, and every Jewish patient knows why he, Karl Solomon, left the Jewish faith. Next, Karl took the Board exams in general surgery, neurosurgery and cardiothoracic surgery. He is the only person in the city who has Boards in three specialties, and he has been known to remind the full-time professors that his qualifications are better than theirs. Next, he is a superb surgeon. He is very gifted. Besides, he has never let a resident do surgery on a patient of his. At most, he may let you cut a suture. He won't even let you remove an appendix. The word got around—when you go to Karl Solomon, he does your operation. When you go to a university faculty professor, the resident operates. Karl has never turned away a case. He has never had a malpractice suit. His patients adore him. He has an enormous practice, of course. The full-time general surgery faculty have to keep busy with emergency surgery. Karl sees all the good elective cases. Does it embarrass the faculty to have the busiest, best surgeon in town *not* on the full-time faculty? You bet it does, and Karl loves it."

Dr. Solomon must have been quite rich, but he lived modestly, had a plain office, and drove a ten-year-old Chevy. He read every surgical book and every journal and kept them stacked in piles in his office. He particularly enjoyed Surgical Grand Rounds on Saturday morning. He and Dr. Hillebrand would sit together high up in the amphitheater, perched like eagles in the narrow seats at the top. One morning a full professor of surgery lectured on a patient who had died before the right diagnosis was made. The disease was stomach cancer. He had been treated for a stomach ulcer for six years. During the discussion after the lecture, a resident asked if a biopsy should have been done.

The professor looked affronted. "Of course not. The cytology was normal."

The resident turned to Dr. Hillebrand and Dr. Solomon.

"What would your opinion be? Would you want a biopsy, or would you believe the cytology?"

They murmured to one another, then Dr. Hillebrand nodded to Dr. Solomon, who said, "As everyone knows, cytology is valuable if it shows cancer cells, but if it is normal, you must do a biopsy. If the biopsy is normal but the ulcer does not heal in six months, then I operate."

"A stomach cancer cannot be present for five years," objected the faculty surgeon.

"If I may disagree," said Karl, "I think it can." He paused.

"Yes, yes. Go ahead," said the professor.

"First, there is an excellent review on stomach cancer and its confusion with stomach ulcers in the August issue of the *Annals of Surgery*. I am sure the faculty are familiar with the article, although you did not refer to it, but, for the benefit of the medical students, the article is on page four hundred and thirty-four." He paused again. The medical students made notes.

"Is that all?" asked the professor sarcastically.

"No. In my own small practice, I have seen twenty patients with stomach cancer in whom the cytology was normal, as in your patient, and numerous papers in the surgical literature say the same thing, in the *Annals, The Archives, The American Journal*. Had this man been my patient, or, I believe, the patient of any private surgeon in this room, we would have operated five years ago, when the ulcer had not healed for a year. Perhaps he would be alive today. It seems a pity to me that, in one of the greatest medical centers in the country, a patient with stomach cancer received no treatment for five years and died of it." He cleared his throat. "But I am merely an ignorant surgeon in private practice, struggling to keep abreast of all the new developments in surgery. Perhaps the learned professors of the surgical faculty could teach us more?"

There was an embarrassed silence.

"Thank you, Dr. Solomon. I do not think there is more to say."

Grand Rounds were over.

Dr. Solomon bowed politely and said "Good morning" to the surgical professors on his way out. Later I heard a professor telling a resident angrily, "How many times do I have to tell you? Karl Solomon is *not* always right. Yes, I admit, he was right this morning."

After his morning surgery, Dr. Solomon would eat a lunch of milk and graham crackers in the operating room kitchenette. He removed huge rectal tumors, rare liver tumors, did pelvic exenterations and bile duct surgery—and he always finished before lunchtime. He usually did three operations a day. Even now, when an operation is not going smoothly, I ask myself, "What would Dr. Hillebrand do here? What would Dr. Solomon do?"

Years later, as a chief resident, I was doing an operation on the liver ducts, surrounded by cement-hard scar tissue from previous operations. I have seen surgeons give up after looking in vain for the common duct, the main liver duct. After two hours, the attending surgeon said, "We had better quit," and left the operating room to smoke a cigarette. I remembered Dr. Solomon saying, five years before, as he operated with his gold-handled scissors, "Know the anatomy. The rest is easy. Anatomically, the duct has to be anterior and medial to the artery."

I pulled the overhead light into better focus and told the tired intern to hold his retractor steady.

"Long-handled Metzenbaums and vascular forceps."

The nurse put them in my hand.

Standing straight with my head out of the light, my mask falling down off my nose, just like Dr. Solomon's, I spread and cut the amorphous scar tissue where I knew, anatomically, the duct had to be.

"Don't move," I said sharply when the intern leaned forward to look.

Very delicately, cut, spread, cut, and there was the fragile duct. I dissected it from the liver, where it begins, to the intestine, where it ends, in silence, just like Dr. Solomon, who rarely spoke when he operated. The attending was astonished when he returned from his cigarette break.

Shortly after Dr. Hillebrand was forced to retire from his position as chief of the private surgeons, Dr. Solomon retired, without warning. He was sixty-seven, but we all expected him to operate till he was eighty. One Monday he walked into the office of the new chief.

"Dr. Hillebrand is gone, and today I am retiring. Dr. Kennedy will take over my patients. Good-bye."

After that, he went swimming for a month. Then he entered law school. Today he is a lawyer. He and Dr. Hillebrand still come to Grand Rounds, to the distress of some of the university faculty, and presumably he is an expert witness for the plaintiff in their malpractice cases.

Saving Time

After seven weeks as intern on private surgery, I was tired. I had gone forty-five hours without sleep when at 3:00 A.M. on the Sunday night of my fourth weekend on call, a nurse screamed down the hall "Stat Page!" I jumped up and ran across the corridor to help her, and the new senior resident, Pete Holland, ran to help me. The problem was minor, a little bleeding around a recent operation incision, but the nurse was inexperienced and had panicked.

"Don't let it bother you," said Pete. "We'd rather you called us for a minor problem than not call when you need help. Right, Elizabeth?"

I felt a little queasy and the lights seemed painfully bright. I closed my eyes. I did not want to answer immediately. I wanted time to think about his question.

"Right, Elizabeth?" I heard Pete say. "Are you all right?"

"Right, right," I said. This was confusing. I felt as though I was lying on something hard.

"What?" said Pete. "Take your time."

I opened my eyes. I was lying on the floor and the nurse was wiping my face with a wet washcloth. I felt embarrassed. My skirt had ridden up around my hips.

"She fainted," said the patient in surprise, looking at me from his bed. I stood up.

"I am all right," I said. "Perfectly all right. I don't know what happened."

"Don't worry about it," said Pete. "You're just tired. It happened to me when I was an intern."

I dozed in the O.R. all the next day, Monday. I tried to stand up straight but found I was leaning on the scrub nurse's shoulder. I tried to watch the operation but my eyes went out of focus. The surgeon told me to cut the sutures and I could not get the sutures between the blades of the scissors. They seemed very far away. I leaned my head down to get a closer look at the suture.

"Get your head out of the belly," snapped the surgeon, "and give me the scissors."

I gave them to him. My eyes fell shut. I yawned and swayed backwards. A firm hand pushed me upright. It was the circulating nurse.

"Hold on," she said. "I am getting you a stool to sit down on."

"How do they expect me to operate when the only help I have is a sleeping woman? Don't give her a stool."

My eyes closed. I shook myself. "I am wide awake. I'm sorry," I said defensively. It wasn't because I was a woman, and I wasn't weak. I just hadn't slept for three days.

"Do you want her sitting on a stool or lying on the floor? You can choose," the nurse asked the surgeon.

"Goddammit, get her the stool. We're wasting time."

When I got out of the O.R. I still had work-ups to do, but on the ward I discovered they had all been done. Pete Holland, the senior resident, had done two for me, and Zach Bernard was finishing a third. Zach looked slightly rested after his weekend off.

"We had nothing to do," said Pete. "Our cases were canceled."

I could not begin to thank them, especially Pete. Senior residents almost never did work-ups for the interns. Scut was scut.

"Are you anemic?" Zach asked.

"No, why?"

"You look terrible."

I sat down.

"You should go home," he added. "Everything is under control. You let me go home early last Friday."

It was five o'clock.

"Maybe I will," I said, slowly. My voice sounded like a 45 record played on 33⅓ rpm.

"Now," added Pete.

"I'm going."

"You have to stand up first," said Pete.

"I will. Give me time."

Zach took my arm and pulled me up.

"Go home!"

I walked to the stairs and met Mark, who was going home too. A nursing supervisor passed us on her way up. "You two look terrible." We were too tired to answer. The cumulative sleep loss, plus three days awake, made it hard even to speak.

At the front of the hospital, Mark turned right and so did I.

"Where are you going?" he asked after a while.

"Home."

"I didn't know you commuted." He stopped and scratched his head.

"I don't." I stopped too.

"I thought you lived in the Madison Apartments."

"I do."

"You're going the wrong way."

"No, I'm not."

"Yes, you are."

"Yes, I am."

"You should have turned left."

"Yes, you have a point. Good night." I turned slowly to the right direction.

"Do you want a ride home?"

"No," I said indignantly. "It's only a block."

"Call an ambulance if you get lost."

It took me half an hour to walk home. I could not walk straight, and collided with several trees and trash cans. I arrived at five-thirty and went to bed immediately, setting the alarm to wake me at six-thirty the next morning. When the alarm went off, it seemed impossible that it should have been morning again so soon. I was about to get out of bed when I fell asleep again. When I woke up it was 7:45. It was light outside. I panicked. I was going to be late for surgery. Why me? Zach would never do a thing like this. I leaped out of bed, ran to the kitchen, drank some orange juice, and ran to the hospital.

It was eight o'clock. I was already late for surgery, but I had to stop by the ward to be sure my patients were all right.

"Where is Miss Libby?" I panted, out of breath.

"Home," said the ward secretary. "Do you need her?"

"I didn't know she was sick," I said, looking for a nurse to check with.

"She isn't. She just went home," said the secretary. I pounced on a passing nurse. I had to get to the O.R.

"I'm terribly sorry to be late. Is everything all right? I have to go to the O.R."

"Is there a case?" she asked.

"There are lots of cases. It's a very busy schedule."

"I didn't know you were on call. Weren't you on call this weekend?"

"Yes, but it's an every-other-night schedule," I told her.

"Why this trivial chitchat," I thought irritably as I ran down to the O.R. I was scrubbing with Dr. Eton and I knew he was going to be angry with me. In a good mood, he teased and flattered me, but in a bad mood he shouted, which terrified me. I ran into the locker room. None of the nurses was around. They must be in the O.R.s already, I thought frantically as I changed into a scrub dress. I ran to the O.R. front desk. A couple of nurses were making phone calls.

"I'm late, I'm late," I said as I looked at the schedule. Dr. Eton was operating in room eight.

"No, you're doing fine," said the nurse. "Your case has not started yet."

"Room eight hasn't started?" I asked breathlessly.

"No, room six." I was out of luck.

"I'm in room eight," I called as I ran down the hall to the O.R. I almost ran into the anesthesiologist, who was coming out of room six.

"What's the rush?" he asked.

"I'm late. It is almost ten past eight."

"That's right. We haven't started."

"But I am sure Dr. Eton has."

"He doesn't have a case."

"It must have been canceled."

Pause.

"I thought you were on call last night," said the anesthesiologist.

"No, I was on the weekend."

"That's what I said, yesterday—Sunday."

"It was Monday yesterday."

"No, Elizabeth, today is Monday."

"It is not Monday. I was here Monday morning."

"Yes, and now it's Monday night."

Zach walked down the O.R. corridor.

"Elizabeth, I told you to go home."

"Is this Monday night?" I asked suspiciously. They both said, "Yes."

"But I've just had breakfast."

"No, Elizabeth," said the anesthesiologist. "We call the evening meal dinner."

"You had dinner. I had breakfast." I leaned against the wall. "I went to bed at 5:45 and I set the alarm for 6:30. That was the problem."

They waited. The nurses came down the hall to listen. "So I overslept, till 7:30, and then I had breakfast and came to work. This means I can go home and sleep. This is wonderful news."

"You need it," said Zach.

As I walked home it was getting dark. Having spent the entire summer indoors, I had forgotten how late it stayed light. Life was beautiful. I was going to sleep for ten and a half more hours.

Cosmopolitan

My brother called me at home one night.

"Elizabeth, I have a great chance for you."

"What's that?" I was suspicious. Jimmy can sell me any idea.

"I've been talking to Roberta Ashley, an important editor at *Cosmo*. She wants you to try doing an article for them about physical check-ups. What the Cosmo girl should look for to be sure her doctor is thorough."

"*Cosmopolitan?*"

"Yes, *Cosmopolitan*. They wanted me to do an article on women's tennis. I thought it should be about how to build up arm strength and stuff like that, but it wasn't what they wanted."

"What did they want?"

"Women's tennis personalities, which doesn't really interest me. I can't write about what kind of bloomers Billie Jean King wears, and what she uses for make-up."

"What kind does she wear?"

"Are you kidding? Anyhow, I told Roberta Ashley you might want to do an article for them on a medical topic. What do you think?"

It was absurd. *Cosmopolitan* had over two million readers. Helen Gurley Brown was famous. Becoming an overnight *Cosmo* writer didn't happen in real life.

Roberta Ashley sent me an outline for my proposed article. I wrote what I thought was a helpful, cheerful eight-page piece, "You and Your Yearly Physical." It took me my entire weekend off. Mrs. Ashley sent it back.

> Dear Elizabeth, We have reviewed your piece in our weekly conference. This is not bad for a first effort. You have tried hard and there's good information. Alas, tone is too "flip." Health is a serious matter to most of us. Would you like to try again?

I was embarrassed to have seemed to take medicine lightly. Tired as I was, I forced myself to spend six hours on my next free weekend rewriting it. Mrs. Ashley wrote to say that Mrs. Brown approved the article, and *Cosmopolitan* paid me for it. For the next six months, I checked *Cosmopolitan* in the hospital gift shop hopefully, but my article was not published. After six months, I decided I was being silly, and tried to forget about it.

After ten weeks as an intern on private surgery I was tired and irritable. I was also a lot more confident. All my med school fears about not being able to survive were gone. I had endured. Ninety percent of what I did was mindless repetition, difficult only because there was so much of it. I had seen a lot of "pathology"—patients with cancers of the stomach and rectum, ulcers, appendicitis, infected gallbladders—and I was learning about stomach pain: when to operate and when to wait. I was learning to operate. I could repair groin hernias and take out an appendix as long as I wasn't hurried and the attending surgeon was there to remind me what to do if I forgot. Technically, I was average to good but a bit slow. Under pressure from a male surgeon I operated even more slowly, especially when I had been awake all night. Criticism from Dr. Janet Rome, the neurosurgery chief resident and the only woman surgeon I knew, was not so unnerving. I needed a rest. Fortunately my next internship rotation was pediatric surgery, a quiet service.

Many children came and went quickly after a tonsillectomy or appendectomy, and many lay in bed as broken legs healed; but as these children were otherwise healthy, it was not they who took most of the doctor's time.

During my weeks on pediatrics, I took care of Andrea, an eight-year-old girl born with almost no brain and with abnormal legs, kidneys and heart valves. She was also born blind. Because of the severe deformities, her parents had agreed with the obstetrician to set the child aside and let her die. She did not die, but she stayed in the state institution and her parents forgot her as best they could. She was sent to the hospital when the staff at the institution noticed that she cried more than usual and could not keep food down. When I first saw her she was lying in bed. She was less than three feet long. She whimpered and at times moved her head from side to side. That was all. She needed diapers. If food was put in her mouth, she swallowed. She lay on her back, with her legs splayed out like a frog. This was all she had ever done.

The neurosurgeon, Dr. Janet Rome, came onto the ward to see her. As the neurosurgery chief resident and the only woman member of the surgical department besides Leslie and me, she was someone I admired enormously. She was detached and solemn most of the time but very good-humored. She rarely criticized, never complained or fought with other surgeons, and carried on calmly no matter what disasters befell. She had been an O.R. nurse until her father suddenly needed a brain operation. This galvanized her to go to medical school and then into surgery.

"You're not planning to operate on Andrea," the pediatric chief resident said to Dr. Rome. The chief resident knew Andrea well, having cared for her intermittently since he was an intern.

"Why not?"

"You should ask 'why.' The girl is eight years old, born with almost no brain, and there's no hope of change. Why are you keeping her alive by shunting fluid away from the brain?"

"Do you want me to kill her?"

"No. I'm just asking what right you have to prolong a hopeless life. Without a shunt she will probably die, correct?"

"Correct."

"You agree she will never change. She will lie on her back, swallowing, for the rest of her life. Correct?"

"Correct."

"What are you trying to accomplish as a surgeon?"

"I have no choice. She is under the care of the state. They are her surrogate parents. They sent Andrea here and you asked me to see

151

her. The state could have chosen not to send her. You could have chosen not to consult me. Once they have sent her to you, and you to me, I do not think I have the right to refuse to treat her as I would treat any other child." She shrugged. "There is no happy solution but this is the only clinical possibility."

Andrea was in the hospital for months after her surgery. The state institution had given her bed to another retarded child while Andrea was in hospital, and she had to wait for another.

"At two hundred dollars a day," grumbled the chief resident. "No wonder the welfare system is bankrupt."

A week later, a nurse looked into the conference room.

"Elizabeth, is it your turn for a work-up?"

"Yes, why?"

"We've just gotten an emergency, but don't rush. It's a social emergency. You worked up Andrea, didn't you?"

"Oh, no. There can't be another Andrea."

Andrea's bed was at the front of the ward. Every time we walked down the hall we passed her, turning her head, whimpering, drooling, occasionally giving a loud scream.

"Yes, only his name is Bertie." The nurse smiled. "You'll come to love him, because if you don't, Bertie's mother will kill you with her bare hands." The nurse turned around and gave an embarrassed laugh. "Hello, Mrs. Lewis. This is Dr. Morgan, the nice lady doctor I was telling you about. She is going to examine Bertie. She is very good with children."

"She can't be nicer than the doctor we had last time. I wish we could have him again. I don't think Bertie will like a lady doctor. He's always had men before." She went away.

Bertie was a vegetable. He was fourteen years old and had been severely brain-injured at birth. He couldn't walk, talk or move. He lay in bed and his eyes roved left, then right, then slowly left and quickly right.

His mother stood on his left as I walked in. "Look," she said to me. "You see, he knows I'm here. I explained to him about your being a woman."

Bertie's eyes roved quickly left, then right, then left again, then Bertie said "Aaugh," and his mouth had a spasm which distorted the lower lip. "He doesn't like you," said his mother. "He never takes to strangers, do you darling?" Bertie drooled some saliva onto his bib. "Tut, tut, what a messy mess we make, don't we?" said his mother, as she wiped his lips.

Since birth, Bertie, like Andrea, had had excess fluid pressing on the brain. Neurosurgeons put a plastic tube in his brain to channel the fluid out. His mother insisted he was sick with an infection and pleaded to have him in the hospital for studies. "He is paler than usual," she told me, "and in a lot of pain. He is just not my same darling. You have no energy left, do you, Bertie?"

Energy for what? I thought.

I examined Bertie thoroughly. His mother repeatedly told me how important Bertie was to her, and how much Bertie loved her. "You see," his mother said when Bertie had another spasm. "That proves he loves me, doesn't it? Darling is thirsty, isn't darling? Just a teeny weeny bit of grape juice. Don't be messy, sweetheart, you're in public, dear. Right in front of a great big important doctor." She giggled, and said to me, "He knows you are just an intern, not a real doctor. I told him."

I did not bother to insist I was a real doctor. I had to take blood samples to see if there were bacteria in Bertie's blood from an infected tube. Every day for a week I woke up knowing I had to take blood from Bertie while his mother was there. She refused to leave him.

"Dearie, dearie, sweetheart be brave for the bad lady doctor. She doesn't mean to hurt you, but I know it hurts terrible bad. Oh, she didn't get enough blood. She must hurt you again with the needle. She is so cruel, Bertie darling. Be brave, just like Mommy. Lady doctors can't be perfect all the time." She giggled. Bertie said "Aaugh," and his mother explained to me that it meant the needle hurt.

I felt sorry for Bertie. He was pathetically retarded, but he could not hear or respond to his mother, and I could. Every day she made a point of asking one of the men on the ward, not me, about the results of the blood cultures. When one of them pointed out that I was in charge of Bertie's case, she feigned surprise. "She's not a real doctor, is she? I'm sorry," she giggled, "from your manner, I thought you were just learning."

I drew twenty blood samples looking for bacteria in his blood and the blood sat in the incubator but never grew any bacteria.

On Bertie's tenth day, after all his tests were normal, the resident sent him home with some iron pills to build his blood. He was a little anemic. The next morning, we made lab rounds and went to check our cultures. Bertie's blood cultures were ready to be discarded, but we noticed a fine white cloud rising from the bottom of the first six bottles. "Oh, diphtheroid bacteria," said the bacteriologist, when we asked him to examine them under the microscope. "Very hard to culture. They take forever to grow."

So Bertie had an infection after all, and was called back to hospital the next day. His mother was excited. "See, sweetie, you never can tell with these wonderful doctors, dearest. They never do what they say—out one day, back the next, and I know you're badly upset about it. Bad doctors, but baby won't cry, baby won't mind. Mommy will stay right next to you for always."

Bertie's infection disappeared after the infected tube was taken out in surgery. He went home in three days.

"Oh, he's just wonderful," his mother said to the neurosurgeon. "He's perky and happy and has so much energy you'd never believe he was the same boy."

Bertie's eyes roved left, right, and his face had a spasm.

The neurosurgeon had coffee in the doctor's room after Bertie's mother left.

"The woman is crazy. Did you know she has three other children under fifteen at home? Her husband refuses to have anything to do with Bertie. He says the boy should be in an institution and that his wife neglects the three normal children. She understands Bertie, though. I don't know how she knew he was sick when he didn't have any signs of infection."

"She certainly doesn't like women doctors," I said bitterly.

"She's working through guilt," said the pediatric resident. "You have to understand that she feels responsible for Bertie. She carried him for nine months and she feels a failure as a woman. By rejecting you she is externalizing her own self-rejection."

"Maybe," I said. "But it doesn't make it easier for me."

The neurosurgeon laughed. "Liz, you're a surgeon. You can't let these things bother you. You've got to be tough."

And I was changing. I didn't realize how much so until five years of general surgery residency was over, but I was being trained by good male surgeons to act like a good male surgeon.

"VAH-SPA"

It came as a relief to return to the world of adult surgery. My next intern rotation was the Veterans Hospital, known as the "VAH-SPA." At the University Hospital patients were either respectable working citizens, or drug addicts, pushers, prostitutes, and derelicts. The Veterans Hospital, I was told, had a "different population." They were almost all men and, contrary to my image of veterans' hospitals, few of the men were "war heroes." Many had been drafted and almost immediately had psychiatric disorders or medical discharges for minor injuries. Many of them had avoided life as well as the army, and had become alcoholics. Every one was a heavy cigarette smoker. Few had jobs. Winter was beginning as I started on the V.A. Mark Lehman, who had just been there, said that all the regular bums were now coming to the V.A. for the winter season, so that they wouldn't have to sleep outdoors.

I soon learned how to ask an alcoholic or smoker how much they drank or smoked. It is not easy for an unemployed disabled veteran to tell a disapproving doctor that he drinks a fifth of whiskey a day, especially if the doctor is a woman. If I simply asked "How much?" my patients would say they did not smoke or drink. At first I believed them. One patient said he did not drink. I asked him when his last drink had been. He said, "This morning, but I quit when I came to

155

the hospital." I don't like to humiliate patients so I tried asking, "How much do you drink? Three cases of beer a day? What about smoking—four or five packs a day?"

"God, no," my patient replied in horror. "I couldn't drink *that* much. I only drink a case a day, and I stop after two packs of cigarettes. It's too expensive."

Tobacco smoking was the worst health problem in the V.A. Something in the tobacco injures blood vessels and after twenty years of smoking a pack or two a day, atherosclerosis from the tobacco is bad enough to block arteries to the brain, the heart and the lower limbs, causing stroke, heart attack and gangrene of the legs. The stroke and heart attack victims were on the medical service. The patients with gangrene came to us on surgery to have their blood vessels repaired, if possible, or the leg amputated.

One patient, Mack, had one leg amputated because of gangrene, and I admitted him to the V.A. when the toes of his other leg turned black ten months later. Mack had no family, no job, and was an alcoholic. When I asked him if he drank three cases of beer or smoked four packs of cigarettes a day, he smiled sympathetically. "No, I'm not like some of the bums you get in this hospital. I never drink the hard stuff, just beer, and never over a case and a half a day. I just don't have the money. I smoke four packs a day, but recently I've been cutting down." Dutifully I told him smoking was bad for him, and had contributed to the gangrene of his legs, and I explained the risks of cancer and heart attack from smoking. Mack seemed horrified.

"No! You're joking. Why didn't the other doctors tell me about this?"

Of course every resident had told him not to smoke, and the same day I saw him wheel himself into the hospital canteen to buy cigarettes. These were federally subsidized cigarettes sold at cut-rate prices, tax-free, in unlimited quantities to all V.A. patients. Mack was accompanied by a large, black, blind friend with diabetes, who also had had one leg amputated for gangrene from atherosclerosis. It is shocking policy for a government hospital, but cheap cigarettes are sold in every veterans' hospital, and candy-striper volunteer hospital workers wheel them in carts onto the wards for patients confined to bed—twenty-five cents a pack, bedside service.

Mack's leg had to come off, and I had to do it. Tim Mann, the junior resident, patted me on the shoulder the afternoon Mack came back to the hospital.

"Study the anatomy of the leg tonight, girl. An amputation is an intern's case, and you'll do Mack's right leg tomorrow. I did his left leg as an intern last year." An angiogram of the leg arteries had showed that there was no blood flow in Mack's lower leg. His whole lower leg was red and swollen and most of his foot was black. The leg had to come off above the knee. With both legs gone Mack would be a wheelchair case—his lungs were so poor from tobacco smoking that he did not have the stamina to walk with artificial legs.

At 7:30 A.M. after rounds, I went to the O.R. as Tim Mann and my chief resident, Rick Trudeau, went to breakfast. The V.A. nurses were friendly but never hurried. It was eight o'clock by the time Mack was on the table. He was sedated, and without his dentures he looked much older than his age—he was only fifty.

The nursing supervisor called on the intercom: "Dr. Black, your attending, is in the house and says you can go ahead."

The anesthesiologist impassively placed a mask over Mack's face. "Big breaths. This is just oxygen."

Mack breathed in under the mask, but his eyes opened in anxiety and he squeezed the hand of the nurse standing by him. The anesthesiologist injected the pale yellow Pentothal in through the I.V. line. Mack's eyes quivered and closed halfway. The anesthesiologist touched his lids. There was no blink reflex. He injected curare. A few moments later Mack's muscles quivered, a sign that the curare had worked and his muscles were paralyzed. The anesthesiologist set aside the mask, opened Mack's mouth and inserted the metal laryngoscope, an L-shaped instrument that holds up the jaw so the tube can be passed into the windpipe. The nurse passed him the endotracheal tube, a curved plastic tube about a foot long. He lifted up the laryngoscope, pushed in the tube, and attached the tube to the anesthesia machine. A few trial breaths showed that the tube was in the esophagus and not in the lungs. Ninety seconds had gone by without Mack's being given oxygen, and I expected the anesthesiologist to give it to him by mask before trying to pass the tube into the lungs a second time. He didn't, but put in the laryngoscope again. Mack was faintly blue.

I saw a P.V.C. on the heart monitor—this one abnormal heartbeat was a sign of too little oxygen. Mack was now quite blue.

"You have to give him some oxygen," I said anxiously to the anesthesiologist. People with atherosclerosis are especially susceptible to brain damage from too little oxygen. They have no reserves. The anesthesiologist passed the tube into Mack's lungs, attached the oxygen–halothane tube in a leisurely manner and gave Mack a few breaths. The blue faded to a healthy pink.

"Don't tell me how to do my job, dear," he said. "Just concentrate on learning yours. Now go and scrub. You're holding things up."

After I scrubbed, I went back into the operating room, put on sterile gloves and washed Mack's upper leg with iodine soap. The smelly gangrenous lower leg was wrapped in a green towel.

"Towel, clips, drapes, come on, let's get going," said Tim to the nurse when I had finished. He was gowned and gloved and put the sterile drapes around the upper leg where we would operate. The circulator took my prep gloves off. The scrub nurse handed me a gown and helped me on with a new pair of gloves while the circulator tied the gown on me. I walked to the right side of the table and from there on I had no chance to think about the anesthesiologist. Tim Mann stood opposite me. I marked with blue surgical ink where I would make the incision.

"Too high," said Tim, "make it further down the leg."

Rick Trudeau, the chief resident, walked in with Dr. Black, the attending.

"Curve your incision more," said Rick. "It's too sharp."

"Further down the leg," said Dr. Black. "It's much too high. Give her a knife. It's eight-thirty. You've wasted too much time already."

The nurse handed me the scalpel, and I cut down on the skin. The flabby muscle beneath made it hard to cut except right over the bone.

"At right angles—keep your blade at right angles," ordered Rick.

"Faster," said Dr. Black. "Don't stop to listen to him. Keep cutting. This isn't fancy surgery; just get the leg off."

"Don't undercut," said Tim. "You're tunneling—you're cutting muscle before you've cut the skin over it."

"I'm trying," I said.

"Don't talk, just cut," said Dr. Black. "And stand up. Your head's in the operating field."

Suddenly blood spurted from the leg, spattering Rick and Dr. Black at the foot of the table.

"Goddammit," said Dr. Black, "don't just slice through the

femoral artery. You have to get that mother and tie it off. You can't cut a major artery in half."

Tim got a clamp around the artery and I tied it off, then the nerve and then the vein. All three travel down the inner and back part of the leg. Finally the skin and muscle were cut through, and all that kept the lower leg attached was the bone.

"Give her the Gigli saw," ordered Dr. Black.

The nurse handed me a heavy-braided wire saw, with detachable handles at either end.

"This is the saw," explained Tim. He passed it under the bone. "Just pull up on it and run it back and forth till the bone is sawed through."

I had to stand on a low stool as I pulled back and forth, back and forth, with the cutting wire.

"Faster," said Tim.

"Put some oomph into it," said Rick.

Dr. Black laughed. "Now you find out surgery is hard work—you have to be strong to do this."

I ignored them and just kept pulling back and forth. My shoulders ached. My fingers felt numb with the handles digging into them.

I glared at the bone, bit my lower lip and kept pulling. A sudden crack and the bone was sawed through, and I almost fell off the stool.

"Rasp the bone, smooth it, and sew it up," said Dr. Black, and he and Rick left the O.R.

"Specimen, please," said the nurse, and I had to hand her the severed gangrenous limb so she could send it to the pathology lab for examination.

"That is gross," said Tim. "Just cutting a whole leg off. I hate this operation as much as I hate mastectomies. They are so crude."

"But now I know how to do one," I said. I had surprised myself. Tim was right, amputation was a sad and crude operation, but it was my first, and I was proud that I had done it right.

The medical care at our V.A. was very good. There were full-time professors assigned to the V.A., and residents to take care of every patient. It seemed a wasteful system, bogged down by paperwork and by the government policy that employees are never fired. Some nurses and some salaried full-time doctors were excellent. Others were rude and incompetent, like the anesthesiologist, but they were never fired, just promoted. Many of the best nurses resigned after working a few years at the V.A. They were demoralized by the paperwork and the routine promotion of incompetents. They preferred to work elsewhere for less pay.

Lack of physical strength is a woman's greatest disadvantage in surgery—not only in the O.R. but on the ward. One day I had to discharge a big man of forty-five who had had a hernia repaired three weeks before. He had always smiled at me and said how nice it was to have a lady around. Three weeks was a long time to stay in hospital after a hernia—the usual University Hospital stay was five days—so I told him he could go home. I gave him a prescription for a mild painkiller and told him to come to the clinic next week.

He was in a chair reading the newspaper with his feet on the bed. He put his paper down and stared at me, chewing gum slowly.

"Doc, I guess they forgot to tell you. I'm staying in for some more tests, for my back pain. And would you check out my diabetes while you're at it? And I need a new prescription for glasses. And I need my dentures fixed." He picked up his paper again.

I went to find Tim Mann, the resident, and told him what Mr. Saunders had said.

"That's all baloney. He doesn't have diabetes. His back is fine. He knows the V.A. won't pay for new glasses or new dentures. He pulled the same stunt on me last year when I was an intern. His wife just threw him out of the house because he won't work and he drinks all the time and that is why he decided to have his hernia fixed. Just tell him he goes home."

I went back to Mr. Saunders.

"Mr. Saunders, I have just spoken to Dr. Mann, and he says that you are to go home today."

"But if I go home, the V.A. won't pay for my glasses."

"Then you'll have to pay for them."

"But I don't have any money. You can't do this to me. Just let me stay till Monday. You see, Doc, my wife is mad, and I have to make up with her before she'll let me come back. Give me the weekend to work it out."

It was now Wednesday morning.

"You are to go home today," I persisted. "I'm sure your wife will let you come home."

"But then I can't get my glasses. I told you I'm out of work."

"What was your job?" I asked.

"I was a truck driver."

"Why did you quit?"

"I didn't quit," he said angrily. "I was fired."

"For what?"

"For drinking. You see, Doctor, I have this need to drink. A psychiatrist explained to me once that it goes back to when I was a child." He looked at me hopefully.

"Then stop drinking and get a job."

He jumped off the bed. "You smart-ass doctors. I'm leaving here. This place stinks. I wouldn't stay another night if you paid me." He spat his gum into the sink and glared at me with his fists clenched.

Suddenly Tim was behind me, pulling up his sleeves.

"If you speak to me like that, Saunders, I'll punch you out and I'll do the same if you speak to Dr. Morgan like that."

"All right, all right. I didn't do nothing to the lady. I'm going. Good-bye."

Tim protected me from my patient but seven years later as a plastic surgery resident I had no protector when another plastic surgery resident decided to bully me. He was pudgy and lazy, and in a few weeks I was running the clinics and taking the emergency calls while he rested. When a good operation came up he would rouse himself and elbow me out of the way. Later, a black male resident took my place and the same bullying started. But the black resident was a big man who had played tackle in college football.

"It worked out," he told me. "He started on me because I was black, just as he did to you because you're a woman. But I stopped him. I just told him how it would be and he knew I'd beat his face in if he didn't play fair."

Breathing Pancakes

At the V.A. I had a ward of forty patients to look after—drawing blood, ordering tests, doing admission examinations, discharging patients and checking patients before surgery. There were no medical students to help. After a while, I could manage eight physical exams in one afternoon without enormous trouble. The on-call room was in another building, which made a long cold walk to and from the ward at night. I was on call every other night, alternating with Tim Mann, and I usually got three hours of sleep. The on-call room was used as a coatroom by the chief of anesthesia. He usually barged in just as I was about to get out of bed at 6:15. The chief of surgery was amused when I complained.

"You're not in danger, Elizabeth. He hasn't looked at a woman in years, and probably doesn't even know you're there. All the same, I'll see what I can do."

After that, the chief of anesthesia barged in at 6:15 every morning, said, "That's right—I forgot. You've commandeered my room," and left, slamming the door.

Tim Mann and Rick Trudeau were wonderful to work with, and we were a good team. We did most of the surgery ourselves, with a professor watching or, if it was a simple case, with the professor outside, reading in the O.R. lounge. As an intern, my cases included hernias, amputations, appendectomies and tracheostomies.

"Elizabeth, you're not bad. I don't think I was that good as an intern," said Tim one afternoon as he assisted me on a hernia repair.

"She has good hands," said Rick, who was not scrubbing but watching over my shoulder. "Now we just have to teach her to read. When was the last time you read a surgery textbook?"

"A month ago," I said, turning around to talk to him.

"Don't stop operating! You have to be able to operate and talk at the same time. Like patting your head and rubbing your stomach."

I tried to read on my nights off, but I fell asleep before finishing a single page. Most of my learning was at a weekly surgical conference in which we had to present our cases for the next week to the chief of surgery. I usually had a hernia to present, but I could never remember the name of the hernia operation. There are many different hernia repairs, named after the surgeons who invented them: Bassini, Halsted I, Halsted II, Halsted III, McVay. Each week the chief of surgery would ask me which hernia repair I planned to use and each week I would forget the name.

"It's the one in which you . . ."

"I don't want to know how to do it. I want the name."

"It's the McKay repair."

"No, it isn't."

"It's the McPhee repair."

"No, it isn't."

"I can't remember."

"The McVay repair, Dr. Morgan. I will ask you this question every week until you remember."

The third week, when the chief asked me the name of the hernia repair, I cried "Oh, no," clutched my head and ran out. I had been trying to charge my car battery, which had run down after I left the lights on one day, and I had left the motor running, planning to turn it off after morning rounds, but I forgot. Now it had been running since 6:15 A.M. I could never have afforded to replace my car, and I felt sure someone had stolen it. I found it in the parking lot, running quietly with the battery fully charged. I turned off the car, and suddenly realized the chief of surgery would be furious. I ran back to the conference room—down three corridors and up four flights of stairs—and sat down breathless.

"I'm very sorry," I panted.

To my surprise, the chief of surgery smiled. "Elizabeth, you win. This week I will tell you the name of the hernia repair, if you tell me why you ran out."

"Yes, sir." I was still panting.

"The hernia repair is the McVay. Now it's your turn."

He waited.

I began. "You see, it's about my car. I had left the lights on last night for a while and the battery ran down, so this morning I thought I would leave it running to charge up during rounds, and I did."

"And then what did you do?" asked the chief of surgery.

"I didn't do anything. I mean, I forgot to turn the car off because I had to go to the O.R."

Rick Trudeau sat up, aghast. "Woman—you didn't leave your key in the car and the engine running all day, did you?"

"Yes. I just forgot about it." Everyone laughed.

"I find it reassuring," said the chief of surgery. "You're just like my wife. It's probably easier to teach women surgery than teach them about cars. Next week, Dr. Morgan, no excuses."

One of our new V.A. patients, Mr. George, surprised all of us by turning out to be a real war hero. He was anxious that we should know—it set him apart from the others. Mr. George had served as a Marine in the Pacific in World War II, and among his acts of heroism was to fight up the hill on Iwo Jima under heavy fire and bring back two injured buddies. He lost his left leg from a Japanese grenade.

After the war he worked at his plumbing business and raised four sons, all of them Marines. Mr. George smoked heavily and was admitted to us with gangrene of his right leg from atherosclerosis. He kept his Purple Heart and decoration pictures over his bed. Rick Trudeau told him his right leg would have to be amputated.

"Can I walk with two false legs? You know I already have one gone. I have to walk."

Rick said it would be a struggle, but it was possible.

"Then chop this leg off as fast as you can. I'm tired of looking at it."

His leg was my second amputation. After the operation Mr. George spent hours in physical therapy, strengthening his hip muscles. Six months later, smiling triumphantly, he visited the ward to show off. He was walking on two false legs.

Most of our patients who had amputations did not walk again. Mack did not, and neither did Andy, a friendly man who had served as a kitchen helper in the army, and then supported himself working as a maintenance man. After an amputation of his gangrenous left leg he had a stroke that partly paralyzed him and permanently injured his swallowing so that he needed to be fed slowly by a nurse or nursing aide.

One morning a new nursing aide was assigned to feed him. I am nearsighted, and I was quite close to Andy, changing the next patient's dressing, before I realized something was wrong. Andy sat on the side of the bed and the aide fed him pancakes soaked in maple syrup. She was impatient and Andy, who was sensitive, struggled to eat fast enough to please her. He opened his mouth and she shoveled in more pancakes, but he could not swallow them. His mouth was stuffed from cheek to cheek with pancake mush. Now that his cheeks were full, he was breathing in pancake mush and turning blue. I abandoned my other patient and scooped staggering quantities of pancakes out of Andy's mouth, allowing him to cough up all the mush that had collected in his lungs. He turned pink again, but the incident was traumatic for him. He refused to eat and would not keep a feeding tube in his nose. He came down with pneumonia and continued to lose weight. We decided that to keep him alive, he needed a gastrostomy, an operation to sew a feeding tube directly into his stomach.

The attending surgeon for the month was Dr. Ford. He had not operated with me before and decided to scrub on the case to see how I worked. I had been awake all night and Tim took me aside just before the operation to brief me.

"Liz, this one is easy. Ford uses a transverse upper abdominal incision. Skin, muscle, peritoneum and you are in the belly. Got it? The stomach is right there, but the colon may be in front so be sure you are in the stomach. You can tell because the colon has taenia— longitudinal bands that indent it."

"Taenia," I repeated to try to remember it.

"Pick it up with a Babcock clamp. Sew in two purse-string sutures of 3-0 chromic around the clamp."

"Okay, 3-0 chromic."

"Dr. Morgan," said the head nurse, "you're keeping Dr. Ford waiting."

"Just a sec," said Tim. "Then you incise the stomach, take off the clamp, pick up the stomach with toothed pick-ups, push in the tube, tie down the sutures, bring it out through a stab in the skin, sew the stomach to the abdominal wall and you're all set."

"Thank you," I said, and hurried off to the O.R. Dr. Ford was already scrubbing his hands at the sink and Rick Trudeau was scrubbing Andy's abdomen with antiseptic soap. Andy was awake. His pneumonia was too severe for us to anesthetize him safely, and we would use only local anesthesia.

"I'm sorry I'm late, Dr. Ford," I said, taking a sterile brush from the wall rack.

"One strike against you. You don't keep attendings waiting. Strike two, you don't keep chief residents waiting. Rick shouldn't be washing that skin. You should have been here half an hour ago and done all this. I've told Rick what I think about it. A late intern means a bad service. When I was an intern, if I was late I didn't operate. I have half a mind to do this operation myself to teach you a lesson."

"Yes, sir." It was my own fault, I thought. I finished scrubbing and followed Dr. Ford into the O.R.

"Elizabeth, you have got to get in here on time," said Rick Trudeau severely.

"Yes sir." I was a failure as an intern. All I could do was carry on. I watched Dr. Ford put the sterile towels around Andy's abdomen. Andy tried to sit up and watch.

"Goddammit," said Dr. Ford to the anesthesiologist, "keep him still. That's what you're paid for."

Rick walked over to me and muttered, "Don't let the bastard steal your case. Nip over to the right side and ask for the scalpel. Right now."

I walked over to the right side.

"You're on the left side today," said Dr. Ford, clipping on the drapes.

I walked back to the nonoperating side and suddenly remembered that Andy needed Novocaine before anyone operated on him.

"Scalpel," said Dr. Ford.

"Novocaine," I said.

"That's right," Dr. Ford said, tossing the knife back on the nurses' table. "I forgot."

I took the Novocaine, put the needle through Andy's abdominal skin, and Andy jumped.

"Look," said Dr. Ford to the anesthesiologist, "I told you once to keep him still. I don't want to have to tell you again."

"I'm doing what I can. I've given him Valium and—"

"Don't cry on my shoulder. Just do your job," said Dr. Ford, and to me, "Go ahead. Inject."

I started to inject. I was almost done when behind Dr. Ford's back, Rick Trudeau pulled down his mask and mouthed "Scalpel."

"Scalpel next," I said, and Rick mouthed "Good girl."

I incised the skin just as Tim had told me. Operating from the left side was awkward but not impossible.

"Good," said Dr. Ford. "Use your fingers to split the muscle apart."

I did, and Andy's thin, weak muscles spread apart.

"Two right angle retractors to me," said Dr. Ford, and with the retractors pulled the muscle further apart and out of my way.

"You hold this retractor," he said to the scrub nurse, "and give us both rat-tooth forceps. She needs a scalpel, too." With the forceps we picked up the peritoneum—the thin membrane that encloses the intestines like a plastic bag.

Andy tried to sit up again.

"It's going to hurt him," said Dr. Ford. "Just move along as fast as you can."

I incised the peritoneum with the scalpel and with scissors cut it open the full length of the skin incision. Andy tried to sit up again. Dr. Ford put down his forceps, reached into the belly and pulled out a flat, slippery, pink-brown piece of something. I had never had to identify the stomach before, and as far as I could tell, this could have been a stomach, small intestine or colon. I was about to look for taenia, which would tell us if we had the colon by mistake, when Dr. Ford said, "Stomach. That's what I like about this incision, the stomach lies right under it." I wished I could identify it so easily. He put a Babcock clamp on it and pulled it up. I sewed two circular purse-string sutures around the clamp. With forceps, I cut through

167

into the stomach. A few drops of clear watery fluid came out.

"Has to be stomach," said Dr. Ford. "If we were in the colon, we'd be seeing stool."

I pushed in the soft plastic feeding tube and pulled the sutures tight, then tied them carefully so they would hold the tube in place.

"Hurry up," said Dr. Ford.

I made a stab with the scalpel through the skin above the skin incision. Dr. Ford handed me a long clamp.

"This is a Schnit. Poke it right into the belly. Get the tube and pull the free end out through the skin."

I did that, and then, because I couldn't see from the left side of the table, he put in sutures to hold the stomach to the peritoneum so the tube would not slip out of the stomach and be free in the belly.

"You're done," said Dr. Ford. "Sew up the peritoneum with a continuous chromic, silk on the skin. Don't dawdle, and next time if you're late I really will do the case. Just because you're a pretty girl doesn't mean I have to be nice to you."

"Dr. Ford," said the intercom, "the operating room downtown wants to know how late you will be."

"I'm on my way now," and he left the room.

The first time we fed Andy through his new stomach tube he got diarrhea. An x-ray study showed that Dr. Ford had shown me how to put the tube into the colon instead of the stomach. The tube was useless, and despite a second, successful, operation, Andy was so thin and his pneumonia so severe that he lapsed into a coma.

"You'd better hang crepe with the family," said Dr. Ford. "He's falling apart."

In a few weeks Andy was dead.

There was another kind of toughness on the surgical wards. Residents must learn to operate, and at times the desire to do a new operation is as strong as the desire to help a patient.

Dr. Edwards, chief of surgery at the Veterans Hospital, was a good teacher. A Southerner with a dry sense of humor, he made us think about every operation we planned to do, and he always made me tell him how many operations I had done the week before. He wanted to be sure I was getting my share, and being properly taught by Rick and Tim.

"Tim Mann will operate on anything, living or dead, and I want to be sure he's not stealing your cases," he said sternly. "How many hernias have you done now?"

"Ten, and I've also done eight tracheostomies."

"Good. Where do you do them—in the patient's bed or in the O.R.?"

"Usually in bed. They're all in the I.C.U., and we haven't had any problems."

"Did you ever see Dr. Hillebrand or any private surgeon do a tracheostomy at a patient's bedside?"

"No."

"Why do you think they do it in the O.R.? Because it is cheaper? No. Because it is easier? No. Because it is safer? Yes. Tim is a good resident but he's been a surgeon for only a year and a half. This may come as a surprise, but he doesn't know everything."

He sat down to start the weekly preoperative conference. The most interesting case that week was presented by the chest resident. "My patient, Mr. York, is a seventy-nine-year-old man who came to the Veterans Hospital with back pain. His admission chest x-ray showed that his aorta had developed an aneurysm"—a dangerous thinning and weakening of the blood vessel. "Mr. York developed this aneurysm from a syphilis infection contracted during the First World War, before penicillin was discovered to treat it. X-rays over the sixty years since then show that the aorta slowly weakened and enlarged." The chest resident turned to the x-ray viewboard. "These are some x-rays to show the aneurysm."

The chief of surgery puffed on his pipe, peered through his bifocals at the x-rays and asked the chest resident what he planned for Mr. York.

The resident sat down and lit up his own pipe.

"We'll cut out the aneurysm and replace the blood vessel with a Dacron tube."

"You hope," murmured the chief of surgery. "What is his risk? Fifty percent?"

"Yes, he probably has a fifty-percent chance of leaving the O.R. alive."

The chief turned to another resident. "Does that bother you? Doing an operation on someone with a fifty-percent chance of coming off the table?"

The chest resident answered instead. "The man came into the

hospital with one foot in the box. He's been here two weeks and the aneurysm gets bigger every day. Now he's coughing up blood, which suggests that his aorta is leaking blood into his lungs. On the other hand, it could be his tuberculosis. This is a very sick man. The way I see it, if we operate, he will probably die. If we don't he will certainly die. His family wants him to have the operation. If he dies from surgery, so what? He will be dead from his disease in a few weeks or months, regardless. On the plus side, as a resident I have the experience. Aneurysms are rare. If I learn on York, I can't make him worse than he is, and when a salvageable guy comes in, who might live twenty years, I've had practice."

"That's one point of view," said the chief of surgery.

Later, as we made our rounds, Tim Mann asked me if I would have agreed to the operation.

I shook my head. "I'd rather live out the six days or six months."

"That's a very bad attitude for a surgeon," said Rick Trudeau. "Where did we go wrong? I'll have to work on you."

We were on our way to see one of Tim's patients, a patient with gallstones which Tim had been trying to persuade him to have removed. A gallbladder removal is a junior resident's case, and Tim was on the alert for patients with gallstones whom he could operate on. But he wasn't just making work for himself. Even gallstones that cause no symptoms should be removed. The chances are high that, if neglected, they will cause severe infection and eventually need emergency removal.

"He doesn't want his gallbladder out," said Tim. "Now what do I do?"

"Talk to him some more," said Rick. We went into the patient's room.

"You really need your gallbladder out," Tim began. "I can't let you go home with those gallstones. You could be risking your life."

"Listen, Doc, I'm scared of surgery. I don't want it."

"You need to have it done," persisted Tim. "You have a lot of stones. They could get into your liver duct. They could give you jaundice or a terrible infection."

"Doc, I told you already. I want to think it over. Don't rush me. You push me too much."

"You ought to have the surgery," said Rick. He had been standing in the doorway, listening.

"Now there's two of them ganging up on me," said the patient, turning to me. "I think I'm back in the army. Do this. Do that. What do you think?" he asked.

I took a deep breath. "As your doctor, I would recommend the surgery. On the other hand, you don't have to do anything you don't want. You can always go home and think about it. You're unlikely to get sick from the gallstones within a few weeks, so you don't really have to have it now."

Rick took my elbow and pulled me out of the room.

"Elizabeth, you should never say that. Tim won't get his case and the man will just go home and get drunk."

"If he doesn't want the surgery, he doesn't have to have it. He has a right to make up his mind."

"He doesn't have a mind to make up. You—me—Tim—we are the doctors. We know he should have his gallbladder removed, for medical reasons. You can't leave him to make up his mind. The man is an idiot. Did you see what he's reading? Comic books! And you leave it up to him to decide about surgery?"

"Hey, Doc," said our patient, standing in his doorway. "I thought about it. I'll stay to have the surgery. Like you say, it makes sense."

"Another life to be saved," said Tim as we walked away. "If I had lost that case, Elizabeth, it would have been the end of a beautiful friendship."

Hut-One

My rotation at the V.A. ended and Tim and I rotated back to the University Hospital. Tim was going to work in the E.R. and I went to orthopedic surgery—surgery of bones and joints.

"You're ready for them," said Tim as we left the hospital our last evening. "You've done thirteen hernias. That could be an all-time V.A. record. It's slow, but this is how you learn to operate."

The orthopods were a big group. There were two teams of four residents and each team had an intern. One team operated when the other saw patients in the clinic, and vice versa. As the intern I did not have to go to the clinics, and I was not often needed in the O.R. There were four residents and they all wanted to scrub on the cases. When I did go, I did not necessarily see the operation.

"We need you in the O.R. this morning," announced my chief resident one day. "We have two operations at once. Those two are doing the back. We need you to help on the total hip replacement. Eat your Wheaties. We need you to be strong."

The patient was a fat lady of fifty with severe arthritis. Her hip was going to be replaced with a metal joint so that she could walk again. I washed my hands, put on the gown, and looked forward to seeing the operation, which was a new one then.

The chief resident looked at me doubtfully as he started to operate.

"I hope you're stronger than you look." He weighed 250 pounds and had been an All-American fullback.

"Elizabeth will be fine," said the senior resident, who weighed 225 and had been an All-American halfback. "It's all a matter of position and strategy. You don't have to be strong. All you do is take the knee and hold the leg up. When we say 'pull,' you pull so the hip comes out of the socket. It's easy."

I held up the leg. It was heavy. The scrub nurse piled folded sterile sheets under the knee to support it and help me hold it up. In the next half hour my shoulders began to ache but I kept the leg up.

"We're almost ready for you," said the chief resident after thirty minutes. "You can pull now." He was concentrating on the operation. "Pull. Harder." He looked around for me. "What happened to her?" I was on the floor. I had pulled so hard that I had lost balance and fallen down.

"I guess we're asking a lot," the chief resident said. He grabbed the patient by the hip bones. The senior resident took the thigh. They crouched for the snap.

"One—two—three—*pull,*" said the chief resident.

"Wait—you're pulling her off the table," complained the anesthesiologist. They readjusted.

"Elizabeth, you help me," said the senior resident. I had changed my gown and gloves, after falling on the floor.

"Pull," said the chief resident.

"It's coming out of the joint—not quite. Keep pulling. Pull. Relax. We'll have to try again."

The attending orthopedic surgeon scrubbed in to help. He had been an All-American quarterback.

"You're the new intern, aren't you?" he said to me. "All I want you to do is stand back." He took the leg, with the senior resident.

"Hut-one, hut-two, hut-three, pull. Slow and steady. Go team—keep pulling. It's coming. Pull. More. Relax. The hip is out of the joint. Good work, men. You can come back," he said to me, breathing heavily, his brow sweating. "Just hold the leg up by the knee like so. Relax. It isn't heavy. We'll let you take a look when the interesting part comes."

They forgot to let me look until I reminded them, so I had time to reflect on my own physical limitations. Any woman is strong enough to do any surgery except surgery on the shoulder, hip and knee joints

173

of an adult. Then she needs two or three men to help her. A man also needs help from other men but a woman needs more. I couldn't bench press 250 pounds and in bone surgery there are times when you need a couple of men who can. I know two successful woman orthopods, and they are no stronger than I am, but they have had to learn when to corral strong male doctors or strong male orderlies to help them during surgery.

Tim Mann used to call me at night to see if orthopedics was slow and to tell me to come down to the E.R. to see what was happening.

"You'd love it down here, Elizabeth. A lot of action."

Usually I could not go because I had too much scut work, but occasionally I had time to visit the E.R. or join other interns and residents for dinner and talk. It was at dinner that we told medical stories, talking freely once the cafeteria was officially closed and patients' families had gone. I tried to be careful, because Dr. Hillebrand had once told me of a woman who learned that her sister was dying from cancer by overhearing two residents talking at lunch. Sometimes I had a chance to talk to Leslie, the other woman surgical intern, but we could rarely arrange to meet. We were always on different rotations, usually in different hospitals. The women pediatricians were friendly but it was hard to get to know them. They never ate dinner as late as I did and I never had time to meet them at lunch in the cafeteria. At dinner I might see Susan O'Donnell, a woman intern in medicine with whom I became good friends. The only other woman doctors I saw were the female medical students who occasionally ate dinner in the hospital instead of in the dorm. Janet Rome, the chief resident in neurosurgery, never had time to eat dinner.

I missed talking with other women, and I would stay up late at times, chatting with the nurses, whose company I enjoyed.

One evening at dinner Susan and I and the surgical residents and interns on call were entertained by "Speedy" Sam, a urology resident back from Vietnam, where he had operated on the front lines in the mud for two years.

"Psychiatrists!" he said, and stabbed his rhubarb pie in disgust. "They'll drive you nuts. I was paged one night this week to the psychiatry ward for an emergency. I ran there as fast as I could. I arrived breathless, and gasped to the man behind the desk. 'I'm the urologist. You just called me for an emergency.'

"'Oh,' he says.

"'I was called for an *emergency*.'

"'Oh.'

"'Where is it? Is someone dying?'

"'You can't talk here.'

"'This is the nurses' station, isn't it?'

"'Yes.'

"'Where is the psychiatry chief resident? I was just called for an emergency.'

"'He's not on the ward,' the man tells me.

"'Where is his office?'

"'Down the hall.'

"'Is he in his office?'

"'You can't talk here.'

"'Well, goddammit, one of your patients is supposed to be dying.'

"'You mustn't swear. It upsets the patients.'

"'Is there any other doctor around?'

"'Yes.'

"'Where?'

"'I am the psychiatry resident in charge.'

"'Where is your patient?'

"'You can't talk here. This area is reserved for visitors.'

"'I am a visitor. Do you have a patient called Smythe? I received a consult for a patient by that name today. Maybe it's the same problem.'

"'Yes, Mrs. Smythe is with us.'

"'Is she sick?'

"'I can't discuss that. It's confidential.'

"'Where is she?'

"'Visiting hours are over now. It's eight o'clock. Your patient is probably in group therapy.'

"'Why was I called for an emergency if she's in group therapy?'

"'Her doctor will tell you.'

"'Where is he?'

"'At home.'

"'You mean a psychiatrist has me stat paged when he's sitting at home reading? Do you know what you can do with this consult requisition? You can fold it up and—'

"'You can't talk here.'

"I gave up," said Sam, "but the next day I'm called out of the O.R. to the phone for an emergency. It's a psychiatrist.

"'Hello,' I say.

"'We have a patient here.'

"'Right.'

"'Her name is Smythe.'

"'Right.'

"'She has not passed any urine for three days.'

"This did not surprise me, because a lot of drugs the shrinks use cause urinary retention. 'Is her bladder distended?' I asked.

"'What?'

"'Is she distended—is her abdomen bloated by a bladder full of urine?'

"'I don't know.'

"'Go and examine your patient and then tell me. Do you remember how to examine a patient?'

"He doesn't answer. Ten minutes later, he comes back to the phone.

"'Hello,' he says.

"'Is she distended?' I ask him.

"'I don't know.'

"'Fine. I'll come down to examine her.'

"I see the lady and her bladder is ready to explode. This pissed me off, because untreated distension can cause kidney damage. I tell the psychiatrist, 'Your patient is distended. May I show you her abdomen so the next time you can make the diagnosis?'

"'I can't examine her. It would ruin our therapeutic relationship.'

"'Are you a doctor?'

"'Yes.'

"'Your patient has to have a tube in her bladder to drain the urine.'

"'She can't have that. It would destroy her mental self-image.'

"'She hasn't voided for three days. She must have a catheter.'

"'She can't have that.'

"'She won't void without a tube. She can get kidney damage.'

"'Psychologically, she could not tolerate a bladder tube.'

"'You make the decision. You are her doctor.'

"'Aren't you going to help her? We called you for advice.'

"'I told you my advice. She has to have a tube.'

"'She can't have one.'

"'Good-bye.'

"No wonder the patients are crazy," Sam went on. "They have to talk to psychiatrists all day. At eight o'clock that night the psychiatrist called me again."

"'She hasn't voided.'

"'I know. She won't be able to void without a tube.'

"'She can't have that.'

"'Good-bye.'

"'Wait! Does she really need a tube?'

"'Yes.'

"'Will you come now to put it in?'

"'The nurses can do it.'

"'No. It would interfere with our professional rapport.'

"'Have them get things ready for me.'

"'They can't do that, it would . . .'

"'I'll take care of everything.'

"I bring a bladder tube and put it in. Four gallons of urine pour out. The patient feels more comfortable. I tell the psychiatrist to leave the tube in. No one can void normally for three days after urinary retention."

"'I can't do that—mentally she is unable to cope with such a body-image alteration.'

"'You have to.'

"Three days later he calls me at home at four in the morning. He must have insomnia.

"'She hasn't voided.'

"'Did you leave the tube in?'

"'No.'

"'Did I tell you it was necessary?'

"'Yes.'

"'Good-bye. You can find a new urologist.'

"'Aren't you going to help us? I'll tell the nurses to leave the tube in. You have to come to do it now. I'm at home, but the nurses called to say she is uncomfortable.'

"'You turkey. It's four in the morning. I'm at home, too. I just finished an operation. Tell your nurses to do it. This is routine nursing care . . .'

"'We can't have them . . .'

"I give up, go to the hospital and put in the tube. Next morning he calls me to ask if the tube can come out now, and I told him that if he had it removed, I'd strangle him with it. He decided to leave it in. What a turkey."

Susan O'Donnell shook her head. "You surgeons really have it in for psychiatrists. You never give them a break, but when it's your patient who goes off his head, hallucinates and gets violent you scream for the psychiatrists louder than anyone else. Surgeons aren't perfect either, you know. At medical school we had a surgical resident who was a kleptomaniac. The cops found him one morning holed up in his on-call room with hundreds of typewriters, wheelchairs, hospital stretchers—everything. He had stolen thousands of dollars of equipment from the hospital, and the psychiatrists locked him up—said he cracked under the stress of a surgical residency. It could happen to you, too, Sam."

We all laughed and got up from the table to go back to work.

"Susan's in medicine, isn't she?" Sam asked me later. "She belongs in surgery. She is one tough lady."

Mr. Wonderful

After orthopedics, I went to neurosurgery. Janet Rome was my chief resident and there were three other neurosurgery residents on the service. My first night on call, a man was found beaten up on a sidewalk and was brought to the hospital in a coma. A cerebral angiogram was done. This is an x-ray study to see if there was bleeding in his brain. He had a subdural hematoma—blood clots on one side of his head that needed to be removed if he were to live.

Janet Rome and Brian, the senior resident, took the patient to the O.R. At 8:00 P.M. the operating room nurse called me. "Dr. Rome wants you up here."

When I came into the room, Janet was standing by the patient's head. He was asleep, covered by sterile green sheets except for his head. Even his face was covered. The skin of the scalp had been cut and folded back, the bone removed and red, swollen brain was bulging out. Brian, the senior neurosurgery resident, stood beside Janet with suction.

"Careful, Brian," she said and with a broad metal spatula moved the brain gently to one side. The whole side of the brain, I could see, was black with blood.

"Suction there gently," she told him. He put the tip of the suction gently near the damaged brain and with an abrupt, slurping sound

179

the mixture of blood clot and torn-up brain was sucked up and I was looking at a hole where part of the brain had been.

"There goes high school, down the tube," said Brian.

"Not to mention speech, memory, walking, and a few other essential human actions," added Janet. She saw me for the first time.

"Elizabeth, I'm glad you got here. I wanted you to see what bleeding within the brain can do. We are now operating on what is practically a corpse. We didn't expect to see so much damage when we started the operation, but as you can see, almost the entire brain is shredded and mushy from bleeding everywhere. This man will stop breathing shortly after the anesthesiologist removes the tube from his lungs at the end of the operation. He may hang on for a few hours, or even a few days, but the brain stem injury makes breathing impossible for long. In any case, the rest of the brain is so torn up he would be a vegetable if he survived. Brian was up all night with me yesterday and I want him to go home and sleep. You scrub in and help me close."

I scrubbed, and when I was gowned and gloved Brian backed away from the table. The nurse helped him off with his gown and gloves. "Thanks, Janet," he said. "I'll see you tomorrow at six."

I wondered how Janet managed. She had been awake for three nights in a row, and yet she stood up straight, her eyes red, her skin a yellow-white, working slowly but methodically. She fitted the piece of bone from the skull back into place, and unfolded the scalp skin over it.

"We're just going to sew up the skin. You start on this end of the incision. Use 3-0 silk."

The man would be dead as soon as the anesthesiologist stopped breathing oxygen into his lungs. I decided to test myself to see how fast I could put in sutures. It wouldn't matter if they weren't neat. I had tied six sutures when Janet leaned over and looked at them.

"No good, Elizabeth. You have to take them out. I know you're tired. I am, too, and I know he's as good as dead but never do sloppy work. Always do your best. Especially as a woman. You have to try even harder. You can't be satisfied with being as good as the men. You have to be better. Otherwise they won't respect you." She clenched her teeth and I noticed her jaw harden behind the mask. I cut my sutures out and started again. A few moments later she looked over again. "Better. Much better."

She wrapped a white bandage around the man's head when all the sutures were in. We took off the sterile drapes, and with the nurse's help lifted the man from the table onto the stretcher. I wheeled him into Recovery where Janet removed the tube from his lungs. He did not breathe.

"Pronounce him dead in three minutes," she told me, taking off her mask. "Then meet me on the ward. I'm going to start rounds."

There were only two patients on the service who could speak. One was a man who had to be tied in bed. He screamed obscenities all day and once, when his hands were left unbound, he hit his wife, threw a water pitcher at a nurse, and bit the professor of neurosurgery on the arm.

The other patient who could speak was a black woman doctor in her forties with a cancer in her spine which had paralyzed her legs. She was dying. "Another woman surgeon!" she said when she met me. "I thought Dr. Rome was the only one. I have a friend, another black woman, also a doctor, and dying from breast cancer now. It seems such a waste after those years of struggle. I'm glad to see you two going into surgery now."

The rest of our twenty patients were unconscious. A few would groan if their faces were pinched. A few made grunting sounds if the nurse shouted loudly at them. Many of them had frequent seizures which made them shake all over. The nurses had to wedge their mouths open to prevent them from biting their tongues in half during a seizure.

Janet had seen most of the patients before I got to the ward, but it was my job to go around after she left to make sure that Mr. X was not in a deeper coma than he had been in the morning, that Mrs. Y did not have a fever from a brain infection, and that Mr. Z had not untied his hands and strangled the night nurse. From habit, my first night on, I said to every patient, "Hello, how are you tonight?" None of them answered, and I could hear my voice echo in the hallway as I spoke to them. The only sound was the breathing machines, breathing for the two new comatose car-accident victims.

My last visit was to a patient in the I.C.U. who had had a tumor in his brain removed during surgery that morning. I turned on the light over his bed and startled the patient, who sat up, his head wrapped in a white turban bandage. He smiled at me broadly, wide awake. He looked alert and happy, not at all as though he had just had brain surgery. I smiled back, and said, "I'm sorry to wake you. You look great. How do you feel?"

"Wonderful!" exclaimed the patient and shook hands with me.

"I suppose you feel pretty tired, though," I went on.

"Wonderful!" was the reply.

"That's nice to hear."

"Wonderful!" smiled my patient.

I paused.

"Excuse me, sir," I asked, "but could you tell me your name?"

"Wonderful!"

"Do you know where you are?"

"Wonderful!"

"What year is this?"

"Wonderful!"

"Now, I want you to think hard. Where exactly are you? Do you know?"

The patient's smile faded.

"Tell me your name. Do you know your name? It isn't Wonderful. Tell me your name." I had to know if he knew.

The patient sank back and began to cry.

"I'm sorry. It's hard, I know, and you're doing very well. I hope you don't mind my coming and asking a lot of silly questions?" I patted his hand to comfort him.

"Wonderful!" said my patient, smiling happily.

"Good night, sir. I'll see you in the morning." I switched off the light.

I heard him say "wonderful" to himself three more times before he fell asleep again.

After that first night, I decided not to become a neurosurgeon.

Neurosurgery was my last rotation as an intern and it was made much more difficult by an enthusiastic neurosurgical professor who was doing some research. My job as intern included assisting in research whenever needed, but after Oxford I knew my talent for research was limited. Besides, the ward was back-breakingly busy as it was: I had thirty patients on one ward, twenty on another, two in the adult I.C.U., two in the pediatric I.C.U., and nine other patients scattered around. Sixty-three patients altogether, not counting the research patient, and I had had ten hours' sleep in seven days. I was so tired that when I smoked a cigarette it made me giddy, but I still smoked almost two packs a day. Something in the tobacco made me not care so much about being tired. And now I had to do research.

The professor handed me a sheet of instructions for the tests I had to perform and went away to a week-long conference. I read the research sheet. It did not sound difficult. I had to draw blood samples from the research patient and do other tests on Tuesday, Wednesday, and Thursday, exactly five, six, and seven days after the first four days of baseline studies, which were blood samples drawn every six hours, day and night. The research depended on precise timing. "Not a day earlier, not a day later. Timing is of the essence," said the professor before he left.

Many of our patients were very sick, but in between looking after them I tried to remember the research, and found I had lost the research sheet. "Two, three and four days after. No, six, seven and eight days. That's a day off. The tests began four, six and nine days— no, that's not right." I called the head nurse on the research floor, who knew the project. "On days five, six and seven you do the tests, Doctor." She was friendly the first time I called to check the days, but soon my calls became routine. She called me every four hours during the first three days to remind me to come to take the baseline blood studies.

On the third day, when the baseline studies were being done, the head nurse had the flu and went home. Her assistant forgot to call me, and I had 63 patients to care for and forgot to call her. But despite being awake all night for two days in a row again, I had it down in my notebook that the research tests were to be done on days five, six and seven.

With my lack of sleep I began to get confused. On Monday morning, day four of the research, a new dietician served Tuesday's menu (farina, bacon) instead of Monday's (oatmeal, bacon, eggs). I ate breakfast and concluded from the menu that it was Tuesday, day five of research. Janet Rome was in the O.R. and there was no one else who knew enough about the research to correct me. To add to my confusion, the hospital administrator had posted notices about standard time and daylight saving time. I did not read it carefully, but it seemed time would not be the same time in the near future.

After breakfast I became somnolent instead of comatose, and realizing that it was day five of research, I chugged off to the research ward and did the test, which consisted of injecting the patient with glucose and taking blood samples every ten minutes for three hours. Twenty-four hours later, after only two hours' sleep, I repeated the test. I was rather proud of being such a reliable research assistant. I went home that night and slept eight hours. The next day, in the middle of the "last research test," I realized that it was not Thursday but Wednesday, the fourteenth.

I had finished the test and had used all the special glucose so I could not do it again the next day. I was so appalled by my incompetence that I could not confess to anyone, not even Janet. The professor returned and liked the results of my research. He said they were just what he expected, and that I was a credit to the department. I told him the timing might be wrong, but he was not interested. He never listened to the intern.

He was disappointed that not all the patients gave the same results as mine, but six months later he presented his findings at an international meeting. All his research had been done by interns, and when I discussed it with Mark and Zach, we all ended up confessing to each other than *none* of us had done it right.

A year later the professor was appointed chairman of a department on the strength of his research.

Coming of Age

Residency

The Case of the Vanishing Bullet

On June 24, the internship year ended and I took the new intern, a short cocky young man, on rounds to introduce him to the patients on neurosurgery and brief him on how the service was run.

"Don't worry about it," I told him. "You probably think you can't do it, that you can't operate, but as long as you do what you're told and ask when you don't know, you'll be fine."

"Shit," he said, "I'm okay. I'm not going to bust my ass for anyone. I can take care of patients. I want to learn how to operate, make them let me do a few of the big cases."

"Good luck," I said and left him to start his internship. His confidence impressed me. I wished I could have been like him a year ago, but I had been a surgeon for a year and I knew how the system worked. I was a woman, but I had worked hard, taken orders and criticism, and done the scut. I didn't demand to operate; I was happy to be allowed to do cases. In return, I had learned I could survive more fatigue and stress than I would have thought possible a year before. I was getting tough. I could diagnose many surgical illnesses, and knew what studies were needed and what operations should be done. I could operate well enough to remove moles and warts, drain abscesses, remove appendixes, and repair simple hernias. Janet Rome had even let me make the skin incision and remove part of the skull for a brain operation. I had been abused, taken for granted and treated like the cheap labor that I was. But I was confident to the point where I didn't have to put M.D. after my name every time I wrote out a check to pay a bill. I had survived, and unless I misunderstood the system completely, this new intern would not. (It turned out I was right. After one year, he quit and went to work in a general clinic.)

After I left him, I went to my on-call room to get my overnight case, and found Leslie Andrews in the hall. "Leslie, can you believe it's over?"

"It's amazing."

"Incredible!"

"Congratulations!" and we hugged each other.

My internship ended with five days' vacation before our first-year residency began on the first of July. I took a limousine to the airport and went home, where I announced I did not feel tired, and slept most of the next five days.

When I returned as a resident I started in the emergency room rotation. We would spend over four months working in the E.R. as first-year residents, working two twenty-four hour shifts every five days. It looked much easier than being an intern. Mark Lehman was to work with me. Leslie was to work with Eric. Mark and I looked at the schedule in the E.R. the first morning.

"Lizzie," he said, "lend me a cigarette. We have just had bad news."

"I stopped smoking last week. What's the bad news?"

"You stopped? That isn't fair. Now who do I steal cigarettes from?"

"Buy some."

"*Buy?* Never. I've been smoking for ten years and haven't bought a pack yet. It keeps me from smoking too much."

"What's the bad news?"

"Look at the schedule. We're on July Fourth. Do you know what that means? Gunshot wounds and car accidents by the dozen. Liz, do you have any enemies in the surgical office who would do this to you?"

"None that I know. Do you?"

"Sure. Last week the chairman of the surgery department asked me what I thought of my internship. I told him. I said I agreed with

Hillebrand. The program has potential, but the full-time faculty are lazy and don't teach, and the best surgeons are the private surgeons. I said this wasn't a teaching program, it was an immigrant labor camp. I offered to buy the program. I said my father could use the cheap labor in his business. The chairman frothed at the mouth and walked off. I have plenty of enemies. If you and I can survive July Fourth in the emergency room, we can face anything."

Our first day in the E.R. was July second. Mark and I worked from 7:00 A.M. on the second to 7:00 A.M. on the third, and we learned a lot. We could save patients from dying, but we did not know what to prescribe for a stubbed toe. We had worked with hospital patients, and no one is admitted to the hospital for a stubbed toe. We consulted each other.

"Liz, what do you do for anal warts?"

"Send them to dermatology clinic. The dermatologists burn them with podophyllin. What about sunburn?"

"Calamine lotion. That's what my mother used."

We treated fractured bones well, but we had to call the orthopedic resident for advice about a sprained ankle. At 9:00 P.M. the red emergency ambulance phone rang. It was the triage nurse.

"A man is coming in an ambulance, shot in the neck. He will be in your code room."

A code room is a disaster room, stocked for all emergencies, including emergency surgery for gunshot wounds to the heart. It was my turn for a patient. Mark was still sewing up a man with a face laceration from a broken beer bottle. I frowned, thinking of everything I had read about bullet wounds of the neck—they were often fatal. A few minutes later a policeman escorted in a talkative young man on an ambulance stretcher.

"Listen," said the man, "I was just standing there. I didn't see who it was, man. I was just standing there outside the bar minding my own business."

He was surprised to find that I was a doctor but he recovered quickly. The policeman ordered him to remove his shirt so I could see where he was shot. The entrance wound was just above the collar bone, a bad place to be shot. He would probably collapse at any moment. I started an intravenous line and sent off emergency blood tests. I checked the carotid artery and jugular veins in his neck. There was no neck swelling from major bleeding. No nerves seemed

189

to be damaged. He could move his arm and shrug his shoulder. I relaxed slightly. The man said he thought it was a .38-caliber pistol, though he still denied to the police that he had seen his assailant. His blood pressure and pulse were normal. I decided it was safe to send him across the hall for an x-ray. There was no exit wound; the bullet had to be in him. That was dangerous. Bullets can travel under the skin and end up in strange places, even in the lung, heart or liver.

The x-ray of his neck was normal. There was no bullet. An x-ray of his face was normal. There was no bullet. An x-ray of the chest and another of the abdomen were also normal. The policeman was happy to wait while all the x-rays were taken. He read the newspaper and drank coffee in the doctors' lounge in the E.R. The radiology resident looked at all the x-rays with me.

"It's funny. We ought to see the bullet. Should we x-ray his arms and legs?"

George, the evening director of the x-ray department, looked at the x-rays with us. He was not a doctor. He was in charge of the x-rays, seeing that they were filed away properly. I knew him well because during the day he was director of the x-ray file room at the Veterans Hospital. If an x-ray at the V.A. was lost and needed for an operation, I would just ask George to find it. He would look at the floor and say, "That's a familiar name. Is your patient on 4 West? The new radiologist took that film two days ago. I bet it's still in her private file." This time he looked at the x-rays and shook his head. He walked to my patient, who was lying on a stretcher, and peered at the wound in his neck, then motioned me to follow him into the hallway, which was empty. He lit a cigarette and asked me, "Liz, have you found the bullet?"

"No, but it may be in his arm."

"You're sure he was shot with a bullet?"

"I can see the wound."

"I saw the wound, too. Liz, you know I'm not a doctor, and please don't get mad . . ."

"Tell me what you think, George. I don't mind."

"I don't think there was any bullet to go through his skin. It looks like an air gun injury to me."

I looked at him in horror, and went back to check my patient. He was right. The wound was ugly and bloody, but when I pushed aside the shreds of skin over the "bullet hole," I could see the deeper skin was not injured. George motioned me back into the hallway.

"Elizabeth," he whispered between drags on his cigarette, "just tell him he was lucky not to be hurt worse, that the x-rays are normal and the bullet didn't go into him. It's true, isn't it? And he'll be happy. It's good news."

The man was happy and went with the policeman to police headquarters to make a report. I told Mark about it afterwards.

"Lizzie, think what a mess it would be if it was the other way 'round. Yesterday one of the guys sent a man home with a broken leg! I heard an orthopod calling him this morning, asking him to come back right away."

Two days later on July Fourth the city celebrated with a fireworks display on the beach. Mark and I had worked July second, and had no sleep at all for those twenty-four hours. We did not even sit down. The nurses ordered pizza for us at lunch and take-out hamburgers for dinner. We ate them standing up while we wrote out prescriptions and emergency room notes. July Fourth began the same way. We started work at eight, and found Leslie and Eric were still seeing patients who had signed in at 5:00 A.M. They went home, and Mark and I took over. We drank quarts of coffee. Already we found emergency work unsatisfying. We rarely saw our patients again, and had no way of knowing if we had done the right thing or not. We were entirely on our own. The other residents referred to us as "the poor bastards in the Pit." At ten in the morning on July Fourth we had twenty patients waiting with broken legs, cut hands, cut feet, dog bites, and cut faces from car accidents. By two o'clock there were forty surgical patients in the waiting room and we had no time to care how long patients had to wait to see us. We were sewing up patients on stretchers in the hallways, and after one day in the E.R. we were almost twice as fast at sewing up skin. Our biggest rooms—the code rooms, each meant for one serious case—had four patients in each. In my code room, one patient had appendicitis and was admitted to the hospital for surgery. One patient had his leg torn apart. A car had run over it. The skin and muscles were in shreds, and both bones were broken. He was admitted to the hospital for surgery. The third had run across the beach in bare feet and had broken glass in his foot.

I dug the glass out and sent him home on crutches. He had waited six hours to see me. It took me an hour to get the glass out. In the other code room, Mark sewed up a girl's wrist, cut on the windshield in a car accident. A year later she came back to the E.R. Mark had missed a piece of glass, and it was now coming through the skin in her palm. Amazingly, no tendons or nerves had been cut as the glass worked its way to the surface.

At five o'clock on the evening of July Fourth, I was eating cold pizza and scribbling a patient note. Jerry Tamourean, the senior surgical resident, came down to the E.R. to visit Mark and me.

"Have you two seen the waiting room?" he asked in astonishment. "What did you do? Run a color ad in the newspaper?"

"They've seen a hundred and eighty patients in the past nine hours," said Sandy, the triage nurse, looking at her clipboard. "You have some beauties waiting in the cubicles. One girl there has taught me some new curse words, and I thought I had heard everything." She slapped a stack of papers in front of us. "When you're finished in the code room, start on these. They've been here since noon."

Jerry ate the rest of the cold pizza on the counter.

"I've never seen anything like it," he said. "You ought to have some help. We're about to take the appendix out on the patient you sent to us, Elizabeth. That's our third case from you guys today. After that, I'll come and give you a hand."

The intercom crackled and a nasal voice announced, "X-ray says they have forty patients waiting in their hallway. They won't accept any more patients in x-ray for the next half-hour."

"Ambulance," shouted Sandy. Every patient that came by ambulance was seen immediately, ahead of everyone else. The ambulance man wheeled in a stretcher carrying a lady in tears.

I followed her into the code room, where there were three other people waiting. She did not look injured. I introduced myself.

"I'm going to die," she sobbed.

"What is the matter?" I asked.

"I should have come in a month ago."

"Tell me the trouble, and don't cry," I said, patting her shoulder.

"My cat scratched me." She was still crying.

"Show me where."

She pointed to her left leg. I saw a healed abrasion.

She continued, "And my friend next door said I could die from lockjaw."

"When was your last tetanus shot?"

"Six weeks ago."

"You won't get lockjaw. The shot can protect you for five years. Why did you come in now?"

"I just remembered, and I had nothing else to do."

"Why did you take an ambulance?"

She looked indignant. "I always take an ambulance to the emergency room. That way I don't have to wait in line."

"That isn't right," I objected, "and it's expensive, too."

"I don't pay for it. Welfare does. They always pay for the ambulance but they won't always pay for a taxi."

"You're free to go home now, at any rate. I have quite a few seriously injured patients to see."

"Call me a cab before you go, and fill out my cab form so welfare will pay."

"How far away do you live?"

"Three blocks."

"Why don't you walk? You don't need a taxi for medical reasons."

"I can't walk."

"Why not?"

"I just won't."

"Fine. Then call a friend and sit in the waiting room."

"Sign my cab form, Doctor. I'm too busy to wait."

"I won't sign the form. You don't need a taxi ride for medical reasons. You may walk or wait, but not here. We need the room for patients."

"You can't treat me like this," she shouted, getting off the table. "I'll tell my social worker. I'll have a lawyer. You mother-fucking shithead doctors!" She stormed out.

"So that's where my tax money goes," said a man sitting on a stool with a bloody bandage wrapped around his hand. "And that's why I've been waiting three hours."

"I'm sorry. We just see people in turn, except for ambulance cases, and we have to see them first."

I went to the surgical cubicles where my next patients were. The first patient was an alcoholic, asleep on a stretcher. A friend had hit him over the head with a lead pipe in a barroom fight and I had to check to be sure he had not suffered a brain injury. Then I turned to a black girl who had been thrown from a cab and had a scraped leg. She had a beautiful face. She was about twenty, heavily made up, with very high heels, a short low-cut silky dress, and costume jewelry rings on every finger.

"You dirty honkies," she screamed at me. "You hate blacks so much you won't even treat them. I was in a car accident and I been here waiting for four hours."

"I am very sorry," I said, "we just see people in turn."

"In turn! I've heard that shit before. You're so low you are disgusting. Don't touch me," she shouted. "I want to see the surgeon in charge."

"I am the surgeon in charge down here."

"You're a liar! You're a honky liar!"

One of the hospital security officers walked in and stood by me. He was six feet two, very strong, and black.

"Young lady," he said in a deep voice, "this is a hospital. I want you to keep calm. Answer the doctor's questions. She will look after you."

"Don't hit me," she screamed at him. "Don't touch me! Leave me alone! Don't beat me!"

A small crowd of people, black and white, started to gather around the cubicle, and Sandy, the triage nurse, told them to go away. A thin, elegantly dressed young man pushed forward, his hat balanced at an angle over one eye.

"Shut up, girl," he said to her very quietly. "You're working for me. I don't want you ever to leave work in a cab without a man beside you. When the doctor is through, I'll take you back."

The security man looked at them both in disgust and walked away. A black woman with two children was sitting on a stretcher next to them.

"Excuse me," I said to her, as my patient asked her boyfriend if he still loved her. "If you would like, you can wait in the hallway. I'll call you when I'm through."

"Thank you," she said, taking her children by the hand. "It bothers me to have my children around folks like that. We'll just wait outside."

After I had taken care of the girl, and then the mother and her children, Sandy brought in two more groups of patients, both white this time. There were two young men together and two teenage girls in cut-off blue jeans.

I left the room to look for some more suture kits. By the time I came back there was a fight brewing.

One of the young men minced up to me.

"Doctor, these young ladies are being rude to my friend. Please tell them to apologize." His friend was sitting on a stretcher, examining the rings on his hand.

"You're nothing but a pair of pansies," said the younger girl, who looked thirteen. "I'm not nice to pansies."

"Karen, don't say things like that," said the other girl. She seemed to be her elder sister.

"Why not? I can talk, can't I? It's a free country. You don't have the right to stop me. They *are* pansies. Look at him look at his rings. A fairy."

"You just shut your mouth, little child," said the first young man. "You are so ugly I don't want to look at you. You make me want to vomit."

"You can't talk to my little sister like that," yelled the older sister.

"It's a free country, isn't it?" mimicked the first young man.

"I want all of you to be quiet, please," I said, loudly and firmly. "This is a hospital. You can't fight here. I will see each of you in turn. Who was here first?"

"The snotty fairy flew in first," said the thirteen-year-old girl.

"You old hag," said the young man with the rings. "Your mother ought to wash your mouth out with soap, and I hope you choke on it, you little bitch."

"Go fuck each other," screamed the older sister.

"Go fuck yourself," screamed the first young man.

"Darling, ignore her," said the young man with the rings. He stood up and brushed himself off. "I can see we're not wanted here. We don't have to listen to this motherfucking shit. Let's go somewhere else where we are treated properly."

"Yeah," screamed the little girl. "Go fuck your cat, fuck your mother. Fly away, fairy fucker."

"You have to sign out before you go," I protested.

"Go fuck yourself, nurse," said the first young man, and they were gone.

I counted to ten, washed my hands, and turned to the thirteen-year-old girl.

"I'm sorry," she said smiling sweetly. "I hate fairies."

"You were very rude."

"I know. I can say a lot of dirty things."

"Show me what's wrong with your hand." She unwrapped a dirty, bloody handkerchief from her left hand.

"What happened?"

"I got angry so I stabbed myself with a knife. I do that when I'm angry."

"It will need some stitches," I said, looking at the gash across her palm. Only the skin was cut. The nerves and tendons beneath were unharmed.

"No nurse is sewing me up."

"I'm the surgeon, not a nurse."

"Well, no shit-faced asshole motherfucking doctor is sewing up my fucking hand. You can't push me around." She punched at me with her fist. I dodged. The emergency room psychiatrist came up behind me. His counseling room was next door and he must have heard her shouting.

"Commit her. You don't have to take that language."

"I can't commit her."

"I can. She's crazy. Will she let you sew her hand up?"

"No."

"Do you mind if I commit her? She's obviously uncontrollable."

"Please go right ahead."

"Come to my office, both of you," he said to the sisters.

"You twerp-faced asshole. I'm not taking orders."

The psychiatrist smiled. "You will come to my office. Either you walk, or eight security guards hold you down, put you in a strait jacket, and drag you there."

"I'll come. Just don't commit me to the state hospital in Anderson. I like the other one better."

They walked out. "Never," I vowed to myself, "will I ever complain about psychiatrists again."

Sandy came in running. "Elizabeth, in about two minutes the ambulances are bringing two bad gunshot wounds from the fireworks on the beach. Can you be ready in the code room?"

"I'm coming."

By now Jerry Tamourean, the senior resident, had returned to help us. He joined Mark and me in the code room as the siren scream came closer and then stopped. In a moment two ambulance men came running down the E.R. ramp with a stretcher.

"I'll take it," I said to Mark. "You take the next."

As I pulled the stretcher into my code room, the second stretcher passed by. There was a young girl screaming on my stretcher, and an angry boy on the other one.

The girl was asking hysterically, "Is my boyfriend all right? Is he all right? Is he all right?"

I checked her rapidly. Her left cheek was grazed by a bullet wound. Her right wrist had a bullet entrance and exit wound. One bone was broken—I could feel it—but the blood vessels and nerves were unharmed. There were no other wounds. I grabbed a nurse next to me by the arm.

"She needs an x-ray, and before that, wrap it in a sterile dressing and tape it to a splint so she can't move it. I'm going to help Mark."

In the other room the boy was dead white. A nurse had just finished cutting his clothes off. There were three bleeding bullet wounds in his belly. He was coughing and vomiting blood. Two orderlies held him on the table. He was trying to climb off to see if his girl friend next door was all right. At the same time, a nurse, checking his blood pressure, shouted, "Lie down, you idiot. You have no blood pressure." And Mark, feeling for his pulse and finding none, yelled, "Lie down, you idiot. You're bleeding to death." He and Jerry were putting in two large intravenous needles while an E.R. secretary stood by with a clipboard, asking the boy his last name, his home address, if he had Blue Cross/Blue Shield, and if he knew the insurance policy number.

"Leave me alone," he shouted, trying to get off the table. "I want to kill the bastards who shot my girl friend."

A police officer standing on the other side of the room was trying to get his attention, asking if he could describe and/or recognize the man who shot him. I took a stomach tube and shoved it down his nose into his stomach. Blood spurted out of the tube. Mark was taping the intravenous needle and tubing to his left arm. The head nurse was taping down the second one that Jerry had inserted into the jugular vein. I drew blood from the needle in the jugular vein and sent the orderly running to the blood bank—he would leave that blood to be typed and bring back untyped emergency-release blood.

As he left, Jerry called to him, "If the turkeys in the blood bank don't give you four units of blood stat, I'll take them to court for murder. This boy will die without blood." Then he looked at me and shrugged. "He ought to be dead already."

I put a tube through the boy's penis into his bladder. A technician slid an x-ray plate under his chest and another under his belly and x-rayed him while we were working. In an emergency room the staff is repeatedly exposed to x-rays. There is no way to avoid it.

Jerry looked down at the boy, who now lay flat and shaking. "How old are you, kid?"

"I'm eighteen. I'm not a kid. I don't feel good."

"I'm thirty, and you are a kid. You listen to me. You are going to the operating room now." The orderly returned with the blood, and Mark and I pumped it through the intravenous lines. Mark had placed a third needle in the left jugular vein.

"You're bleeding to death. We'll try to save your life."

"I want to see my girl friend," said the boy, as Jerry wheeled the stretcher into the corridor.

"She's next door. She's fine," I told him. Jerry ran down the corridor pulling the stretcher, while a nurse pushed the other end. An oxygen therapist ran by the stretcher with oxygen. An anesthesiology resident met them halfway down the hall carrying his resuscitation kit with lung tubes. The boy was vomiting blood, and it gushed out on the floor as he was wheeled.

The police told us the story the boy had told them in the ambulance. He had taken his girl friend to see the fireworks on the waterfront. He played baseball, and his baseball bat was in the back of his car, an old Chevy convertible. They looked for a place to park for a long time. The beach was hot, crowded, and dark except for the fireworks and neon road lights. He finally found a place and started to pull in, but two men in a car next to his were also trying to park there. They told him to get out of their way. He told them to get out of his way. He and the other driver got out of their cars to fight it out. The passenger in the other car noticed the girl, made obscene remarks and gestures to her, got out of the car and walked over to her. The boy ran back to the car and pulled his baseball bat from the back seat. The passenger from the other car pulled out a gun, shot the boy three times in the abdomen and shot twice at his girl friend's face, but she had crouched down with her arm up to protect herself. Then the two men drove away.

Mark and I were on our feet for the rest of the night. At seven the next morning, when Eric and Leslie came in, there were twenty patients in the waiting room. Leslie looked at me sympathetically.

"You've ruined your dress. It's covered with blood. You really should wear slacks in the E.R., Elizabeth, like me. I know you think it's unprofessional, but at this rate you won't have any clothes left by next week."

I looked in the mirror. The dress had been green when I started. Now it looked like one of Picasso's nightmares.

"Lizzie, girl," Mark said, "if we survive this, we can survive anything. I'm going home."

As we were leaving, Jerry came to the E.R. to tell us about the boy. "Those bullets were right on target. One went through his stomach and his spleen. One went through his liver and his colon. There was stool all over his insides. The third went through the aorta and tore it in half. We had to take out the spleen, part of the liver, half the stomach, the injured colon, and do a colostomy, but before that we had to replace the aorta entirely with a plastic graft. With feces all around the plastic aorta, he'll almost certainly die from infection around the graft, but we're giving him all the antibiotics we can."

Mark and I felt depressed. We had helped to save the boy's life, and now it seemed he would be dead in a few months anyway.

"At least it wasn't garlic," said Jerry.

"Jerry, this may surprise you, but most bullets are not made of garlic," said Mark, taking a cigarette from Jerry's pocket.

"But the Mafia rub their bullets in garlic," replied Jerry. "You don't know that because you're so ignorant. We have a victim in the I.C.U. who was hit with a garlic bullet. He was shot in the stomach, and we sewed it up and he looked fine, but he kept saying it was a garlic bullet. The bullet had lodged in his spine, and we couldn't remove it. Ten days after surgery he had a seizure, then an abscess in the spinal cord, and then abscesses in his brain. We asked the neurosurgeon to see him and he said there's something in garlic that causes a delayed but fatal infection that spreads to the brain. The man had been an executioner for the Mafia—and look what happened."

"Sure," said Mark, "you went to medical school, and look what happened to you. You're going out of your mind. Next time you'll tell me the Mafia uses voodoo."

"You mean I never told you? I had a patient from Haiti who said she was hexed. She said she would die on the first Monday in April, because her sister had hexed her. She died on the first Monday in April. Don't argue with me. I'm tired."

Mark and I finally went home after more coffee, still depressed about the boy. We did not know that in a year he would be back on the football team. He recovered from the surgery in a month, and wondered why the doctors made such a fuss over him.

As Mark and I became used to the emergency room, we worked out a routine. We never had lunch. We each took fifteen minutes off for dinner. There was an emergency room follow-up clinic each day in which we had to take stitches out and change dressings. At midnight, if the waiting patients had all been seen, we divided the next seven hours and slept three-and-a-half hours each.

One night at 3:30 Mark called and woke me up. It was his turn to sleep, and a new surgical patient was signing in.

I got out of bed and dressed, yawning. I had taken Leslie's advice and now wore pants in the emergency room. I had two pairs of bell bottoms, one brown knit pair and one purple satin pair. I put on the purple satin ones, which I thought looked particularly dashing in the middle of the night, and walked down sleepily from my on-call room.

The patient was standing in the examining room. He was a stocky man in his mid-forties.

"Hi, Doc. I've never had a woman before."

"Good morning. Sit down and tell me what the problem is."

"Pain. I have a terrible pain."

"I'm sorry to hear that. What kind of pain?"

"Sometimes it's bad; sometimes it isn't. It aches. It's a bad pain."

"I see. What I meant to ask was, where is the pain?"

"In my back."

"I see. Where in your back?"

"All up and down." He ran his hand over various places in his lower back.

"What makes it better?"

"Nothing. It hurts all the time."

200

"Not even an aspirin or something like that?"

"Maybe I take an aspirin if the pain is bad."

"It doesn't sound too bad. Let me examine you."

"What do you mean 'not too bad,' honey? The pain is terrible."

"Let me examine you."

"You don't have to. Look, I can lean left, like this, and right, see? But when I lean over it pulls." He bent over and touched his toes four times.

"You look fairly limber."

"What do you mean limber? I'm telling you, sweetheart, it feels stiff."

"I see." I was waking up slowly, and I didn't like this man. His pain was no emergency.

"Don't just stand there, dear. What are you going to do about it?"

"First of all, don't speak to me like that. I am Dr. Morgan. It is here on the name tag. M-O-R-G-A-N. Would you like me to write it down?"

"Don't get sore. I'm just asking. I was teasing."

"Don't. How long have you had this pain? Just answer my question."

"Twenty years."

"Twenty years? Why did you suddenly decide to see a doctor now?"

"I was watching the late show. I couldn't sleep. I figure, why not? If I come now, I get seen quickly. I don't have to wait."

"Who pays for it?"

"The company I work for, as long as I get seen in an emergency room. They don't pay for regular doctors' visits."

"And your pain has not been bad enough for the past twenty years for you to pay to see a doctor?"

"Oh, no. It's not that bad."

"You can leave now."

"What do you mean, I can leave now? This is an emergency room. You have to diagnose me."

"I have. The diagnosis is that your back pain is not an emergency. The emergency room is for emergencies. You come in here, and I get out of bed to see you because your back has pulled whenever you touched your toes for the past twenty years, and you decide to come because you stayed up late watching TV. Tomorrow, you call a doctor and have him examine you."

"You have to give me a prescription. You're just the intern. You have to do it."

"I am a resident, not an intern."

"Same thing."

"And I don't have to do anything. I am a state-licensed physician, and I say you can leave."

"So you won't help me?"

"You can leave by yourself, or I can call in security."

"No, I'm going. The pain isn't that bad. It doesn't bother me. I figured I might get a general physical while I was here." He walked out.

The head nurse watched him. She had been checking dressing supplies in the hallway. After he had gone, she laughed.

"What does he want—a tune-up and grease job at four in the morning? He wouldn't speak to his car mechanic the way he speaks to you. Watch him call his lawyer tomorrow to say he was refused emergency treatment."

I went to the kitchenette to pour out a cup of coffee, and sat down to think. The man had been stupid, provoking and rude, I told myself. All the same, I wasn't proud of the way I had behaved. It didn't seem right for me to speak like that, although all the men surgical residents around me talked the same way whenever they were tired and irritated.

I resolved to be a better doctor. I didn't like to think I was becoming unfeminine, but I knew I would not have spoken like that a year ago.

"Elizabeth, long time no see. How does it feel to be a surgeon?"

I looked up and saw Marshall, a psychiatry resident I had dated a year ago. As an intern, I had no time to see him and we had parted more or less friends.

"Fine."

"You look unhappy. Pretty, but unhappy."

"I'm tired."

"It's more than that. It's something about being a surgeon. Come out to dinner with me tomorrow and tell me about it."

Damn psychiatrists. Damn Marshall. How could he tell what I

was thinking about? I would never tell a male doctor that being a surgeon was hard for me as a woman. Never.

"The woman in you is struggling to come out," said Marshall. "Tell me about it tomorrow night."

"No," I lied, "I really can't. I have to work."

He nodded. "I thought you'd say that. Surgery is changing you. You're very closed, very defensive. You're trying to protect your psyche."

I laughed. "I'm just tired. I'm going to bed. Good night."

I was *not* defensive, I was *not* closed. I was happy, goddammit.

Stab Wounds for Breakfast

Once the summer passed and school started again, the emergency room became quieter. Although we were busy, we did not always have patients waiting, and occasionally we had time to eat dinner. Neither of us could sleep during the morning after being up all night. Mark would usually go home for breakfast and then play golf. I went swimming at the gym, or had a piano lesson, or wandered around in a daze thinking it would be more sensible to try to sleep. My eyes felt gritty and my reactions were slow. Occasionally I cleaned the apartment I was sharing. My roommate was Suzanne Ryan, a friend from Harvard who was a pediatric intern.

Back at work, Mark and I tried to guess whether the day would be a good one. Rainy days were bad because of car accidents. Sandy, the triage nurse, said that crazy people came into the E.R. when it was a full moon. One Saturday morning it was raining *and* full-moon time. It had been a very quiet morning. Mark was reading the sports pages. I was eating a powdered doughnut. One of the secretaries had come to work with fresh bagels and doughnuts, a gift from an ambulance driver who also had a job as a baker.

About ten o'clock, when I had powdered sugar all over myself, a thin young black man walked into the E.R. with his arm around a girl who was crying. He made her sit in the waiting room, and walked over to the E.R. secretary. "I think I need to see a doctor," he said.

"Name?" she asked. "I need your name, date of birth, employer, insurance number." She wrote all this down. "Now tell me what the problem is."

"I've just been stabbed."

"You what? Just been stabbed?" She jumped up, but he leaned over the counter to reassure her.

"It isn't serious. I don't want my girl friend upset more than necessary. It's nothing. I probably don't need to be checked, but we live so close to the E.R."

"Have you reported it to the police? You ought to."

"No, that isn't necessary. I won't press charges."

Sandy brought him into one of the code rooms and told me, "He looks cool for a stabbing victim. I wish they were all like him. He probably stabbed himself with a toothpick."

I went in to see him. He was embarrassed to have a woman doctor examine him but finally he took his shirt off to show me his wound. It was two inches long, in the middle of his back, through a rib.

"You certainly have been stabbed," I said. "Tell me, what happened? Who stabbed you?"

"His blood pressure and pulse are normal," said Sandy. "Do you want to send him for an x-ray?"

"No, tell them to come here. It isn't a good place to be stabbed and I don't want him moved."

"My girlfriend stabbed me," said the man when Sandy left. "She didn't mean to do it. We were having breakfast, and we had an argument about last night. I said something to another girl I shouldn't have, and my girl friend is her best friend. I got up to pour myself some coffee and she stabbed at me with the bread knife. It didn't go deep, but she insisted I come over here. She worries a lot."

"Take a deep breath," I said, listening to his lungs with a stethoscope. They were fine. "How long is the bread knife?" I imagined a short, blunt knife that explained his lack of alarm.

"Like so," he stretched his hands apart twelve inches. "It's a real butcher's knife. But it didn't go deep."

I put in a large intravenous needle, sent off routine blood tests, and ordered two units of blood for him. It seemed wasteful, because he looked so normal, but a twelve-inch butcher's knife must have done some harm. I waited in the room with him. There was no one else to see, and I felt uneasy about leaving him alone. The stab wound was right over his lungs and not far from his heart, but it seemed to be a fuss about nothing. I checked his lungs, his pulse, and his blood pressure again. They were normal. I began to feel foolish. I remembered my panic over the air-gun bullet. The x-ray technician came and took the films and I left the room, to avoid being exposed to unnecessary x-rays. When she came out, pushing the awkward x-ray machine, she said to me, "He doesn't feel well all of a sudden."

He was lying on the stretcher, with sweat on his forehead. His pulse was 120, almost twice what it had been, but his blood pressure was still normal. "Just lay down for a catnap," he explained, trying to smile although he was breathing heavily. "I have a hangover."

I called Sandy and asked her to order four more units of blood and to bring me the two units I had already ordered. I was unwrapping the chest-tube kit.

"What's that for?"

I told him I thought the knife had cut his lung and probably an artery, and he was bleeding inside.

"No way, man." He looked at me in dismay as I put on gloves and arranged the twelve-inch-long steel rods sharpened at the end. These rods are for making a hole into the chest so a drainage tube could be put in. Otherwise, blood and air from the damaged lung would collapse the lung so that he could not breathe.

"I'll call the nurse to help me, and I'll give you medicine to calm you." His eyes widened. "You're having trouble breathing, and you need this tube."

Sandy came in. His blood pressure had fallen from 120 to 100. His pulse was now 130. I asked her to hang a unit of blood and then give him an intravenous sedative.

"Doc, you have a point. I do feel a touch short of breath."

Sandy turned him on his side. I washed off the side of the chest to put in the tube. The stretcher was too high, and I had to stand on a stool to control the tube. Strong male surgeons have been known to push the steel-pointed trochar vigorously into the chest, and by accident on into the heart. I had to struggle to position it properly and get it through the muscle. I leaned on the tube. It plunged forward about an inch and was in the chest. I widened the hole with an instrument, pushed in the plastic drainage tube, removed the steel one, sewed the plastic tube to his skin so it would not move out of place, and attached the end to the collecting bottle. For a moment nothing drained out, and I thought I had made a terrible mistake. Then Sandy said, "Look at that!" Blood and air bubbles rushed out through the tube. The gallon collecting bottle filled with blood in a few minutes and Sandy attached a new bottle as I began a new blood transfusion. I called X-ray over again to take a film to make sure the tube was positioned properly. His pulse and blood pressure improved. I told the E.R. secretary to call the chief chest resident. My patient would have to be admitted. The chest resident was Rick Trudeau, who had been my chief resident at Veterans. He arrived fifteen minutes later. The x-ray had come back, showing the left lung almost collapsed with air and blood. The second x-ray showed the tube was in the correct position, not lying on the heart.

"What have you got for me, Elizabeth?" Rick asked.

I handed him the x-ray. "His girl friend stabbed him with a bread knife at breakfast."

"God, don't tell my wife. It might give her ideas. He needs a chest tube, low down, to get out the blood."

"I put it in already."

"And he needs some blood."

"I've given him two units and there are four more ready for him."

"Did you wait to see the x-ray before you put in the tube?" Rick asked me.

"No. His pulse was up, and he had some trouble breathing, so I went ahead."

"I'm not criticizing you. You did the right thing. I must have trained you well." He patted me on the back and went in to see how much blood was draining.

"There's a lot of blood coming out of the tube," he said. "You couldn't have gone into the spleen?"

"No. I only advanced the trochar an inch, and the chest x-ray shows the tube is in the chest."

Rick smiled. "When I was a resident in the E.R., I could put a chest tube in faster than anyone, only I tended to aim low. I put one chest tube in the spleen, and we had to remove the spleen because it wouldn't stop bleeding." He turned to my patient.

"Look, my friend, you are bleeding a lot. Your girl friend has an undiscovered talent. If the bleeding doesn't stop soon, we may have to operate."

"That would really upset my girl friend."

"The one who stabbed you?"

"She didn't mean any harm."

Mark and I finished the first E.R. rotation in September. I went next to orthopedics. There was a crisis coming in December for us and the other first-year residents. The surgery department had hired more interns and first-year residents than it could train as general surgeons. There were thirteen first-year residents, including Mark and me, who wanted to train as general surgeons and the department would hire only four as senior residents at the end of the year. Although I wanted, out of pride, to be asked to stay, I was not happy with the teaching, or lack of it, from the full-time faculty. The V.A. teaching was good, the private service was good, but there was only one full-time general surgery faculty professor who taught us anything. The chief of surgery rarely operated, and came to lectures even less often. Mark Lehman had also been thinking of leaving, for the same reasons. Leslie Andrews wanted to stay. She had recently married an assistant professor on the orthopedic faculty, so she would certainly not be cut.

There was one rather pompous resident, just back from two years' leave, who had ingratiated himself with the chief of surgery. He would not be cut. He, Leslie, and two other residents would stay; nine others would leave. The cut letters were sent out in October. Mark and I were out, as we had expected, but even though I didn't want to stay, I was upset.

"I thought you didn't want to spend the next three years in the surgery program here," said my roommate Suzanne. We were eating dinner together in the hospital cafeteria.

"I don't."

"You just don't like being cut."

"No, I don't."

I was not certain why I had been cut. It may have been partly because I kept my distance from the faculty surgeons, all of whom were married. Hospital gossip loves to link any woman—nurse, medical student or doctor—in a love affair with a married man on the faculty, and there were many such affairs. I knew that if I had a love affair with a surgeon, I would no longer be part of the surgical team, but labeled "so-and-so's girl," a woman who got ahead by sex, not ability. As a consequence, few of these men knew me well. Besides, all thirteen residents in my year were unusually good doctors; the intern group behind us didn't have anyone as good as we were. The faculty had to choose five of us. Leslie would stay because she was not only good but was married to a faculty surgeon. They had to have one woman to qualify for certain federal grants, but they didn't need two. I was not surprised to be cut, but I was surprised that Mark was cut. He was an exceptionally good surgeon, but he had fought with the chief of surgery. The three men invited to stay were all tall, handsome, solid surgeons who had been careful not to make any enemies.

The next day I talked to Dr. Ford, the faculty surgeon in charge of residents, about finding a position at another teaching hospital.

"You won't have a problem. There are nine of you who need positions, and you're all good. At the American College meeting next week, we will just make contacts. Half the teaching hospitals need residents. The other half, like us, have too many good ones. I can find you a good residency. Don't worry."

Mark saw me in the hallway the next week.

"Lizzie, you got cut too, didn't you?"

"Yes."

"Who have you asked for help in finding a residency for next year?"

"Dr. Ford."

"What did he say?"

"He thought he could find us all good positions."

"Don't believe anything that rat says. Rick Trudeau told me that his first-year residency, they cut three residents. Ford told them the same thing, but then didn't do anything to help them, and at the end of the year not one of them had a job. He told me yesterday he could find me a job, too. I laughed at him.

"I went to Hillebrand. He trained at Harvard. He knows everyone. Everyone respects him. They kick him around here, but he has the highest national reputation of all the general surgeons on the faculty. He likes you. Ask him. If you don't find someone to help you now,

Liz, you'll never find a surgical residency. Hillebrand said no good surgical program takes a resident at our level just through an application. It's done entirely through personal contacts. Talk to him today."

"I can't. I have ortho clinic."

"Tell them to go to hell. What can they do to you now?"

I went to talk to Dr. Hillebrand that afternoon. The chief resident was not pleased when I said I wouldn't be in orthopedic clinic.

"You have to come to clinic, Elizabeth. You know that. You can't just take time off the job."

It didn't matter to me how he felt. If I didn't talk to Dr. Hillebrand, I might never finish my surgical training.

Dr. Hillebrand was wonderful. We sat in his office and his secretary brought me coffee.

"Elizabeth, what may I do to help you?"

"Dr. Hillebrand, I don't know if you know, but I've been cut from the program."

"So I heard. I was sorry to hear it."

"Mark Lehman told me that you very kindly offered to help him find a place for next year. I was wondering if you could possibly help me too?"

"I'm very glad you asked me, Elizabeth. Have you asked anyone else to help you?"

"I spoke with Dr. Ford yesterday. That's all."

"Yes. I hope this is not indiscreet, but Dr. Ford has not in the past been as successful as he might be in helping to place residents he cuts from the program. Where would you like to do your surgical residency?"

"I didn't know I had a choice. I'll go anywhere that will take me."

"There's always a place for someone good. Philadelphia or Boston might be places to look. Would you be willing to live in those places?"

I couldn't believe he had to ask. Boston is the Mecca of medicine. When I heard that someone had trained in Boston, I always felt he knew more than I did.

"I would love to go to Boston."

"Good. Let me make a few phone calls and see what I can do. Mark is interested in Boston, too. That wouldn't be a problem? You seem to get along fairly well."

"Oh, yes. We survived the E.R. together this summer. Dr. Hillebrand, I don't know how to thank you. I really don't."

"Please," he was genuinely distressed. "It's a privilege for me to be able to help any good surgeon. This is the surgical tradition."

A week later Dr. Hillebrand called to ask if I could be interviewed by two hospitals in Boston in a week.

"One is the Brigham. They have a very good program, but I think they want you for their surgical research lab. I don't want you to take a year off to do research. As a woman, you will find it hard to get a residency position if you take a year off. If they offer you a research position, turn them down."

The second was another eminent teaching hospital in Boston. The orthopedic chief resident was staggered when I said I would be in Boston next Monday, and not at work. Alf, the orthopedic resident who had taught me the "Q" sign, was also there when I broke the news.

"I didn't hear you correctly," said the chief resident. "I thought you said you were going to take a day off, but it's ridiculous. You can't have said that."

"Don't be smart, you dummy," said Alf, who was glancing idly through an old copy of *Woman's Day* lying on the nurses' desk. "The kid is going to Boston for a residency interview. Don't give her a lot of grief. We can manage without her for a day. What do you think of this cake recipe—a cup of grated carrots, a cup of butter, it sounds disgusting. I like this one, Brandy Nut Cake. Could you make this one, Liz?"

The chief resident folded his arms in anger.

"On this service, Alf, I am the chief. Get that straight?"

"Big deal. I could beat you up any time. Look at this." He flexed his biceps. "You may be bigger, but I have speed. You should work out on the punching bags, Liz, and pretend it's Chief Groucho here. Do women really spend their time making these things?" He showed me a picture of macramé baskets in *Woman's Day*.

The chief resident gave up, and we started evening rounds.

The next Monday morning I had my interview at the Brigham. They did want a resident to do surgical research, although the surgeon who interviewed me said there "might" be a residency place for me the following year. I thanked him and explained I was looking for one now. We ended by talking about the good old days as undergraduates at Harvard.

In the afternoon I arrived at the other teaching hospital, near Chinatown and the Danger Zone. I met Mark Lehman going in. We were interviewed together by Dr. Norland, a tall, aristocratic surgeon with a handlebar mustache. He was friendly with Mark and polite but guarded with me. We passed a portrait on one of the hospital corridor walls. The name was an unusual one, and I thought I recognized it as that of Mark's grandmother, who, I gathered from the inscription, had given money to build a hospital wing. It began to seem unlikely that they would have two positions open for the same year. Dr. Norland showed us the x-ray department and introduced us to four surgical residents there. One was a girl called Patsy, a first-year resident like me. That finished my hopes. No surgical program wanted two women residents in the same year. It was still new for them to admit any. Dr. Norland then took us to the office of Dr. Tobey, chief of surgery, a high-ceilinged, wood-paneled room lined with books. Dr. Tobey asked us if we liked the hospital, thanked us for taking the time to come, and then had to leave to go to the operating room. Dr. Norland talked with us each for a few minutes alone. He asked me if I liked the program.

"It's very impressive," I said. "Boston is a superb place to be trained. If you had a place, of course I would love to come."

"We might have two places. One of the residents we had planned to keep has just been drafted, and the second has decided to spend a year in Pago Pago with the World Health Organization."

"You wouldn't want two women in the same year, though."

"What's wrong with that? We've only trained one woman in the past ten years or so. Women don't apply. Patsy is great—I'd rather have a good woman than a second-rate man." He smiled. "The program you come from may not want women surgeons. In fact, I know they don't. But Boston is different."

I returned home. The orthopedic intern was on vacation, and the next day I was doing scut work on the wards. The ward secretary called me to the phone. It was Dr. Hillebrand.

"Elizabeth, what did you think of the programs in Boston? I know the Brigham offered you a research position. I hope you said no."

"Yes, I did."

"I'm very glad. What about the other place?"

"Dr. Hillebrand, it was wonderful. The residents have teaching conferences every week with the faculty. They make rounds every day with the faculty."

"Would you like to go there?"

"Yes, if they have a place, but I don't think they do."

"Why not?"

"They already have a woman in the program. Dr. Norland was nice about it, but there's no escaping that it counts against me."

"There's always room at a good hospital for a good surgical resident. If you want to go, they will make room for you. What I want to be certain about is, if they wrote to you, would you accept?"

"Immediately."

A month later Mark and I were both offered places, and we each wrote to Boston accepting the offer of a second-year surgical residency.

I told Dr. Ford the day I accepted that I'd decided where to go next year.

"To go? Where? Oh, yes. I forgot, you were looking for a new residency, weren't you? Fine." He turned to go, then whipped around. "Who helped you find it?"

"Dr. Hillebrand."

"Where?"

"Boston."

"Boston? They're an inbred, conservative bunch up there." He walked away, displeased.

Two of the nine residents who were cut had not been interns with us, but joined us in our first year of residency. I talked to one of them and suggested Dr. Hillebrand might help.

"I can't ask him. I don't know him. I've only been here six months, and I haven't worked on the private service." He sighed. "Did I tell you why I'm here this year? Dr. Ford promised me that the program cut no one, and that I could count on finishing my residency here. I hate that man. He's told others the same thing, too."

"But not in writing." I was learning how surgical politics worked.

In July, when the residency year was over, Mark and I went to

213

Boston and another resident went back to Chicago, where he had been an intern. The other five went into the army. They were all good doctors and good surgeons, from a "famous name" surgery program. But they had nowhere else to go. Dr. Ford had forgotten to help them at the American College meeting in October.

Cosmopolitan for Christmas

At Christmas I was back at work in the E.R. with Leslie and Mark again. We were a good team. We all arranged to work for each other so each of us had three days off. I flew home. My mother met me at the airport. Jimmy was home; Rob would be home the next day. In the kitchen I found Jimmy reading *Cosmopolitan*.

"How does it feel to be published?"

"Where?"

"In *Cosmopolitan*."

On page sixty-eight was "You and Your Yearly Physical" by Jean E. Morgan, M.D. (I had decided that using my first name was pseudonym enough.) It was a wonderful issue, and it was hard to believe that I was part of it. I asked Jimmy if he thought that *Cosmopolitan* might want me to write another article. He suggested that I call Mrs. Ashley, but I couldn't face making a call, so I wrote to her instead.

Christmas ended on Christmas Eve when my family put me in the overnight Pullman for New England. There had been a snowstorm and the planes were grounded in Washington, but I had to get back or Leslie would have to work for me instead of spending Christmas with her husband.

By 7:00 A.M. Christmas Day, when I relieved Leslie, it had stopped

215

snowing but it was very cold. No one came in all morning, and Mark and I and the nurses sat around drinking coffee and eating doughnuts. Then the door to the emergency room opened and a big, elderly black man wrapped up in a coat and scarf came in. He seemed vaguely familiar, but he was not a surgical patient. The medical resident looked irritated. The elderly man, who was very large, was slowly undressing himself behind the curtains of a cubicle.

"What's the matter?" I asked.

The resident scowled, and whispered, "An old fathead. He refuses to take his medicine. He comes in here every month in congestive failure. We treat him and send him home but he doesn't do what we say. All he'll ever take is cherry cough syrup. He ought to be dead by now."

I went into the cubicle and the nurse drew the curtains. The elderly man filled the bed, and looked quite happy with the white sheet pulled up to his neck.

"Hey," he shouted, wheezing a little. "It's Doctor Morgan. You must be a doctor by now. You don't remember me, but you looked after me when you were in medical school."

It all came back to me. He was the man I presented to the Boston cardiologist when I was a student. His name was Joe Brown, and he had outlived three doctors.

"What are you doing here?"

"Honey, you remember when I was in the hospital?"

"Of course I do."

"You were nice to me, but those doctors worked me over. They dried me up, and they put me on a diet, and they took away my pipe, and my liquor, and I felt terrible. They told me to cut out fat, can you imagine? I was a short-order cook till I was seventy-five. You can't cook sausage and eggs and beans without fat. That was too much. I never would go back in hospital. Now I come to the emergency room whenever I get wheezy. I drive these young boys crazy." He pointed to the medical resident. "But they don't understand. You can't reform when you're eighty-four."

"You aren't!"

"I am. I got a little wheezy this morning and my lady friend is bringing some Christmas dinner to my place this afternoon, and I want to be in good shape for her."

"Did you walk here?"

"Yes. Eight blocks. It's nippy out there."

"Mr. Brown, you really are wonderful. I hope you have a very merry Christmas."

"I'm sorry you have to work, honey." I didn't like patients calling me "honey," but Mr. Brown was different.

"And I'm sorry you have to come to the emergency room. Take care of yourself."

I kissed him good-bye and Merry Christmas.

"Some boyfriend!" said the medical resident.

"I met him in medical school. Be nice to him. Do you know why he started not to take doctors' advice?"

"Why?"

"Three doctors gave him the same advice you did, and they all died."

The intercom crackled.

"Dr. Morgan, you are needed up front."

I left to see what was happening. Patty Flanders, a friend of mine, had come in with a turkey dinner for me and a fruitcake for the emergency room staff. It was a nice Christmas.

Dear Elizabeth, Thank you for writing. We do not plan any special pieces on medicine for *Cosmopolitan* just now. Will contact you when we do. Happy New Year. Roberta Ashley.

I was disappointed, but not surprised. *Cosmopolitan* was probably swamped with people who wanted to write for them. A few days later I received a long distance call in the E.R.

"Dr. Morgan? This is *Cosmopolitan*. Would you hold for a moment?"

It was Mrs. Ashley. She explained that the present *Cosmopolitan* medical columnist was finding the column too time-consuming, what with her busy Manhattan practice. Was I interested in trying out for *Cosmopolitan*'s monthly column?

I was thrilled.

"You don't have the job yet," warned Mrs. Ashley. "I'll send you four sample questions. Your answers should be a hundred and fifty to

217

two hundred words each. I will enclose our 'Guidelines' for *Cosmopolitan* writers. But above all, we need medical information that is new, accurate, and helpful."

The next day I received the sample questions and surrounded myself with medical books and journals. I did not know exactly how much vitamin C was safe. I did after I wrote two hundred words about it. I stayed up until eleven typing the final. I mentioned my *Cosmopolitan* offer to no one at the hospital. I regarded writing for the public as an aspect of medicine, but the faculty surgeons might have disagreed with me.

There was a telegram in my mailbox two weeks later. "Good girl! You got the job. Congratulations! Roberta Ashley."

I called Jimmy. I called my parents. I jumped up and down, and I called Roberta Ashley to thank her.

My column would begin in May 1973. My editor would be Barbara Hustedt. My try-out questions would be used in the May column.

Every month after that Barbara Hustedt sent me the questions and I sent her the answers. It took me, on the average, eight to ten hours to write a column, sometimes much longer. I would go to the library and look up all the most recent references in the medical literature and in the textbooks. I never had fewer than five references for each article, and sometimes twenty or more. After I did the research, and copied the articles I used for my file, I sat down to write the answer. It was usually much too long, and I then had to rewrite it so it was clear and accurate, but short. After that, Barbara would pore over the answers, rearrange and edit my writing, make notes about everything that was not absolutely clear, and often ask for more information if there had been many articles in the press about a medical topic, for instance, birth control pills.

Barbara would then call me, and we would have a discussion of the column that rarely lasted less than an hour. After that, Helen Gurley Brown had to approve it. It all seemed glamorous to me, and different from anything I had ever done.

I wanted to tell someone at the hospital that I was writing for *Cosmopolitan,* so I decided to tell Dr. Chase. He had been the surgeon in charge of Mr. Homer, my first patient on my first day on surgery as a medical student. Some time after that I had sewn up Dr. Chase's mother when she came into the emergency room with a minor laceration, and he had taken a personal interest in me ever since. As I'd hoped, he was enthusiastic about the column. But Dr. Hillebrand, who was with him, looked surprised and said he was not sure it was a wise decision. I didn't mention it after that, and most of the surgeons never knew because they did not read *Cosmopolitan*.

By the end of June I had letters from readers of my column. It would have been unethical for me to give them individual medical advice by mail—a doctor has to know his own patients personally—but I wrote to as many as I could, advising them how to find the right doctor through their medical society or a teaching hospital. After several years of caring for patients on wards, it was hard for me to grasp how many readers the column was reaching.

I was anxious to leave for Boston. I would miss my friends, especially Susan O'Donnell, Patty Flanders, and my weekly piano lesson with Tina Monterose, but I was looking forward to a change. Besides, there seemed to be a hex on the hospital residents. Everyone was having bad luck with his health.

For me, it began with a headache so violent I could neither move nor open my eyes. Suzanne had to call my ward to say I could not come in. When she left, I tried to get up. I fell out of bed and had to crawl back with my eyes closed. Every time I moved, my head felt as though it would explode. For the next twelve hours I lay motionless, but throbbing pain kept me awake. It was a week before I had recovered, and by then Suzanne had developed a bacterial throat infection that put her in bed for three weeks and off work for four.

During the next four months, the surgical service had unending bad luck. An orthopedic resident crashed his car into a tree along the highway. He had had no sleep for days. One hip and a hand were smashed.

Then the wife of one of the residents came to the emergency room with bleeding from an abnormal pregnancy. The gynecology resident was in the operating room. No one else was called to see her. Suddenly, she bled massively. There was no blood ready for her, and she had a stroke from lack of oxygen. She recovered slowly, but her left arm and leg remained partly paralyzed.

Then two gynecology residents went lobster fishing one weekend in their dinghy. Their Labrador retriever went along. The sea was rough and they were both drowned. The dog was found perched on a rock a short way from shore.

Then Leslie Andrews and another surgical resident at the V.A. caught staphylococcal infections in their legs from a patient. They were unable to work for two weeks.

Then another orthopedic resident developed a swelling in the artery in his leg. The artery was repaired surgically, but became infected. His leg was amputated.

Then a resident developed a melanoma cancer in the skin of his back. It had already spread to his liver. He died.

Then another orthopedic resident developed Hodgkins' disease, a cancer of the lymph glands. He had to give up his surgical training.

Then Eric caught hepatitis during an operation on a drug addict, who had been shot in the stomach. No one knew the addict had hepatitis until after the surgery. Six weeks later Eric was jaundiced and started to vomit. After three months he was well enough to work part time.

Then Leslie had to spend a week in the hospital with a herniated disc.

Then Dr. Chase had a heart attack.

Then the chairman of the medical department was found dead in his office from a heart attack.

Then the chief of pathology at the private unit developed lung cancer. He was one of the best pathologists in the hospital.

Then an ENT resident died one night of bleeding in his brain from a weakened blood vessel.

And a urology resident suddenly developed severe diabetes.

I could not get to Boston fast enough.

Meet the Count

I arrived in a sweltering July heat wave. I didn't expect to be nervous but Boston overawed me. I felt—irrationally—that every surgeon in Boston would know more than I did. There was some justice in this. My past year had drilled me into being competent in the emergency room, and I had learned how to take out a gallbladder, but I hadn't had time to do much studying. Boston's surgical tradition was education, not just surgery and emergencies.

My new residency began with a 7:00 A.M., Sunday morning breakfast to meet the attending surgeons, a formality which Mark and I thought was pleasantly civilized.

I liked the new program. My chief resident, whose name was Jack Fine, told me that I was not on call for that Sunday, and I could go home for the day. After the breakfast, I took the MTA back to Harvard Square to continue unpacking.

I had moved my belongings in a U-Haul truck in ninety-degree weather, with the help of two undergraduates. We did it in one day. Moving out was bad enough, but moving into my new apartment almost defeated me. My old apartment had been modern and convenient, and I wanted something old-fashioned. With Jimmy's help I rented a one-bedroom place in Harvard Square, where he had lived two years before. It was cheap, convenient, antiquated, and surrounded by bookstores, camera shops and ice cream parlors.

We arrived at four in the afternoon. The apartment was locked, the superintendent out. I ran around Harvard Square looking for a pay phone that worked, and called a number Jimmy had given me for another superintendent. There was no answer. My U-Haul was blocking traffic in Plympton Street, a narrow, one-way, cobbled lane. The apartment building was next to the Harvard bookstore, and I asked for the superintendent there. They knew him, but not where he was. The undergraduates helping me had to catch a train in three hours. An old man in dirty white overalls came to stare at me by the truck.

"You moving in?"

"Yes, I am."

"You have the keys?"

"No. Do you know anything about them?"

"Yeah. I'm the super from the other building. I can give you a door key and open your apartment, but I have to keep the apartment key. The other super will give you yours tomorrow."

I didn't argue. He let us in. The walls were a faded gray, but the lobby was clean. The elevator was tiny, and had a heavy door that slammed shut unless you held it open. I was on the third floor. In two and a half hours, I was moved in. By Sunday night I had unpacked everything. I discovered my table did not fit in the kitchen, and the stereo did not fit in the living room because of the piano. This apartment was small. There was a fireplace, and a huge enamel bathtub on bronze feet, which filled most of the bathroom. In the afternoon there was a curious sweet smell that filled the apartment. I could not identify it. I looked out the window and saw two Chinese cooks drinking tea at the kitchen door of a restaurant. My apartment was over the Hong Kong Restaurant, and the smell was sweet-and-sour sauce. I smelled it every day for three years, and I was cured of my liking of Chinese food.

I walked around the tiny apartment, and looked out on the busy street below. It was a dump but it was cheap, and best of all I didn't feel isolated. I had lived in a modern apartment for two years and even with Suzanne Ryan as a roommate, it often felt lonely. No one was friendly, and every night everyone crept back to their own solitary boxes. This dilapidated building in the middle of Harvard's bustle suited me.

Monday morning at 6:30, rounds began at the hospital. I was now a senior resident, which made me feel grand. Two years were over, three were left before my general surgery training was done. I had come a long way, and barring disaster, I would finish. Jack Fine arrived the same time I did, and introduced me to Sean Stewart, the intern, and Pierre Renard, the junior (first-year) resident. Sean was from a Chicago medical school, and Pierre was from New York but had done his medical training in France.

At seven, Jack told me I had better go to the operating room. "Dr. Sharman is resecting a melanoma. I want you to assist him. He won't like it if you are late."

"Where's the operating room?"

"Oh, down the elevator and then around the corner. You can't miss it."

I knew I would get lost. I arrived first in the hospital kitchen, then in the mailroom, and finally found myself in a back street of the Boston Danger Zone on the hospital delivery platform. I did get to the operating room, but a few minutes late. It was 7:35 and Jack had said 7:30. Five minutes late is forgivable the first day when you are new in a hospital.

I did not know that Dr. Sharman had a "late" routine. Whenever he worked with a new resident, he arranged with the nurses to start operating early so he could be angry when the resident arrived late. He had started the operation at seven. The patient was asleep and Dr. Sharman was already scrubbed when I scurried into the operating room.

"You're the new resident," he snapped. "You're late. This is a hospital. I operate on time. If you're ever late again, don't bother to come at all. Don't just stand there. Are you a surgeon or a bystander? Go and scrub! Where did you train before? There? There are no decent surgeons there. My training program was different. I was taking out the pancreas as an intern."

The melanoma was on the chest of a thirty-six-year-old man. By the time I had scrubbed and was back in the O.R., gowned and gloved, Dr. Sharman had cut a three-inch circle of skin around the tumor. The nipple was included in the specimen and blood dripped from the cut skin and down the side of the chest. This should have been my case to do. I had never taken a melanoma off before. Feeling cheated, embarrassed and humiliated, I struggled to assist him during the operation.

"Get out of the way. Get out of the way," Dr. Sharman shouted when I tried to clamp a bleeding vessel. "Number ten blade," he said to the scrub nurse, and then he sliced, cutting skin plus nipple and melanoma off the muscle of the chest wall. Blood spurted from a cut artery in the muscle and hit me in the face. I jerked my head back and Dr. Sharman snorted.

"Haven't you learned yet not to jump? Just put a sponge on the bleeder. This is basics. Surgical basics. I shouldn't have to teach you this."

Jack Fine came into the room to watch.

"Scrub in," said Dr. Sharman. "The new resident can't operate."

Jack scrubbed in, and I watched him take a skin graft from the patient's leg. He and Dr. Sharman sewed it over the bare muscle on the chest, while I cut the sutures. The suture scissors were dull and once I didn't cut the suture on the first try when Dr. Sharman held it up for me.

"Go away till you learn how to operate," he snapped, grabbing the scissors out of my hand. For the rest of the case I stood doing nothing, with my hands folded on the operating table like a medical student. If I were capable of blushing, I would have been red in the face. On my first day as senior resident, I felt a complete, miserable failure as a surgeon. I thought of resigning, and then I thought of Dr. Hillebrand, and decided that if he thought I was good enough, I should stick it out a little longer. Then, a few days later when I made rounds with him, I began to wonder if Dr. Sharman was such a good doctor. One of his patients, a nineteen-year-old girl with ulcerative colitis, had just had an emergency operation to remove her entire colon. For the rest of her life she would have liquid bowel movements coming out onto her abdomen skin collecting in a plastic bag glued to her skin. His conversation with her was like this:

"Hi."

"Dr. Sharman, I feel so depressed, I could kill myself. I feel like jumping out the window."

"Jump out the window. I just wish you had done it before I wasted all my time operating on you. Go ahead and kill yourself. No one would care."

I stared at him in disbelief, but the head nurse was used to it. She and the psychiatric social worker spent the rest of the morning keeping the girl from killing herself.

We continued on rounds, and went to see another patient, an old lady dying of cancer who wished to go home in a wheelchair to look after her fifteen cats. She had broken her leg falling out of bed in the hospital and walking on the leg was still painful. She often refused to go to physical therapy and said she did not care if she never walked again. She wanted to go home, and began by saying, "Doctor, I don't want to go to physical therapy this morning. My leg is killing me."

He folded his arms and glared at her. "I'm telling you to go, and if you don't do what I tell you, I'll have you thrown out of the hospital this afternoon, and you can die in the gutter. I don't want to waste my time looking after a nasty old woman like you."

The old lady began to cry.

"Oh, Christ," said Dr. Sharman, and walked away.

When Dr. Sharman went on vacation that summer, Dr. Baker looked after his patients. Dr. Baker never went home at night until he had seen every patient on his service, talked with their families, and asked after their children. He was an excellent surgeon, though slow. When Dr. Sharman returned, the old lady with the fifteen cats and cancer refused to see him and, to Dr. Baker's embarrassment, insisted that he take over her care.

The only people Dr. Sharman disliked more than his patients were the residents. He once confided to his nurse during a party that the greatest pleasure in his life was watching a resident squirm. He was nasty and bullying to me, but just as horrid to the men. Sean Stewart did his first hernia repair with Dr. Sharman, and I came in to watch. It was curious to see Sean hesitate over cutting the skin and cut the muscle awkwardly with the Metzenbaum dissecting scissors. It seemed impossible that I had operated like that two years ago. I was no dazzling maestro, but I could take out a gallbladder, and with some help do a modified radical mastectomy.

Suddenly Dr. Sharman laughed at Sean. "If you can't cut the skin you'll never be a surgeon. No talent. You have clumsy hands." I left the operating room quietly. I loathed the grating sound of Dr. Sharman's voice when he began to dig at people.

"Sean," I said later when we were gathering in the I.C.U. for evening rounds, "I don't know how bad you feel after operating with Dr. Sharman, but ignore it. I thought I would die the first time I operated with him, but you just have to block him out."

"Really?"

"Really. You'll be a good surgeon, but if you knew how to operate already you wouldn't be an intern. Right?"

After a month, I decided never to speak to Dr. Sharman again except to say "yes" or "no." I was a senior surgical resident and felt entitled to be critical of the doctors teaching me. I knew Dr. Sharman for what he was—an adequate surgeon but a nasty man, a bad teacher and foul to his patients. Patsy Glover, the other woman surgical resident in the program, and Mark Lehman agreed with me, and Mark gave Dr. Sharman the nickname, "Count Maligno."

Sean asked Mark what he planned for "The Count."

"Don't worry," Mark said. "Someday you'll see Count Maligno curl up into a ball and roll away."

Patsy Glover was pretty, agreeable and, like me, anxious that everyone should recognize her as a competent surgeon. We were wary of one another, though, and never became close friends. She looked on me as an invader into her territory, but I felt that what she was also afraid of was competing with another woman surgeon. There were no women surgeons on the faculty and until I arrived Patsy was the only woman surgical resident. She would burst into tears when she was criticized, and complain bitterly when she had to work late on her nights off. I knew I was getting more critical and impatient of people I worked with but crying was ridiculous. Part of being molded into a surgeon was learning the courage to make a fuss and insist that things be done right, no matter how tired the team was. A woman had to demand just as much from herself and the team as a man, and I felt betrayed when another woman surgeon, just as capable as I was, wept and complained when things got tough.

Dr. Baker was at the other extreme from Dr. Sharman. No doctor could have been kinder to his patients or to his residents. He made teaching rounds with us every day, as most of the surgeons did. The first day I made rounds with him, he said it was a pleasure to have me on his service. Then he rubbed the back of his left hand, and looking down said, "According to Jack . . . maybe I misheard, please don't be offended, but Jack said you write an article, column—is that the wrong word?—for a women's publication or magazine."

"Yes, I write the monthly medical column for *Cosmopolitan*. I hope you don't think that's wrong?"

"No, no. What is it called?"

"'Your Body.'"

"My body? Oh, yes, 'Your Body.' A good title."

He stopped scratching his hand. He was allergic to the powder in surgical gloves and had a constant rash.

"I like having a celebrity on the service. Would you mind if I told my patients? Not the men, they don't read *Cosmopolitan,* but the women would be interested."

It was difficult at first making people believe I was a surgical resident. Everyone knew Patsy but they did not know me. It was asking for trouble not to wear a white coat, but I hated those coats. I spent most of my spare money on clothes, and I wore low heels, not flat shoes to work. I needed to feel feminine and different from the male surgeons, and besides, those long white coats were always too big. When I wore a white coat I felt ugly and unfeminine.

One day a nurse pounced on me when I was reading one of my patient's charts. "Who are you?" she demanded. "You're not supposed to be here."

"Oh yes, I am," I said, nettled. "I'm one of the new doctors."

"Doctor? You're a doctor? You mean you're an intern. I didn't know they let in women doctors. We've never had one of them."

"No," I said. "I am a surgical senior resident."

She peered at me over her half-lens bifocals. "Don't you know your professional behavior is very bad? You should never walk onto a ward without a white coat. How am I supposed to know you're a doctor when you come around in street clothes? Carrying all those germs. You ought to know better. There's a hospital rule that says you have to wear a white coat and name tag, so people know who you are."

"But I am wearing my name tag."

"Oh that," she said, peering at it. "I can't read that. The writing is too small. Where's your coat?"

"I've lost my coat."

"Lost your white coat? You'll never be a good doctor if you can't even keep a white coat. I remember now, we did once have a woman doctor here. She couldn't take it, walked off the job in the middle of the night." She turned to the secretary.

"This is the new intern. A woman. Give her the charts of the new admissions, so she can see them. She has a lot of work to do today— at least five new admissions are in already. You can't be hanging around doing nothing." She marched off, but turned back again.

"You don't look like a surgeon to me." She went into her office and shut the door loudly.

The secretary smiled at me. "Don't mind her, she's very old-fashioned. She doesn't like male nurses either. I think it's neat to have a woman be a doctor. The women doctors I've known have been easier to work with than the men. They don't do so much ordering around." She handed me the charts.

"Thank you," I said. "And by the way, I'm a senior resident, not the intern. Sean Stewart is the intern."

The first chart I looked at was a dentist, admitted for surgical removal of a colon cancer. He had had several heart attacks, and I went to his room feeling properly sympathetic. I walked down one corridor looking for his room. On the door was a scrawled sign saying, "Do not disturb. Go away." I thought about this for a while, and decided to go in and see him regardless.

He was a gray-haired, thin man, lying on his bed, reading a paperback. Seeing me, he sat up, and shouted, "Go away. Who are you? Can't you read? You must be from the kitchen. This cheese sandwich is disgusting. 'A nutritious snack' the label says. Look at this." He shook a cellophane wrapper containing a slice of pre-packaged bread with a slice of soapy cheese. "This is garbage." He flung it across the bed.

I said, "I'm not from the kitchen. I'm Dr. Morgan and I've come by to talk to you."

"You can't be a doctor. You're too young to be a doctor. How long have you been a doctor?"

"For three years. What brings you into the hospital, sir?"

"Nothing brings me into the hospital. I came. You must be young enough to be my granddaughter."

"You know you're here for an operation tomorrow on your colon. Have you had a change in your bowel habits?"

"I feel fit as a horse. My doctor just told me to come in so I came. I don't know why. You say I'm going to have an operation? It's the first I've heard about it. You're not going to examine me, are you?"

"Yes, sir, I am."

"You're a woman, you can't examine me. Where did you go to medical school?"

"I went to Yale."

"Yale? Do they take women? God, times have changed. When I

was in medical school, they wouldn't let woman into the building, let alone let them be dentists. What's wrong with being a wife and mother? Are you married?"

"I would prefer to ask you the questions. We need to know about your health before your surgery."

"You'll never catch a man with that attitude, my dear." But he let me do the asking. He insisted his only health problem was a weak golf swing.

His surgeon came up as I left the dentist's room.

"Have you been examining him? He's a strange man, but he has a huge cancer in his colon. Some nurse told me about you this morning. You are quite a curiosity."

In a few weeks the nurses became used to me. One morning our surgery was canceled, and Sean and I were sitting at the secretary's desk making notes in charts and ordering lab tests. The secretary was gone for morning coffee. An angry medical resident, about six feet two, marched up to me, grabbed the chart I was reading, threw it down, and grabbed another one. After he had grabbed up and thrown down the five charts in front of me, he snorted, "You have a rotten ward. Why can't you keep the charts in the rack so the doctors can use them? You called me this morning"—he shoved his face at me—"and asked me to come right away to see a surgical consult. Here I am, and I can't find the damn chart. I don't suppose they teach you these things in South Boston High School, do they? Get me Clarkson's chart and get me his recent lab data immediately. I don't have time to waste."

Sean had been reading the chart in question. He stood up. "Allow me," he said, "to present you with Mr. Clarkson's chart. Allow me, also, to present you to Dr. Morgan, our senior surgical resident."

The consultant looked around for Dr. Morgan.

"Dr. Elizabeth Morgan," said Sean. *"She* is our senior resident."

The consultant suddenly realized that I was the doctor. He jumped back in dismay. "Oh, I'm terribly sorry. Dr. Morgan, I really must apologize. I thought you were just the secretary. I don't know what you must think of me. I'm so embarrassed. I don't suppose you might spare the time to tell me about this patient Clarkson, would you? How very kind of you."

After he left, Sean turned to me and said, "I don't like the way you mop floors either." We both felt sorry for the secretary; that was the way several of the male doctors talked to any female member of the staff, regardless of whether she was good at her job or not.

I was Dr. Baker's and Dr. Sharman's senior resident, and it was my duty to cover the emergency room. This meant that when the emergency room had a surgical problem they called me.

There were four rotations for the four third-year senior residents—the three general surgery services and the cardiac surgery service. The senior resident on cardiac surgery did not cover the emergency room because the service was too busy. As a senior resident on cardiac surgery, you never slept your night on call, and so were awake for thirty-six hours, "babysitting" postoperative heart patients, keeping track of heart rate, the respirator, blood pressure, and urine output.

On the general surgery services as senior residents, we were on call every third night, not every second. We were not always awake all night, and on occasion slept as much as six hours. Sleep was frequently interrupted with calls from a nurse to ask for anything from a sleeping pill at five in the morning to a laxative renewal order, and we also took calls from the emergency room. The emergency room was not busy, but was getting busier, because the hospital had expanded to take ambulance calls. At first I was called infrequently, but by December I was spending two or three hours a day and most of the night sewing up lacerations. The hospital was in the Danger Zone, and I was treating an increasing number of cheerful drunks with slashes from "conversations" in nearby bars.

My first patient in the emergency room was a thirty-year-old woman with a stomach pain. I examined her carefully, anxious to make the right diagnosis. She had become sick, with nausea and vomiting, after eating a sandwich from a vending machine. Her stomach was slightly tender. I checked all her blood tests. They were normal. I examined her a second time. She had nothing I could find, except mild gastroenteritis, or food poisoning. I was sure she did not have appendicitis. She had no pain over her appendix, and her pelvic exam was normal. Appendicitis always causes loss of appetite but my patient was hungry. I sent her home with instructions to drink fluids, and to return if she got worse or did not improve during the day. I told Jack Fine about her later the same day. I thought I had been careful and had done a good exam.

"How do you *know* she doesn't have appendicitis?" Jack asked me. "You should have called me to see her."

I explained again that her exam was normal but he shook his head and disapprovingly said, "I should have seen her. It's a hard diagnosis to make." She did not return during the day, and I went home at 7:30. The next morning on rounds I found the patient on our ward. During the night she had returned with severe pain over her appendix. Jack Fine, Dr. Baker, and Sean Stewart had operated on her for appendicitis. I felt dreadful that I had made the wrong diagnosis. My confidence was shaken. I had thought I knew how to diagnose abdominal problems that needed surgery. The lady herself was unaware that I had made any mistake. She greeted me with a smile, asked me how I was, and announced in a voice of pleased surprise that she had had to have her appendix removed.

Later that day Dr. Baker took me aside to talk with me about my misdiagnosis. He was the chief of his service, and watched how his senior resident managed emergency room cases. If a resident seemed to be mismanaging them, Dr. Baker would supervise him more closely. I told him the details of my examination the day before. I was afraid that, like Dr. Sharman, he would begin to shout at me and tell me what a bad surgeon I was, but he just scratched the back of his hand.

"I've often made the same mistake myself. I think I would have done exactly what you did, although I might have admitted her to the hospital for observation. In these days of cost control and keeping down hospital expense, I might just as well have sent her home. Appendicitis is called 'The Great Pretender.' I've seen it begin in many different ways. A surgeon who can diagnose appendicitis correctly ninety percent of the time is doing amazingly well." He patted me lightly on the shoulder. "You don't mind, do you? I pat the men on the shoulder when they look gloomy, too."

Later that month, during a busy afternoon clinic, I was called by the emergency room. The nurse was apologetic, but said there was a peculiar madman who had a bad ulcer on his leg. Would I come down to see him? I explained that we were in the middle of clinic, but I would go down as soon as I could. An hour later we finished clinic, about 4:30. Jack Fine allowed me to go to see the madman while he and Sean Stewart started evening rounds. I was not on call that

231

night, so it was not absolutely necessary that I see all the patients for the second time that day. I would catch up on any new patients on morning rounds the next day.

I bought a cup of hot chocolate from the vending machine on the way to the emergency room. I had not had lunch. Nursing shifts had changed, and the nurse who had called me had gone home. My mad patient was still waiting, an elderly unshaven man in dirty clothes with a bandage, black with dirt, wrapped loosely around his leg. He was in a cubicle, sitting on an examining table, rocking gently back and forth, and talking to himself. The only other patients in the emergency room were a Chinese lady with a heart attack surrounded by doctors, a boy with hemophilia who was being given a blood transfusion, and a schizophrenic lady waiting to see the psychiatrist. When I walked by her, she asked, "Are you the psychiatrist?"

"No, I am not."

"You goddamned liar, you ought to be ashamed of yourself," she said, and shook her head angrily.

I walked into my patient's cubicle and introduced myself. He looked up at me and said something. It sounded like a question, but he was not speaking words. It was an indistinguishable mumble. Neither was it a foreign language, but the mumble seemed to mean something to him. I carried on as though I had understood what he had said.

"How long have you had the ulcer, sir?"

He shouted a loud, indignant, unintelligible reply. Obviously I had offended him.

"I'm sorry," I said. "I need to look at your ulcer so I can advise you how it should be treated."

He threw his hands up, muttered indignantly, banged the side of the bed with his feet, and opened his mouth. He shoved his open mouth to me. I shook my head to indicate that I did not want to look in his mouth. I gently coaxed him till he lay down on the stretcher, and I tried to take the bandage off his leg. He sat up and tried to wrap it up again. I pushed him back down. This happened five times, but finally the dressing was off. I am near-sighted, and the light was poor, but I bent close over the ulcer on his leg to get a good look. The ulcer appeared to move. This seemed strange. I frowned and looked again. As I leaned closely over the ulcer, a fat, well-fed maggot crawled out of the stinking dead tissue on the man's leg, walked across the ulcer and started to feed on another piece of dead tissue. Suddenly I realized the ulcer seemed to move because dozens of maggots were crawling over it. I sprang backwards out of the room and landed in the hallway, to the surprise of two nurses.

"There are ten thousand disgusting maggots crawling all over that man's ulcer. It's the most horrible sight I have ever seen."

Both nurses blanched in horror. It made me feel better to have sympathy. I had never seen a maggot-infested wound. I called Jack. "What do I do for maggots?"

"You can choose. You can pick the maggots off one by one and drop them in ether to kill them, or you can put ether on the ulcer and kill the maggots while they are still on the wound. The disadvantage is that this method injures healthy tissue left in the wound."

I picked maggots off the ulcer for an hour. They were hard to catch. After picking and killing thirty maggots, dozens more still crawled to the surface from the ulcer's depths. I gave up, put an ether-soaked pad on the ulcer, and watched with grim satisfaction as maggots rushed to the surface, and curled up dead. The patient had fallen asleep.

Sean and Jack finished rounds and came to find me in the emergency room when I was picking off the last dead maggot.

"Don't move. You have a maggot on your dress," said Sean, picking it off my skirt with a piece of cotton gauze. "Does your mother know you do this for a living?"

For the next week my arm or leg would suddenly itch severely, and I would jump, thinking a maggot was crawling on my skin.

Chinese Tragedy

Our hospital was near Chinatown. If we had the time, we could tell the page operator to ring us on our beepers, walk down the street and get an excellent Chinese meal. Many of the people who worked in the hospital were of Chinese descent, but much more Americanized than their parents. Their older friends or relatives might go shopping, even in winter, in flat slippers and thin, quilted Chinese jackets, while their grandchildren wore Western clothes and worked in the hospital. They all spoke Chinese, even the more Westernized.

I learned that Chinese emigrated to the United States in tongs, which seem to be very large extended families. First, some men from a tong move to the United States. When they have earned enough, they send for the women and the children, until the whole village has come. San Francisco's Chinatown is said to have seven tongs. I never learned how many tongs lived in Boston, but there were at least three, because there were three different Chinese languages spoken: Cantonese, Mandarin and a third, much less common. Many of the Chinese were reluctant to consult Western doctors, but when they did, translation was a problem. The hospital had one social worker who spoke Cantonese and another who spoke Mandarin. A page operator could speak the third dialect, and she was often called away from the switchboard to translate. One day a very old Chinese woman came into the emergency room with her husband, who was equally old. I was called to see her. The husband and wife smiled at me politely. I asked them if they spoke English, and the husband replied at length in Chinese. I sent for an interpreter.

"What dialect?" the operator asked.

"I don't know. They don't speak English."

A social-worker-interpreter came and spoke to the couple.

"I'm sorry, Dr. Morgan," she said. "It's Mandarin. I speak only Cantonese." She left, looking for the other social worker. When the Mandarin interpreter arrived, a long conversation followed between her and the husband. The interpreter then announced to me that the woman was feeling sick. I knew that she must have felt very sick indeed before she would come to a Western hospital. But the interpreter meant that the formalities were over, and I could now ask questions. I learned she was eighty-five. She had had severe stomach pain for two years, and had sought help from herbalists. Her pain had continued to worsen until now she could no longer live with it. Embarrassed, she told the interpreter that her bowel movements had been bloody, painful and liquid for the past two years. After her husband left the room, I examined her. I did a rectal examination and felt a large, hard lump. I examined it with a proctoscope. It was an enormous, ulcerated cancer, growing into the bone of her spine behind and into the uterus in front. I took a small sample for a biopsy.

I admitted her to our surgical service, under the supervision of Dr. Baker. The cancer was incurable, but we planned to give her radiation treatment to deaden the pain. Jack Fine thought she should have a colostomy, too, because the cancer had almost completely blocked her rectum. She agreed to have radiation treatment, but she refused the colostomy surgery. Su, the I.C.U. secretary, was also Chinese and knew our patient. She explained to her the need for a colostomy, but the old lady was adamant. Radiation, yes. Colostomy, no. We asked the radiation therapists to see her. The therapist agreed to treat her, but said that before they would begin treatment Jack had to order a barium enema to "document the extent of the lesion."

Jack ordered the barium enema, and told Sean to be sure it was done that day, to avoid delay in treating the woman. Jack and I spent the day operating with Dr. Baker. At 4:00 P.M. I was holding retractors so Dr. Baker could assist Jack, who was doing a thyroidectomy. The direct line intercom between X-ray and our operating room crackled.

"Jack, are you there?" said the intercom.

"Speaking."

"I'm calling you from the x-ray suite. You wanted us to do a barium enema on a Chinese lady?"

"Yes," said Jack.

"I wouldn't order that, Jack," whispered Dr. Baker. "Those huge rectal cancers are very friable. The barium enema nozzle can perforate the cancer and inject barium into the abdomen."

The radiologist continued over the intercom. "On injecting the barium into the rectum, we immediately demonstrated a large perforation of the colon. Your patient now has barium in the abdominal cavity. Not more than a few cc's, but barium is very toxic. It can cause severe inflammation and the lady already looks sick. You ought to see your patient now. You may want to take her to the O.R. to clean out the barium."

"We'll be right up," interposed Dr. Baker. "We just have to finish this case. It won't take long."

The intercom voice sighed. The radiologist knew Dr. Baker operated slowly.

"Don't take this lightly. You know it will take you hours to finish a thyroid."

Dr. Baker asked the nurse to disconnect the intercom, and in silence he assisted as Jack rapidly cut the remaining attachments of the thyroid gland to the windpipe in the neck. It took him three minutes.

"Elizabeth, I'm sorry to leave you, but would you put in the skin stitches? Jack and I are going to see this patient in X-ray."

I sewed up the skin, took the thyroid patient to the recovery room, and went to find Jack and Dr. Baker. Our Chinese lady did need emergency surgery, and her family agreed to a colostomy, which she had to have now that her colon had been perforated. Dr. Baker and I operated on her that night. We started at ten o'clock because it had taken that long to find her family and get permission.

I was tired, as I always was, but I looked forward to the operation. At the same time I both felt sorry for our patient, and excited because it was a big case, and mine to do. The easy operations were done by Sean and the difficult ones by Jack. I had done only a few operations,

236

and most of them with Dr. Sharman because Jack didn't like him and assigned me to his cases. Our Chinese lady would be my first major abdominal operation with Dr. Baker.

After she was asleep on the operating table, I washed her abdomen with sterile iodine soap. She weighed eighty pounds and her abdomen was sunken in. Dr. Baker came in with his hands scrubbed and when I was done, put the sterile drapes across her chest, across the pubis and down the sides.

"What are you going to do, John?" the anesthesiologist asked him. He looked up in surprise.

"If she can, Dr. Morgan will remove the cancer. If she can't, she'll do just a colostomy, and either way she'll remove as much barium as she can." He turned to me while he clipped a drape in place. "Am I right, Elizabeth? Or were you planning something else?"

I was planning to do whatever he told me to do, but it was pleasant to be treated with such respect. One of the overhead operating lights fizzled and went out.

"Don't worry," said Dr. Baker to the nurse. "Just bring in a spotlight and turn down the side lights for contrast. That will give us plenty of light."

With the side lights down, the room was dark except for the patient's brightly lit abdomen, which made the operation look like a stage performance.

"Use a generous midline incision," said Dr. Baker. "We need lots of exposure and room to move around." The nurse handed me the scalpel, and I incised the skin firmly from above the belly button down to the pubis.

"Not too hard," murmured Dr. Baker. "You don't want to plunge into the belly before it's time. She has no muscle or fat and you might cut into the intestine if you're too vigorous with the scalpel."

I lightened the pressure on the scalpel.

"Here," said Dr. Baker, picking up tissue in the middle of the incision with his forceps, "you made a tiny nick in the peritoneum. Take advantage of it. Slide in the tips of the Metzenbaums and slit the peritoneum. Don't cut. It will give way if you just push with the blades."

I pushed with the scissors and the peritoneum gave way. I slit up, turned the scissors in the other direction and slit the peritoneum down to the pubis. We were in the belly. Instead of normal, thin, wrinkled small intestines, the intestines were swollen, red and patchy white where the barium had stuck to them.

"Pour in a liter of warm saline and see if you can wash any of it off," said Dr. Baker.

I poured in the saline, and sloshed it around inside the belly but only a few flakes of barium came off.

"Suction," I said. The nurse handed it to me and I suctioned out the saline.

"Try to peel off the barium," suggested Dr. Baker and with smooth forceps I tried, but either it would not come, or came off with a piece of intestine, leaving a raw bleeding area behind. Dr. Baker tried with the same result.

"Feel the liver, next." And I slid my hand in the belly up under the ribs on the right. The cuff of my surgical gown above the gloves lay on the intestines and I could feel moisture seep through.

"I can feel tumor studded all over the liver," I said, feeling inch-wide hard knobs of tissue on both lobes of the liver. I finished exploring the abdomen—the stomach and spleen were normal, there were knobs of metastatic tumor scattered over the small intestines and in lymph nodes along the spine.

When I had finished Dr. Baker felt inside the abdomen, too, then turned to Jack, who had stayed to watch.

"A sad mistake, Jack, but the lady has tumor everywhere. She wouldn't have had long to live whatever we did. Now Elizabeth, pack the small intestines aside and let's see the tumor."

Deep in the pelvis, a large mass the shape of a football lay where the rectum should have been.

"Perforation," said Dr. Baker, pointing to a shaggy gray area with the long scissors, which he had picked up when I put them down.

I looked at him. "May I have the Metzenbaums please, Dr. Baker?"

He chuckled. "Never put down the Metzenbaums, otherwise you'll find your attending has stolen your case." He handed them to me. "Be careful, but try to coax this tumor out of here."

The tumor was growing through the pelvis into the muscles of the back. I held the tumor with my left hand and tried to peel it off the muscles, but it wouldn't move. I tried to dissect the tumor from the uterus but it was too deeply ingrown.

"Try getting your hands all the way around it."

I tried everything but the tumor was hard as a rock and had grown directly into the bone of the spine. I gave up and Dr. Baker tried.

"Impossible," he agreed. "Now a colostomy." I placed two long flat clamps across the large intestine above the tumor, and cut the intestine in half.

"Three-0 chromic," I said, and sutured the one end of the intestine closed over the tumor. Then I brought the other end out through a hole in the skin and sewed the abdomen back together.

After the surgery I took our patient directly to the I.C.U. She had a high fever and such trouble breathing that she needed a respirator to breathe for her. The following morning her family came to visit and brought baskets of oranges.

I was astonished when I saw them. "Her family doesn't expect her to eat the oranges, do they?" I asked her nurse. "Do they realize how sick she is?"

"Yes, Elizabeth," said the nurse, mocking me. "Just because they don't speak English doesn't mean they don't know what's happening. The oranges are to feed her when she makes a long journey."

I did not understand. She explained. "When a Chinese person dies, their soul goes on a long journey to the new land and the soul needs to eat. The oranges are to feed her soul on its trip."

"She may pull through," I said. "They shouldn't give up all hope."

The nurse shook her head. "I've worked here five years, and I've never seen a Chinese family be wrong. When they bring in oranges, you know death is coming."

Our patient died two days later.

All surgical deaths were presented each week at a conference called "M and M's"—Mortality and Morbidity. Morbidity was surgical complications. Mortality was surgical deaths. All the professors and all the residents sat around a huge oval table and listened while the chief residents presented their deaths and complications. The week after our patient died, Jack presented her death. There was a brief silence. Everyone in the surgical department had known of our patient, and knew that the barium enema had been a disaster.

Dr. Sharman leaned forward to Jack. "Doctor," he began in his raspy, nasal voice. "As I understand it, the barium enema precipitated the death of this lady?"

"Yes, sir."

"Who ordered the barium enema?"

"I did, sir."

"Why?"

"The radiation therapist wanted it before he began radiation therapy."

"Did he order the enema without your permission?"

"No, sir."

"Then, you agreed with the radiation therapist that the test was absolutely necessary before radiation therapy was begun? You can't blame it on him."

"No, sir."

"What information exactly did you expect to gain?"

"The extent of the tumor, so he could map the area to be radiated."

"As a chief surgical resident do you not know that radiation for rectal cancer covers a standardized area in the lower abdomen? You don't know that?"

Silence.

"Answer me. Do you or do you not know that?"

"I know that, sir."

"So, to begin again, why did you order the barium enema?"

"I believed it might help him narrow the radiation field."

"Impossible in such a large cancer. Are you aware, as a chief surgical resident, that rectal cancers can be perforated, and that barium in the abdomen is usually fatal? You will be practicing on your own in six months. This information is known to a third-year medical student."

"I know that, sir."

"It didn't occur to you to order a Hypaque enema? Isn't that the dye recommended by any decent surgeon when there is any question of perforation, because—unlike barium—it doesn't irritate the intestine? That would've given you the information you were so anxious to get."

"It wouldn't have given the same detail."

"I don't see any detail on these films," said Dr. Sharman scornfully, indicating the x-ray that showed barium throughout our patient's abdomen. "You could have given her a Hypaque enema first, then a barium enema if the Hypaque showed it to be safe. Would you object to that?"

"No, sir. It would have been a good idea."

"Why didn't you do it?"

"I didn't think of it."

"You did not think. Period. A consult suggested a test. You ordered it. You didn't even ask your attending, or are you telling me that Dr. Baker told you to order the test?"

"No, sir. I didn't tell him."

"You forgot. You did not think. You are a surgeon. You aren't allowed to forget. You have to think. Surgeons don't act on inspiration from God. Surgeons are trained to think. To remember. Do you realize that you killed this woman? You killed her. There is no way around it. You ordered the barium. You killed her. I suggest to the Committee that the death be assigned as 'Error in surgical judgment.'"

Dr. Baker objected on the grounds that the woman had been dying from cancer, and there was more discussion between the attendings before the death was signed out. Jack looked as though he had been run over by a truck. Dr. Baker hurried over to him after the conference, scratching the back of his hand vigorously.

"Jack, don't let this throw you. We all make mistakes, including Dr. Sharman—lots of them. Every surgeon makes mistakes all his life. We can't help it. No one is perfect. I've made some much worse than this. It was regrettable, very regrettable. It was wrong, but you've learned never to do what a consultant asks without thinking about it. You took care of your patient in good faith. You did your best. You can't do more than your best. It's all any of us can do."

Heaven and Hell

Dr. Baker was as close to a saint as a surgeon can be. He was kind to his patients, intelligent, and an excellent surgeon. He was slow, and his operations took a long time. I thought he tended to take his time because he liked to be in the O.R. instead of in his office, where his secretary made him do his paperwork. He was a general surgeon, and he reminded me of Dr. Solomon and Dr. Hillebrand—he could do any operation because he knew the anatomy perfectly. Dr. Baker had a particular interest in cancer surgery. He waged war against cancer. He was always hunting for it, and he often found it. I was with him once when he was taken by a chief resident, "just as a formality," to see a lady on the medical service who had a leg ulcer.

"You did a complete physical exam?" Dr. Baker asked the chief resident.

"Not a complete one," he said. "She's already been examined by the medical attending, two medical residents, and a surgical resident."

Dr. Baker did his own complete examination. He slowed down as he examined her breasts, and asked her permission for the rest of us to examine them. There was a hard lump in her right breast. We left her room, and Dr. Baker started to scratch the back of his left hand. "I found out a long time ago that, as a trained general surgeon, I could detect disease other doctors couldn't find. She has been seen by five doctors, and not one of them found that she had a lump in her breast which is certainly a cancer." He stopped scratching his hand. "I always do a complete examination on every patient I see. There is a lot of cancer to find, but you won't find it if you don't look for it."

Breast cancer is the most common cancer in women, and Dr. Baker had many female patients whose breasts he had removed for cancer during the twenty-five years he had been in practice. One was an eighty-year-old lady who played the piano in a suburban hotel. She had had her surgery twenty years before, and came in regularly to see Dr. Baker for her yearly check. Each year she invited him to visit the hotel and have a drink on the house. Not all of his patients were so fortunate. One forty-five-year-old woman had had a mastectomy six years before and had no problems until she noticed a red lump in the scar, but thought it was unimportant. I saw her in Dr. Baker's clinic for a routine follow-up exam and she felt fine. I examined her scar, and the red swelling was still there. The week before, I had removed a "cyst" from a man's back which had proved to be a metastatic lung cancer. This skin swelling looked iike the "cyst" I had removed. I mentioned it to Dr. Baker before he went in with me to see her. He examined her completely, and then examined her mastectomy scar.

"You don't think there's anything wrong, do you, Dr. Baker?" she asked.

"Um . . ." he scratched the back of his hand. "I couldn't say really, you know. I think we'll just biopsy it. Nothing to worry about, my dear. If it is, um, something, um, bad, we can treat it."

He injected the area with Novocaine, and watched me cut out a tiny part of the swelling. We sent it to the lab for a frozen-section examination and in twenty minutes had the report. "Breast cancer, metastatic to the skin." When Dr. Baker broke the news, the woman said she wanted to go home and die. For an hour he patted her hand and said, "Yes, yes," and "I know, my dear," and . . . "but we can help you with x-ray treatment," while she cried. The clinic nurses were frantic because he had ten other patients waiting, but Dr. Baker kept talking to his patient until she felt well enough to register at the hospital desk for radiation therapy.

Most of what I learned about cancer, I learned from Dr. Baker. He never gave up, even when a patient's case seemed hopeless. Usually it *was* hopeless, but he had some remarkable recoveries. I was sorry to leave Dr. Baker's service, but I disliked Dr. Sharman so much that I was looking forward to January when I would start on cardiac surgery. The last operation I did with Dr. Sharman was a gallbladder removal. He was in a bad mood to begin with. At first he concentrated on the nurses. I was still refusing to speak to him.

"Give me a scalpel."

"Yes, sir." Noreen, the scrub nurse, handed him a scalpel.

He tried it and threw it on the floor. "When I ask for a scalpel, I want to see a blade that cuts, not a penknife." Noreen handed him a new blade.

"It still won't cut, but it seems if I want to operate here, I have to use secondhand blades."

"It's a fresh blade, sir. I never give a surgeon a used blade," Noreen said indignantly.

"Shut up. I'm operating. Give me a sponge." She handed him one. He threw it on the floor.

"That's no way to hand a sponge to a surgeon. Where did you go to nursing school?"

"I trained at General."

"No, you didn't. I trained there as a resident, and no nurse ever handed me a sponge like that. You hand a sponge flat—not wrinkled."

She handed him a flat sponge.

"Hurry up, give me another."

She handed him a second.

"Speak to me. Say 'Yes,' otherwise I don't know if you heard me."

"Yes, sir."

Noreen turned to the circulating nurse.

"I need some more scalpel blades, and I want an early lunch relief."

The circulator understood. Noreen was not going to be able to stand operating with Dr. Sharman.

"What's that?" he sputtered. "Lunch relief! I don't eat lunch. Why should you? It's ridiculous for you to leave me in the middle of the operation. You get morning coffee break, lunch break, afternoon coffee break. You're overpaid, you're stupid, you're ignorant. You're no good as a nurse. I could be a better scrub nurse blindfolded. You don't know your instruments. Give me the Mayo scissors." She did, and he threw them on the floor. "Can't you see I need the long

Mayos? You're hopeless. Why do they always send me the worst nurses?"

Another scrub nurse, Hilda, came in and Noreen left. Hilda, the new nurse, was English and excellent at her job. "I will be with you for the operation, sir. What do you need?"

"A nurse with more brains than a clam. I hope you're better. What do you think of that last one?"

"I wouldn't know, sir. What instrument may I give you?"

"Shut up. I'll tell you what I want."

"Yes, sir."

"Schnit. Forceps."

She handed him a Schnit and long toothed forceps, and stood ready with the long smooth forceps in case he needed them. He threw the toothed forceps on the floor. She immediately put the smooth ones in his hands. "Smooth forceps, sir. Please tell me what you need, and I will give it to you."

The circulating nurse picked the forceps off the floor, and said, "Dr. Sharman, these forceps cost seventy-five dollars. They were brand new and you just ruined them."

"It's not my fault," he snarled. "Tell that to the scrub nurse. She gave me the wrong ones." Hilda looked at him with narrowed eyes.

"Scissors," he shouted.

She slapped a pair of long-handled Metzenbaums into his hand, and held three other kinds ready just in case. "Please don't throw them on the floor, Dr. Sharman."

"Why not?" He threw them on the floor. "They're not what I wanted." He grabbed past her at her instrument tray, knocked it off-balance, and the sterile instruments fell on the floor. "It's not my fault," he snapped, "when my nurse can't give me a decent pair of scissors."

"I can give you these, Dr. Sharman," and Hilda showed him the three she was still holding. He grabbed all three. "And I am leaving the room," Hilda added.

"You can't leave unless I say you can." But Hilda had walked out in disgust. He turned to the circulator. "How can a nurse be so irresponsible?"

"Why don't you just operate, Dr. Sharman? There's no point in a scrub nurse being here if her instruments are on the floor." She opened a new sterile instrument tray.

The nursing supervisor came into the operating room. "Dr. Sharman, I am sending you a third scrub. Noreen and Hilda will not scrub with you. If the third nurse leaves, there is no one else I can send. You should understand that."

"It's not my fault you hire bad nurses."

The new scrub nurse walked in. She had a placid disposition and had just started to work at the Center. Surgeons at different hospitals call many instruments by different names.

"Schnit? What's that?" the new nurse asked.

He pointed to the instrument he wanted, making his exasperation obvious.

"I call that a Crile," she said in a conversational tone. She picked it up slowly, gave it to him, and started to chew the gum she had in her mouth. She was not good prey. Dr. Sharman would never be able to get her upset, so he turned on me. "You operate. You're the resident."

I took the scissors he gave me.

"You're holding them wrong. You're holding them wrong." He showed me how he wanted them held—at an angle impossible for me.

"Suture, please," I said. "Five-0 silk." I put in a suture.

"You can't even put in a suture," he laughed. "You're really terrible. You can't operate. I would have been ashamed to be that bad when I was a resident. Why, I didn't go to the O.R. until I could sew wet cigarette stubs under water in the bathtub."

I handed him back the scissors. "You operate, Dr. Sharman, and show me."

He finished the rest in silence.

"Elizabeth, have you met the new resident?" Sean asked one morning just before O.R.

I hadn't, but I had certainly heard about him. Georg Berger was German, spoke excellent English, and was so arrogant that everyone assumed he had to be extremely talented.

As we operated that day Sean and I discovered for ourselves that Georg was technically worse than any American surgical resident we had seen. Sean and I felt sorry for him, because all surgeons struggle through uncoordinated, clumsy periods while they learn to operate. Georg cut the sutures three inches long instead of a quarter inch. At

246

the end of the row of three-inch sutures, Dr. Childress, a new staff surgeon, said, "Georg, I know surgery is hard but I'll help you. Now look at that row of sutures. Don't you think they should be shorter?"

"At home we know this suture material must be cut long or it will absorb."

"Georg, the length of the suture will not slow the absorption of the knot you tie. The suture is not absorbed for several weeks, and the body will heal before then."

"If you order me to cut them shorter I will, but it is not right."

"Cut them."

After the operation Sean said to me, "The guy isn't going to win the Nobel Prize for popularity, but it's rough for him in a foreign country. This is only his second day!"

On Georg's third day he examined a patient admitted for a major liver operation. I read the history-and-physical he wrote on the chart. I knew this patient had a complicated medical history, including jaundice, heart attacks, phlebitis and pneumonia. Georg's note was very brief: "Man is admitted for hospital, 58 years, for surgery. White. Symptoms none, but I have read chart, which is half disordered. Liver is problem. All other normal. Plan—Surgery."

I spent two hours teaching Georg our system for examining patients. I wrote down for him a list of questions he had to ask each patient so he could understand the patient's disease, prevent surgical complications and not overlook other, more serious diseases. Georg was insulted and for two hours he said at intervals, "I know all this. This is just like what we have at home, only ours is much more thorough. Our medical system is much more efficient than yours is here."

"Georg, you examined Mr. Dupres and you have a three-line note that gives no useful information."

"Of course I did. I am being asked to work far too much, and I am not responsible if you assign me to do things that I can't do to my usual standards because there is a lack of time."

"Georg, I don't want you to do anything else for the rest of the day. Just go back and examine Mr. Dupres."

"Again? I just examined him!"

"But you said you didn't have time to do it properly, so go back and do a good examination."

Then I went to the O.R. to assist on a kidney transplant. At three o'clock, when the operation was over, I found Georg asking a nurse to join him for a drink after evening rounds.

"Georg, have you examined Mr. Dupres again?" I asked.

"Who?" he jerked his head sideways at me, annoyed.

"Mr. Dupres. Remember, I spent two hours talking with you about how to do a work-up, before I went to the O.R.?"

"I examined him, but I haven't started writing yet. There was too much noise to concentrate." He pulled open three drawers at the nurses' desk, scrabbling for paper.

"Don't go away," he shouted at me. "I need your pen."

"I need my pen, too. You can find one in the bottom drawer."

"Why didn't you tell me sooner?"

I was annoyed. Junior residents aren't supposed to speak to a senior resident like that.

I walked into Mr. Dupres' room and asked him if a doctor had examined him twice that day or only once.

"I haven't seen any doctor," said Mr. Dupres.

"Didn't a doctor with a foreign accent examine you this morning?"

"Oh, him. I thought he was an orderly. He said I was going to have a chest x-ray, but he didn't do any examination." That night Georg was on call, and I stayed late to watch him examine Mr. Dupres after evening rounds. He went through the motions of an adequate, though casual, examination. I discussed the exam with him.

When I thought Georg was checking for pulses in the feet, he assured me he had been feeling the patient's skin because it seemed dry and he wondered if the man had a fever. I suggested a thermometer should be used to measure that, but Georg assured me that in Germany dry skin was considered more reliable.

After two weeks of Georg, Sean and I had started an underground movement to assassinate him. Dr. Childress still felt Georg would respond to reason and urged me to take him under my wing and teach him. I declined.

Even Dr. Childress gave up the idea of reasoning with Georg after he heard me present our week's complications at the M and M Conference on Tuesday. I sent Georg to the library to do some reading during the conference, because I thought it would be unkind to insist he be present while I discussed the complication he had caused while on call the night before. After the other services presented their complications, Dr. Tobey turned to me.

"Any complications on your service, Dr. Morgan?"

"Yes, Dr. Tobey, we have one."

"Present the case."

"The patient is a sixty-two-year-old man, three years after resection of a carcinoid tumor of the intestine. He was a patient of Dr. Sweet's, and had surgery last week to relieve a small bowel obstruction due to adhesions from scar tissue. A Kantor tube was placed through the nose into the stomach and through to the intestines." The Kantor tube is a long, elastic rubber tube with weights on the end, used to suction out fluid from obstructed intestines. It is long enough to reach the rectum. "The tube moved down the intestine by peristalsis during the week. Last night at three A.M. the patient noticed that the end of the tube was coming out of his rectum. The other end was still taped to his nose. Dr. Berger, who was on call, called Dr. Hopewell, the chief resident, for advice, but then decided his own method would be more effective. First, he pulled hard on the end of the tube at the nose, and then cut it off. The cut end recoiled back into the stomach. At the rectal end, he also pulled as hard as he could, trying to pull the whole tube through the stomach, small intestine and colon with one heave." Dr. Tobey groaned and clutched his stomach. Sean, from the back of the room, whispered audibly, "You ain't heard nothing yet."

I went on. "Having pulled very hard on the rectal end, he discovered he could not pull the whole tube out. He then kept the tube pulled taut, and cut it short." Dr. Baker hid his face in his hands. "The tube promptly recoiled into the intestine." Dr. Mulveney sighed. Dr. Sharman choked on his coffee. I paused.

"What did he do next, Dr. Morgan?" asked Dr. Tobey.

"He went back to bed."

"He went back to bed? With a five-foot Kantor tube coiled inaccessibly in a patient's bowels?"

"He thought it might come out by itself."

"Would you agree with that?"

"I think it would be unlikely, Dr. Tobey."

"Unlikely? Unheard of! What was his plan when he got out of bed this morning? Is he aware that this totally preventable complication may require surgery to remove the tube?"

249

"Fortunately we avoided surgery, sir. An abdominal film this morning did show that the tube had retracted back through the entire length of the large bowel and was in the small intestine. Dr. Sweet, working with a gastroenterologist, miraculously managed to remove the Kantor tube by snaring it with the hook on the end of a colonoscope forceps. It took six hours. The tube end has been brought out the rectum and is being slowly advanced. The whole tube should be out by tomorrow."

"Adventures in the large bowel with gun and camera," murmured Sean in the back.

"Your plans to prevent this in the future?" asked Dr. Tobey severely.

Dr. Sweet intervened angrily, "There is one plan and only one plan. This resident is uncontrollable. I don't know who writes his script, but the Marx Brothers could never have thought of this one. You laugh, Mulveney; you think I'm kidding. Berger hauled so hard on the Kantor tube that a patient in the next bed thought he'd caught a lobster. I had to cancel my entire office hours and spend the whole day with the gastroenterologist halfway up the colon, trying to hook a rubber tube, with the Beast of Dresden standing by complaining that they don't do it this way at home. I'm going to kill him! He's a menace. Send him anywhere, but get him away from my patients."

Soon afterward, Georg was posted to the E.R. to work under supervision. This was not satisfactory, so he was sent back to Dr. Baker's service, but even Dr. Baker couldn't help him. After a rotation at the Veterans Hospital, he took a job as a surgical resident in another state.

Disgraceful

I started cardiac surgery on the first of January. I was beginning to feel fat, because I had gained five pounds since coming to Boston, and I was now one hundred thirty-five pounds. Cardiac surgery seemed a good time to diet because I would not have time to eat, and I was ready to suffer. Dr. Anjou, the chief of cardiac surgery, was well known for his disapproval of women surgeons, on the grounds that they weren't as tough as men.

I assumed the rumors were exaggerated, until several nurses and residents came up to me sympathetically in late December. "Elizabeth, is it true you'll be on Dr. Anjou's service? You poor thing. He'll throw you off the service if he has his way."

A diet, I thought masochistically, would be the perfect complement to all my suffering. Mark had been on heart surgery before me and had been so busy I rarely spoke to him. On January first he signed out to me, telling me about the patients. At the end, he told me, "You'll enjoy the service, Lizzie. Anjou runs a tight ship."

"If he doesn't throw me off his service," I said.

"Why? Because you're a woman? That's garbage. He doesn't care if you're a raccoon. All he wants is someone who will work hard and take care of his patients. It's very hard, almost as bad as being an intern. But you're a hard worker and you won't have a problem.

Listen, I heard a story about a heart surgeon in Houston that makes Anjou look like the Good Humor man. This resident was assigned to the cardiac I.C.U. He had to live there three months, day and night. He couldn't leave to go home for an evening with his wife, and he wasn't even allowed past the I.C.U. doors into the hospital corridor. Toward the end of his three months he went stir-crazy, and arranged to meet his wife for ten minutes out in the hall. The heart surgeon saw him, hit him in the chest, fractured his sternum and two ribs, and then fired him."

January first was a Saturday, and I was on call for the cardiac service from then till Monday night. We had three adult patients in the I.C.U. who had just had heart surgery, and eleven patients recovering on the ward. There was a special team of cardiac nurses to look after Dr. Anjou's patients. In the pediatric wing there were seven children who had had heart surgery. Another resident looked after them. Once a heart patient has survived the first few days there are usually no further problems, but immediately after surgery the heart and lungs are unstable. Patients can develop heart arrhythmias or oxygen problems and deteriorate or die within minutes. After Mark signed out to me I sat in the I.C.U. watching the heart monitors and the urine output, ordering chest x-rays and blood tests, reviewing all the results, ready to change oxygen levels or give heart medicines at the first sign of change.

Mark had warned me that twice a day Dr. Anjou, Dr. Firenze, and Dr. Norland made rounds with the cardiac chief resident, and my first day they arrived at 10:00 A.M.

"You're Dr. Morgan?" asked Dr. Anjou, who was built big enough to have been an orthopedic surgeon. "Tell me about the patients, one, two, three. How are they?"

I was ready. "In the first bed is Mrs. Angles, three days status-post, triple-vessel coronary revascularization. She is awake, alert, and eating a liquid diet. Her blood pressure is 130/80, her pulse is 95, respirations 15. Blood gases on room air. . . ." I knew everything about the patients, their x-rays and lab results.

"Good." Dr. Anjou pointed to Dr. Firenze. "If you have a question, ask him. If Firenze has a question, he asks him," and he pointed to Dr. Norland. "If he has a question, he calls me. That is an unchangeable hierarchy. I don't care how many times anyone gets called, I don't want mistakes. All my patients go home alive. Dr.

Firenze will return at one o'clock after we see the children, to be sure you don't have any questions. Good-bye."

I settled down to monitor my three cardiac patients again. The nurse brought me lunch on a tray. Cold coffee, a piece of fried chicken, canned peas. My diet would be easy.

In five days I lost seven pounds. I sat in the chair all day and all night from Saturday to Monday morning, and stood in the O.R. all day Monday. It was fun. The nurses, the residents, and the attendings worked together in a well-organized team. I was number eight, after the attendings, the cardiac chief resident, and the three cardiologists.

Dr. Anjou decided after a week that I was reliable. He said to Dr. Firenze one morning, "She can look after the children."

The pediatric heart patients were more delicate than the adults, and his high success rate with pediatric heart surgery was Dr. Anjou's special pride. I was very pleased. Despite his apparent fierceness, Dr. Anjou was considerate. During a heart operation, he would send the residents out for coffee, one by one, at times when they were not needed and could not see enough of the surgery to learn from it. Dr. Firenze would correct me constantly during an operation. "Don't hold your forceps that way, Liz. Don't do a backhand stitch. Stand up. Your stitch is too tight. The knot is too loose." After a few minutes, Dr. Anjou would say, "Oh, leave her alone. She's not the intern."

When we gathered in the operating room for the first operation each morning, Dr. Anjou looked around, scowling, checking on the anesthesiologists, the pump team technicians, the nurses, and the residents. Then he would smile. "It's going to be a good day, folks. We've got the 'A' team here."

One evening Dr. Anjou took me and the cardiac chief resident, Charles Longfellow, to see a patient on the medical service. She was a seventy-four-year-old Italian woman with a badly diseased aortic heart valve, as a result of rheumatic fever when she was a child in Milan. The valve was too scarred to close, and most of the blood sloshed back into the heart after each beat. Her heart failure was so severe that she couldn't brush her hair without becoming short of breath.

Dr. Anjou went into her room and Charles and I followed him.

"Mrs. Rosario, I'm Dr. Anjou, the heart surgeon. You're going to have heart surgery tomorrow. I'm going to try to replace the valve. You should know you are a very sick woman. Surgery is your only hope but in your condition it is very dangerous."

"Doctor, do you think I will live through the operation?" she asked anxiously, panting slightly from the exertion of speaking.

"I hope so." He smiled. "We have an excellent team of nurses and doctors to look after you. Three other heart surgeons will be assisting me, to do the very best for you."

"Thank you, Doctor. I have so much faith in you," and she reached for his hand to try to kiss it. He backed away, embarrassed, then patted her arm before he left.

Charles Longfellow and I walked back to the nurses' desk to write orders for her surgery in the morning, but the operation seemed a futile exercise.

"Do you think she'll live?" I asked Charles.

"No. Want some gum?" He handed me a piece. "Her heart is worthless, a flabby balloon."

"Why is Dr. Anjou operating?"

Charles shrugged. "He's got an ego like every other heart surgeon."

The next day at 7:00 A.M., I was in the O.R. with Charles getting Mrs. Rosario ready for surgery. She looked very frightened.

"I'm going to die. I know I'm going to die," she said to the anesthesiologist.

"You'll be all right, dear," he said vaguely, putting the heart monitor attachments on her shoulders.

"Tutti va bene," said Dr. Firenze to her in Italian.

Dr. Anjou signaled the anesthesiologist to put her to sleep. I remembered my heart surgery rotations as a medical student and intern and I didn't want to scrub on Mrs. Rosario. But there was no escape. Ten minutes later I was dissecting out the femoral artery in the left groin; Charles was assisting me by holding retractors and clamping bleeders; Dr. Norland was going over the heart pump with two technicians on the other side of the O.R.; and Dr. Firenze was opening the chest, assisted by Dr. Anjou. I suddenly realized that to Dr. Anjou at least, the operation was no futile exercise but a battle against the odds to save a life. He was being merciless to Dr. Firenze, and he was only like that when he was very worried about a patient.

"Come on, Bill, come on, hurry up. You've been a heart surgeon for four years, you ought to be able to open a chest without my telling you how."

Dr. Firenze frowned and concentrated and Dr. Anjou frowned and badgered him. At nine o'clock the chest was split down the middle and spread open with a metal retractor, the tissue around the heart was peeled back and Mrs. Rosario's heart was going *thump-swish-thump-swish*, because the blood sloshed back into the heart with each beat.

"Get her on the pump, Bill, don't just stand there. This heart's going to stop any minute. Show me the valve."

The nurse gave him the plastic valve to inspect and Dr. Firenze shouldered me away from the groin and checked the vessels.

"Lines up," said Dr. Anjou, and the pump technicians gave Dr. Firenze the sterile tubing attached to the pump. The catheters were placed in the groin, and Dr. Firenze returned to the chest.

"Pump ready?" said Dr. Anjou.

"Pump ready," said Dr. Norland and the pump technicians.

"Aortic clamp down," he said.

"Aortic clamp down," repeated the pump team.

"Femoral clamp down."

"Femoral clamp down," repeated the team.

"Pump clamp off and perfusing."

"Pump clamp off and perfusing," repeated the team.

Chug-chug-chug—the lines from the heart pump quivered and shook with the force of the blood pumping through them. Sterile ice and water were packed around the heart to keep it cool.

Dr. Anjou cut open the heart above the valve.

"Rotten," he said and picked out the hard remnants of the valve.

"Valve up," he said. A circulating nurse dropped something on the other side of the room. "I don't want any noise. No one breathes or moves until the valve is in."

I looked at the tangle of sutures sewn into the side of the valve. The last time I'd seen a valve replaced—when I was an intern—Dr. Bryant had sewed the valve in upside down and had to take it out and start over. Dr. Anjou sewed one stitch into the heart, then a second, until there was a circle of black thread coming out of the heart.

"Hold up the valve, Bill." Dr. Firenze held the valve up, with the black sutures pulled up straight. The valve slid down the sutures into the heart. Dr. Anjou tied the sutures down, cut them, and Dr. Firenze said, "Get ready to come off the pump."

"Ready," said the anesthesiologist.

"Ready," said Dr. Norland and the pump team.

"Ready," said Charles with clamps poised over the pump lines.

Dr. Anjou looked around. "Clamps down, and pray this heart starts again."

He shocked the heart with two electric paddles. It quivered and beat twice, quivered frantically, then with a jolt stopped again.

We went back on the pump.

"This is it," I thought. "She's had it."

Dr. Anjou shocked the heart once again. It pumped and stopped again.

"It wants to start," said Dr. Firenze.

"It won't help by just wanting," said Dr. Anjou and shocked it again. *Thump-thump-thump*, went the heart.

"Coming off the pump," said Dr. Anjou. "Pump time?"

"Twenty minutes," said Dr. Norland.

"Twenty minutes?" I said to myself in amazement. All the heart surgeries I had previously witnessed had required at least one hour on the pump. The longer a patient is on the pump, the more the churning action of the machine damages red blood cells and blood clotting factors. As pump time increases, blood may not clot, and brain damage may result from damaged protein and red cells clumping in the brain. Twenty minutes' pump time greatly increased the patient's chances for a good recovery, but it meant that the cardiac team had worked very quickly and smoothly; twenty minutes was slick work.

At twelve o'clock, Mrs. Rosario was wheeled into the I.C.U. with tubes in her arm, her bladder, her chest, her windpipe.

"Who's on call here tonight?" asked Dr. Anjou.

"I am," I said.

"Don't kill her." He walked away and I overheard him say to Dr. Firenze, "Thank you for your help this morning. You did a great job. I want Dr. Norland to assist you on your case this afternoon. I'll run the pump."

Two weeks later Mrs. Rosario was ready to go home. On evening rounds Dr. Anjou turned to me.

"You thought she'd die, didn't you?"

"Yes," I said.

"We have a good team. You've just never seen first-rate heart surgery before."

After two and a half months on heart surgery I was exhausted and irritable. I could do the work and help at the surgery, but I was jumpy. Dr. Firenze annoyed me because he was such a perfectionist. Everything had to be done his way. He allowed men to disagree with him, but he became indignant if I did. His own wife was an excellent nurse, but he looked upon her as an exception. Three years ago I would simply have tried to stay out of his way, but no more. I was as good a doctor as the male residents I worked with—or better—and I worked as hard as any resident on the heart service. I was getting as tough and quarrelsome as the men, too, and if Dr. Firenze wanted to give me a hard time, I was ready to fight with him.

One morning at 5:00 A.M. I was working in the pediatric I.C.U. I had not slept for two days. Dr. Firenze was there, too, in his custom-made, double-breasted suit. Together we were trying to thread a catheter a tenth of an inch wide into a premature baby's artery. The baby had survived emergency heart surgery performed immediately after birth, and now we were trying to monitor and control his blood pressure and blood oxygen with drugs so he would have a chance of surviving. Dr. Firenze had enough sleep, but he worked under a great strain. Dr. Anjou always wanted to know what was going wrong, why, and whose fault it was. He trusted Dr. Firenze to be perfect, and when he was not, Dr. Anjou was furious.

As Dr. Firenze watched me putting the catheter in, he said, "Your needle holder is held wrong. Stand up. You have the light wrong. You're using the wrong suture. Do you hear me? Are you listening? Let me help you. If you don't do what I say, I'll do it myself. Stand up."

I listened to him and kept working for fifteen minutes. I thought I was being patient. Finally, after I had succeeded in threading the catheter into the artery, Dr. Firenze put his left hand over mine and tried to take the needle holder away from me with his right hand. "You don't have a light enough touch for this fine work. It takes a man to do this right. You better let me take over."

I snatched my hand away and turned on him. "Don't you touch

me. Don't you ever touch me. I'm not your wife. Don't you ever grab anything out of my hand. You ask me for it. Don't ever put your hands on me again."

"What do you mean by speaking to me like that? You're a resident. You wouldn't speak to Dr. Anjou that way. You can't speak to me like that."

I put my hands on my hips and glared at him. "Dr. Anjou doesn't put his hands on me as though I were a tart off the street. He treats me like a doctor, and I respect him. I don't respect you at all, and I'll talk to you any way I want."

The only people to witness this disgraceful scene were babies in incubators and two nurses who looked at us in horror and hurried to the other end of the room, expecting blows to follow. The episode took a few seconds. We turned back to the baby. The catheter was still in good position, where I had left it. Dr. Firenze attached it to a blood pressure monitor and the procedure was over. I watched as, with infinite care, he covered the catheter with a dressing. Then he left, outraged. "You will hear from Dr. Anjou about this."

As it happened, we both did. No one said anything that day. I apologized to the nurses, and told my friends I expected to be fired, or at least thrown off the service. The next day, on evening rounds, Dr. Anjou cleared his throat meaningfully in the I.C.U. before we started. The whole team was there. Gazing at an x-ray, he remarked casually, and apparently irrelevantly, "Attending *and* resident staff should behave like doctors, not children."

We were both in disgrace and Dr. Firenze stiffened. Later on I apologized, and he was polite, but I knew there was still a gulf between him and women surgeons, and I'd just dug it a mile deeper.

Sex and the Single Surgeon

In January of 1974 I was accepted in a plastic surgery residency for 1976. I had decided on plastic surgery because I wanted to learn how to do hand surgery, and facial cancer surgery, and reconstructive surgery. I could not learn all this in five years of general surgery, so I decided to extend my residency to seven years and become a plastic as well as a general surgeon. After various interviews, I was accepted by my first choice. In two years, I would be Board-eligible in general surgery. Two years after that I would finish my residency in plastic surgery, a total of seven years' training, of which I had now done three. In six months I would be halfway through. The last three months of that year and the first three months of the next, my fourth year of residency, I was chief resident on the Third Surgical Service, which did kidney transplants, trauma and some plastic surgery. Transplants and plastic surgery were relatively new sections at the hospital, and we didn't have many patients. We looked after the patients of three other surgeons as well. One of them, Dr. Childress, was just starting practice, specializing in obesity and intestinal bypass surgery to make fat people thin.

Operating with Dr. Childress was a new experience. He was amazingly fast, and forced me to operate quickly. The first time I operated with him was on a ruptured spleen. The patient was hemorrhaging internally and I had to operate fast to stop the bleeding. With Dr. Childress standing over me, saying in his firm, commanding voice, "Faster. Faster," I operated faster than I ever had before.

"Open the belly, Elizabeth. Put your finger in the weak point of the fascia and cut. Faster." I opened the belly, and he put in a large retractor on the left side of the incision, pulling almost hard enough to pull the patient off the table.

"Put your left hand across the ileum to control the bleeding; use your right to pull out the spleen. Don't be gentle. Faster. No one makes you guys work fast enough. Do it!"

I had the spleen out from under the ribs.

"Clamp the artery. Clamp the vein. Clamp the smaller vessels. Cut them; get rid of the spleen and tie the vessels."

I did that.

"Irrigate and sew up. Just use a continuous number-three nylon to close the belly. This isn't plastic surgery."

I did that.

"You're done. Six minutes. Now that's surgery!"

The next time I operated was with Dr. Tobey, and it was an elective splenectomy on a patient with a rare anemia—the spleen was destroying red blood cells.

"Whoa!" said Dr. Tobey when I opened the belly in ten seconds and reached up to pull down the spleen. "Slow down, girl, you're in tiger country up there—the pancreas, the stomach, the colon are all packed up there. Take your time, do it right. I want to see you dissect this, show me the anatomy and do it right."

I was impatient when Dr. Tobey slowed me down, and alarmed when Dr. Childress hurried me up and never could decide which was right. It wasn't until I was a chief resident and operated frequently on my own that I found my own speed. I was happiest at a steady and methodical pace. You need a lot of experience to rush through a complicated operation and still do it well. One senior resident was hurried through a gallbladder operation by his chief resident. In the rush, they forgot to check the abdomen before sewing the incision closed. They left behind a six-inch metal clamp that had slipped behind a loop of intestine. The mistake was not discovered until a few weeks later when the patient went to another hospital for stomach pain, and had to have a second, emergency, operation to remove the clamp.

After finishing my six months on the Third Service, I had an elective rotation and took time off to attend my first national convention, the annual meeting of the American College of Surgeons. That year it was held in Miami. The registration fee was a hundred dollars, but as a resident I could attend for free. I arrived in Miami, and found my hotel was the last one along the beach, about a mile from the Fontainebleau, the main convention hotel. I learned from the porter in the lobby that the surgical convention had brought over ten thousand surgeons and twenty thousand other guests to Miami Beach. I had no idea that it was such a large affair.

It was late October. The weather was hot, but the seas were so rough that I never saw the sand on the beach, although I had a beautiful view of the ocean. I arrived on a Sunday afternoon, and, after consulting the convention map, decided to walk to the Fontainebleau to register. I saw nothing but hotels and resort condominiums along the way, and I soon understood why no one else was walking. I arrived at the Fontainebleau tired and perspiring. I recognized no one there. I had imagined seeing a few professors or residents whom I knew, but among ten thousand surgeons registering in the lobby I was lost. I registered, and as I wandered back through the lobby, I bumped into someone two feet taller than I was. The someone said, "Hello, Elizabeth," and turned out to be Gary Anderson, a classmate at medical school, now a surgical resident in Minnesota. He found the heat of Miami a pleasant change.

"Have you ever been to one of these?" he asked.

"No, have you?"

"Yes, I went last year to the one in San Francisco. The department sent me, because I was presenting some research we had done with kidney transplants. This meeting is much smaller than the one in San Francisco. No one wants to come to Miami Beach."

"I was told there were ten thousand surgeons here."

"There must have been twenty thousand in San Francisco. It's almost frightening to think of so many surgeons in one place, but the girls like it."

"What girls?"

"You can't have ten thousand men in one city, half of whom don't bring their wives, without a few lovelies to entertain them. Haven't you noticed a large number of exotic females hanging around?"

"That's who they are. I thought they were a bit noticeable. There is one amazing creature."

"You mean the six-foot blonde with the skirt up to the waist? Yes, she is eye-catching, but no one's interested in her. She makes you too conspicuous. Join me for a drink."

We spent the next hour talking and watching the action in the darkened hotel bar-lounge, which was lit only by tiny purple candles. I decided to take the convention bus back to my hotel, and we arranged to meet in the morning to attend the symposium on reconstruction of the larynx. A tall, gray-haired, distinguished-looking gentleman followed me onto the bus and sat down next to me.

"Hi, I'm Dr. Atterson, from California." He peered at my name tag. "You're a doctor? Don't tell me you're a surgeon?"

"Yes, I'm a surgeon."

"Isn't that nice." He looked me over. "You're a lot better-looking than the other surgeons I've been talking to today. Did you come to the conference with someone?"

"No. I'm taking an elective now, and I was able to take the time off to come."

"So you're a resident. Good for you. What hotel are you staying at?"

I told him.

"Wonderful. It's the same one I'm at. I didn't think I could make it, so I didn't make reservations, which is why I ended up there. It's not bad, but it's not glamorous. You got stuck there because you're a resident. The housing committee for the convention puts residents at the bottom of the list."

The bus stopped in front of the hotel.

"Would you care to join me for a drink?"

"If you don't mind buying me a soft drink. I've just had one cocktail on an empty stomach."

"Make it two. You'll be surprised how much better it will make you feel." He waggled his eyebrows suggestively and waltzed me into the bar, to a cozy, dark table at the back.

"A whiskey sour for the lady and a Scotch for me," he told the waitress, and, turning to me, "Don't let me frighten you. I'm not as bad as I seem. You don't have to drink it."

"Thank you." I didn't know what else to say. I hadn't met a surgeon like him before.

"Call me Jake," he went on. "I'm a very prominent surgeon on the West Coast. I started before there were half as many surgeons as there are now. I have a wonderful nurse who's been with me for years. When you start in practice, be sure you get someone good to help you. Of course, Mandy and I were more than just a working team. We were good lovers, too. I divorced my wife four years ago. The kids were grown up and in college, and there didn't seem any point in continuing what was a meaningless relationship. Since then, I've moved back into the younger generation. I'm much more with it, as my kids would say. I've begun to explore a lot of new ways of living, looser, freer, more natural. What do you think of that?"

"It sounds very nice."

The waitress served us the drinks.

"Of course, your generation is tuned in to how to live. How old would you say I am? Don't be scared. You won't insult me. Just take a guess."

He looked sixty; I guessed forty.

"Sixty?" I said in pretend surprise when he told me his real age. "I would never believe you had grown children, if you hadn't told me."

He giggled happily. "You really do make a man feel young. Or are you just saying that?"

"Oh, no."

"Well, I do look young for my age. Of course, I run every morning. I'm into jogging. It's the new thing. I work out at the gym at lunch, and I swim pretty regularly. I've been thinking of taking up surfing. All the young kids are into that, but it's inconvenient. I don't live close enough to the beach. Tell me, what do you think of oral sex?"

"Of what?"

"Oral sex. My son is in college, and it's what all the college kids are getting turned on by these days. I sort of like it, too. The old straight vaginal sex is kind of a drag after a while, don't you think?"

"You know, I don't know you very well."

"Be loose. Relax. It's perfectly normal for adults to talk about sex,

263

isn't it?" He smiled and waggled his eyebrows again. "It's no different from talking about any sport, is it, between two doctors?"

"I may be a woman doctor, but I also may be a little old-fashioned."

"You? Old-fashioned? A woman surgeon? You're putting me on. You know all about this stuff. Where are you a resident?"

"Boston."

"Oh, New England. Ye old Puritan stomping grounds. You didn't grow up there, did you?" He sounded concerned.

"No, I grew up near D.C."

"You can't fool me, then. You're a modern lady. You sure are cute. I bet you're a hot number back at your hospital."

"Would you mind if I had a Coke? I really don't think I can drink this whiskey sour."

"Sweetheart, you can have anything you want. Anything you want. So what's your sex life like?"

"I don't discuss it with strange men, as a matter of fact."

"Wow. What an answer. Loosen up, kid, you have the world in front of you. Let me tell you that I know all about lady surgeons. You see, we have a couple of girls in our program back home, and let me tell you, they are something else. In fact, both of them right now are sleeping with the same intern. I don't see what his attraction is, myself. One of the nurses was complaining the other morning that she called the intern during the night, and a female voice answered. She recognized the voice, because it was this woman surgeon.

"'You must have the wrong number,' the lady surgeon said.

"So the nurse, who really needed an intern for a patient, just said, 'Go to hell, I know you're in bed together. Put him on the horn, will you? I'm not fooling around.'

"Have you ever tried group sex—orgies? No? I must say, I haven't either. We could try tonight." He looked around the bar. "It's too dark. I can't see if there's a second gal who is good enough looking." He shrugged. "Too bad.

"I was telling you we have a loose hospital. Very free. One surgeon in our department is married but he's got himself a lesbian girl friend, which is really a new twist. There's me. I left my wife. We tried everything, group therapy, Esalen, meditation, but frankly, she didn't turn me on, and you can't change that. I'm very adventurous, surgically and sexually. You should see me operate." He leered at me.

"The department chairman is very free and loose. He has a whole harem. There's one gorgeous girl running after him, but she's too fat for my taste. I like them firm and athletic, not too luscious. Soft, but not too juicy. Like you. He left his wife a year ago with three kids under ten, which was too bad, but when you have your own life to explore, you can't be held down. It was very tough for him deciding to break up. Frankly, I think he's a sex maniac. He'll fuck anything. I think he must be a sublimated homosexual. You know, if you study sex you learn a lot of things, and one of them is that these sex-maniac types are all of them working through a sexual desire for their mothers. I find it interesting." He tossed off his second double Scotch.

"Do you think that makes a statement about American women being frigid? I mean, why is it that the man needs so many women? It's a deep problem." He ate some peanuts, and put his arm around me. "But not as deep as I could get into you, honey."

I looked at my watch. "It's late; I really must go. Thank you for the drink."

"I'll call you later tonight. Maybe we could get together in my room."

"Would you mind not doing that? Really." He grabbed at my hand, but I hurried off.

He had made me feel squalid and lonely and I wished I had not come to Miami. Many men look on women doctors as an easy lay— you dissected the penis in anatomy class so you must be uninhibited. But I hadn't been treated as common property by another surgeon before.

That evening I met Dr. Sutherland, an eminent Harvard professor, on his way to a committee meeting for the American College.

"Elizabeth, isn't the program exciting? I don't think I've ever seen such a collection of first-rate papers. You mustn't miss this one." He pulled out the conference program. "Here it is. Complications in plastic surgery. Dr. Berenson is presiding and it will be excellent. Isn't it wonderful being part of this society, seeing the new advances in surgery we keep making? The brilliance of some of these papers is humbling." He was genuinely excited, and I was glad once again that I had come.

I spent the rest of the conference dodging tall, distinguished-looking gray-haired men. I was too vain to wear my glasses all the time, and if I noticed any gray, tall form, I entered the nearest dark lecture hall and took refuge among several hundred surgeons, listening to the speaker attentively.

Writing Fever

I spent my three months of elective time at a Harvard hospital, working on Dr. Sutherland's plastic surgery service. I was not allowed to take night or weekend calls because I was only visiting and not employed by the hospital, so I had three months of regular sleep to look forward to, and the chance to study and think. I had already begun work on two surgical papers on decubitus ulcers, and I hoped to finish them and learn as much about plastic surgery as I could. Dr. Sutherland told me I should work on a small project during my three months with his service and give a talk about it at the end.

It was a cold winter in Boston, as usual, and I had to park my car half a mile from the hospital. I was not eligible for hospital parking, and on-the-street parking near the hospital was illegal until after 9:30. Rounds started every morning at seven with the whole "plastic" team: the chief resident, Dean Richards, who was in his seventh and last year of training; the junior resident, Henry Matthews, in his sixth year of training; the intern, Tom Anderson; and all five plastic surgery attendings, Dr. Sutherland and Dr. Berenson; Dr. Revere, who had just returned from Hopkins, Dr. Potter, an oral surgeon, and Dr. Godfrey, a plastic surgeon who did mainly pediatric plastic surgery; and then me and an orthopedic resident from another hospital.

As a team we saw every patient on the service, discussed their operations, and went to the operating room at eight o'clock three days a week, and to clinic two days a week. We finished rounds in time because Dr. Sutherland walked quickly between patients' rooms. He never ran but we did, to keep up with him.

I knew almost nothing about plastic surgery when I started. I had had no plastic surgery except for three weeks as a junior resident at the Veterans Hospital. Many of the patients there had huge cancers on the face and neck, and the plastic resident had taught me a lot about head-and-neck cancer. When I was working in the emergency room, Dr. Mendelssohn had taken time to teach me how to evaluate facial injuries and how to sew up lacerations. That was all I knew. I had a lot to learn.

On Dr. Sutherland's service, one of the first patients I saw had a pressure ulcer that covered most of her back. Dr. Revere showed me the wound with enthusiasm, saying, "This is one of the great challenges in plastic surgery, getting a wound like this to heal." There was a boy with a rare cancer of the nose who needed a new nose created surgically. There were dozens of children with cleft lips and cleft palates, men with fractured faces from altercations in nearby bars, and patients with hand injuries, throat cancers, and face deformities. I thought I knew something about surgery—stomach ulcers, gallstones, colon cancers, reconstructing blood vessels in the abdomen and legs. I had no idea I was so ignorant about a surgical specialty, but I learned solidly for three months. Dr. Potter showed me how to wire jaws together and taught me about jaw growth and function. Dr. Revere taught me about wound healing and skin flaps. He and Dr. Godfrey taught me about cleft lips and palates. Dr. Berenson taught me about cosmetic surgery and hand surgery; and most important of all, how to think again, after three years of learning to operate. Dr. Sutherland taught me about head and neck cancer and reconstructing children with grotesque facial deformities. He had a reputation for being a fearless surgeon.

"Scalpel, please," he said to the nurse the first day I operated with him on a face reconstruction. "You see, I make the incision so," he cut across the scalp from ear to ear, "and once I am in the right place," he pushed with the blunt handle of the scalpel, "the forehead is down, like so, down to the nose. Suction the blood away, please. Now for access to the eyes, we take the bone off the forehead."

Fourteen hours and twenty units of blood later, the child's abnormal upper face had been taken apart and put back together in a normal position. I was exhausted, and so were Dean Richards, Henry Matthews and Dr. Revere.

Dr. Sutherland changed out of his scrub suit, came back to see the child in the recovery room, spoke to the patients, and said good night to us. It was eleven o'clock.

"I'll be in my office if you need me. I have some paper work to do. By the way, Elizabeth, I want you to give a talk for Grand Rounds before you leave the service. Perhaps Dr. Berenson would suggest a topic. He has some excellent ideas. Good night." He strode away.

Dr. Berenson and Dr. Sutherland were each "Chief of Plastic Surgery"—but at two different hospitals. The teaching was outstanding because both of these brilliant and eminent men worked together and set high standards for their residents. Such alliances in surgery are temporary, because one surgeon wants more political power, but while it lasts real advances are made.

I spent the next afternoon with Dr. Berenson in his office, seeing his private patients. He was a remarkable man and somehow managed to have a busy practice and still do surgical research and writing. I saw a girl who needed a rhinoplasty, a nose operation; a girl on whom he had performed a rhinoplasty the year before; and a girl who had developed scarring in the nose so that she could not breathe after rhinoplasty by another doctor, not a plastic surgeon. I also saw a man with a large cancer of his chin, a woman who needed her breasts made smaller, and a child with a hand deformity.

"Plastic surgery is challenging, Elizabeth. There is a great variety of problems, but if you like thinking about and solving the problems, and if you're interested in the patient's psychology, you'll enjoy the field. What topic are you thinking of for your talk?"

"I was thinking of asking you, Dr. Berenson."

"Could you become interested in pigmentation? I have been looking for someone to work on pigmentation. It's a fascinating field. Pigmentation problems are worse in blacks, and haven't perhaps had the attention they deserve. People with dark skin always have darker scars, and thicker scars. It would be interesting to learn about." From his file cabinet he pulled out a folder filled with references on pigmentation.

"You might find this helpful, for a start."

Working on pigmentation meant going to the library. The Countway, Harvard's medical library, was next door to the hospital, so I headed there the next afternoon after surgery was over. It is the biggest and best medical library in the world. There are six floors of books and journals. In the basement there are the old journals, dating back to the early 1800s. On the sixth floor are rare books and journals, as old as the fifteenth century and earlier. There are eight copying machines in the basement. I spent days looking up references to pigmentation and to tuberous sclerosis, a rare inherited defect which one of Dr. Revere's patients had. I made photocopies of everything. I adored the library, it was my first chance to stop and think in three and a half years.

Tuberous sclerosis was confusing but understandable. Pigmentation, after I read my first hundred papers, was incomprehensible. Scientists were studying pigmentation in people, in test tubes, under the microscope, in guinea pigs, chameleons and marmosets.

Plastic surgery Grand Rounds—nicknamed "Sunshine Serenade"—were held every Friday at 7:00 A.M. On the next Friday, Dr. Berenson asked me how pigmentation was coming.

"Do you know what a melanoblast is, Dr. Berenson?" I asked hopefully.

"No. What is it?"

"I don't know, and I thought you might. Pigmentation is confusing. I can't discover if a melanoblast is a melanocyte or not."

"There's a resident in dermatology called Ellen Somerville. Why don't you call her. She's doing research on pigmentation."

Ellen had the answers to all my questions.

"The terminology is confusing," she explained kindly. "A melanocyte is the cell in the skin that makes skin pigment. The melanoblast is an immature melanocyte. The melanophage is a term we don't use any more. The melanophore is found in chameleons. Now the keratinocyte—"

"The what? I've never heard of it."

"Really? It's very important . . ."

After a two-hour tutorial from Ellen, I returned to the library, able to understand what I was reading.

Just before Christmas, I was ready to give my talk. I had spent every evening and every weekend in the library. I had even made slides. Dr. Revere had told me that a plastic surgeon never gives a

270

talk without slides, and that I had better learn to make them if I wanted to be a plastic surgeon. I photographed all my slides, but they looked awful. The color was a horrid yellow-brown but the typing was legible and I had to use them. I also had an eight-page hand-out to help explain pigmentation, photocopied on multicolored paper.

I knew I would be nervous so I had typed up my entire hour's talk and practiced it in my apartment, giving my speech to the wall, the fireplace and the kitchen stove. When I finally gave the talk at Grand Rounds it went surprisingly well. I had forgotten that no one there knew much about skin pigmentation.

"You ought to publish this, Elizabeth," said Dr. Berenson. "If you're interested you might submit it to the *Plastic Surgery Journal*. I'd be glad to help."

Interested? I was jubilant and grateful. Dr. Berenson told me my talk was not quite ready for publication so I spent two weeks in the library, checking out more pigmentation research papers. Ellen supplied me with a list of fifty more. I planned to write the paper during my two-week Christmas vacation, and as I packed to go home I needed an extra suitcase for all my notes, drafts, library books, and photocopies of journal articles.

"Mother, I'm writing this paper and I need your help," I announced, staggering through the airport with a typewriter and three suitcases.

"I'd be glad to," said my mother, who was coming down with the flu.

After Christmas, my mother was laid up in bed for two weeks, which she spent recuperating and helping me write. I had books in one corner of her bedroom and the journal articles spread out all over the floor. Draft one was on the floor behind me; draft two was in front of me.

"Mother, on this paragraph, page three, is this clear now? Let me read it—the melanoblast migrates from the neural crest in the eighth week and—"

"The eighth week of what?"

"Of fetal development."

"You might put that in. It would make it clear what you're talking about."

"Mother, I can't put it in. I have no more room; I have corrections everywhere. The typist will never be able to decipher it."

"Don't put it in then."

"But you said it's not clear."

"Then put it in."

"I can't, there's no room. This paper is a disaster. I hate pigmentation. Why did I ever start this? I'm going crazy."

"I'm sorry you feel that way. Perhaps you should tell Dr. Berenson it's too much to do, and let it go."

"No, wait a minute. If I put it in red ink in this corner, upside down, I can fit it in."

I finally finished the draft, which left the bibliography with all the references to do. I had 120 references and they had to go in sequence of appearance, not in alphabetical order. This went smoothly. I wrote "1" in red on the first article and (1) where it was referred to in the paper. At reference 54, I screamed. My mother sat up in bed, alarmed.

"What's the matter?"

"I just found a reference."

"Yes?"

"It should have been number six."

"No."

"Yes."

"It can't be."

"It is."

"We have to renumber every reference starting from number six?"

"Yes. I can't stand it."

"I don't think I can either. I'm the one who has the flu."

By the time vacation was over, my part of the paper was done. It went through another revision after my coauthors, Dr. Berenson and Ellen, worked on it from the plastic surgery and the dermatology angles, and nine months later it was in print as "Current Problems in Pigmentation."

I had writing fever, and in the next two years I published or co-published nine more scientific papers.

boardinghouse. I ordered throat x-rays and, with Dr. Terrell, examined Mr. Grenville's throat. We did the exam with Mr. Grenville awake, but sedated. Dr. Terrell showed me how to use the esophagoscope, a two-foot long hollow metal tube with a light at the end. The esophagoscope was placed in Mr. Grenville's mouth, then advanced gently down the esophagus.

"If you can't see the lumen [opening] of the esophagus, don't advance the tube, Dr. Morgan," Dr. Terrell warned me. "You can push a big hole in the esophagus that way, especially if a cancer has already eaten away part of the esophagus."

I pushed the esophagoscope forward a few inches, and stopped when I bumped against hard, gray tissue in a narrowed area of the esophagus.

"What's this?" I asked Dr. Terrell, and stood aside so he could look down the esophagoscope. I suspected it was cancer, but didn't want to alarm Mr. Grenville. Dr. Terrell looked, nodded, and murmured in my ear, "Yes. Take a sample with the biopsy forceps."

Microscope examination by the pathologist confirmed that the tissue was cancer but further studies showed that it had not spread. Our plan was to try to shrink it with massive radiation and then remove it surgically. Combined radiation and surgery was Mr. Grenville's one small chance of being cured. We told him his chances were small. We did not say they were as low as ten percent.

During the six weeks of radiation, Mr. Grenville still could not swallow. We fed him intravenously with hyper-alimentation, a high-calorie solution given through a large catheter in a neck vein. Without this he would have starved to death. I had to change the vein catheter about once a week, and Mr. Grenville lay quietly as I stuck needles in his jugular vein. I hated hurting him, and hoped when we operated on him that he would be one of the lucky ones. There was a 90 percent chance that we would find tiny tumor metastases spread all through the lymph nodes of his abdomen. Esophageal cancers often spread in small clumps, and are impossible to detect without taking a sample during surgery. I did not want to believe it would turn out this way for Mr. Grenville, who was a nice man, friendly and anxious to be cooperative in spite of his low spirits. A week after the radiation therapy was over, he was ready for surgery to remove the cancer. It would take nine hours or more, because we had to remove the whole lower throat and replace it with intestine.

I started the surgery, with Dr. Terrell assisting me. I opened the abdomen and felt around Mr. Grenville's liver, which felt smooth, free of tumor nodules, but the lymph nodes around the stomach and lower throat felt gritty. Dr. Terrell next put his hand in the belly, felt around, and shook his head.

"I don't think you'll be doing the operation you were planning, Elizabeth. This sure feels like tumor."

I removed lymph nodes around the liver, spleen, and pancreas, and sent them to pathology for frozen section. While we waited for the report, Dr. Terrell said, "I don't know how many of these cases I've opened and closed up again. It seems like an awful lot of preparation for an operation you can't do in the end. I suppose it's worth it for a ten percent chance of curing him, but I've never seen anyone cured. It's mainly the Japanese who have all the good survivals. In this country, patients usually die in a few months."

The pathologist reported that all the lymph nodes were filled with metastatic cancer. I was too shocked to believe that this was all we could do for Mr. Grenville.

"Why don't we cut out the cancer anyway?" I suggested. "At least he can swallow then, even if it doesn't cure him. The Japanese report good results even with noncurative palliative resections."

"Elizabeth," drawled Dr. Terrell, looking at me over his mask, "you're telling me you want to do a nine-hour operation on a sixty-five year old man to make him feel better? Do the Japanese get longer survivals with their palliative resections?"

"No, not really," I said reluctantly.

"This man has a life expectancy of three months, you know that?"

"Yes, I know."

"Honey, you can't just be a cuttin' surgeon. You have to think before you cut. Now stop stalling and sew him up."

Usually I liked Dr. Terrell very much. He tended to criticize surgical residents, but no more than they deserved. But that morning, standing over Mr. Grenville, I felt unreasonably annoyed. I thought he was being patronizing, but most of all I was angry that I could do nothing at all to help my patient. I sewed his abdomen closed, clenching my teeth furiously, not speaking except to demand an instrument. When Mr. Grenville was off the table and in the recovery room, I cooled down and apologized to Dr. Terrell. He lit a cigarette and smiled.

"You don't have to apologize. I understand. I don't like watching people die from esophageal cancer any more than you do. The only thing is, I've seen more of them than you have."

I presented Mr. Grenville to our Tuesday surgical conference, where we discussed and made plans for every patient with a difficult problem. The radiation therapists had given him a full course of radiation, and they could do no more. The chemotherapists said they had no drugs that would help esophageal cancer. Dr. Egilson, the chief of surgery, asked if there was any way to improve Mr. Grenville's swallowing so he could die more comfortably. The radiation had shrunk the tumor, but the cancer would keep growing, and soon he would again be unable to swallow.

"Sure, we could dilate him," said Dr. Terrell, "or try to. His cancer is so big that we could easily push a dilator through the tumor and into his lungs by mistake. It would be a quick death for him, but I wouldn't like to be the doctor who did it. Liz and I tried to pass a dilator in the O.R. before surgery, but we couldn't get past the cancer."

Dr. Dobson, the radiologist, leaned forward excitedly, peering through his glasses. "Can he swallow a string?" he asked.

"Yes, but he can't live on string."

"I realize that," said Dr. Dobson. "But if you can get him to swallow one end of a piece of string, I can try to dilate him with filiform catheters under a fluoroscopy unit. I can pass the filiforms over the string, and they're small enough to slip around the cancer and through what is left of the esophagus. They're much less likely to perforate the cancer."

Dr. Egilson smiled. "I am always impressed by how much more we can help patients in a conference like this with several specialties working on a problem. I think Dr. Dobson has solved our problem—and we can help Mr. Grenville. Elizabeth, can you have him swallow a string now—and secure it to a tooth? Then let him go home. When he starts to have trouble swallowing, you can bring him back to the hospital. You and Dr. Dobson can dilate him as an outpatient so he can continue to swallow soft foods and liquids. This way he can spend as much time out of hospital as possible, until he wants to come back to die."

276

I talked to Mr. Grenville that evening. He was still sick from his surgery—the incision hurt, especially when he coughed, and he had a chronic cough from years of smoking.

"Dr. Morgan," he asked anxiously, "you don't mean I might not be able to swallow at all, do you?"

"Mr. Grenville, your trouble swallowing will come back again. When it does, you can come back here. We will dilate your food pipe, so you can swallow again."

"Do I have to eat special foods?"

"Anything you want, that you can get down."

"Before I go home, can you call my landlady and explain things to her?"

"Of course."

Mr. Grenville returned to the hospital after a month. He looked emaciated, and his skin was gray. He had lost thirty pounds and did not have the energy to sit up. He had been able to swallow until a few days before, but he was dying from cancer. I dilated him the next day in the x-ray suite. Dr. Dobson came in to help me, and in about three minutes he had passed a small dilator past the cancer. He showed me how to do it, but after passing a dilator only the size of a fountain pen, we agreed it was dangerous to try a larger one. The dilator had wedged firmly into the cancer, which had grown around the esophagus.

Mr. Grenville could not swallow his saliva and had to spit it onto a tissue during the dilation. He hated doing it, and kept apologizing for spitting in front of us. A technician held his hand to encourage him and passed him tissues. After we were done, she and I helped him into a wheelchair and an orderly took him back to the ward.

"He's such a sweetheart," said the technician. "Is he always going to have to have dilations?"

"Yes, but he doesn't have much time left."

He did not have the strength to go home and was too tired to care. He lay flat in bed, spitting into a tissue, looking out his window with glazed eyes. Mr. Grenville's landlady called me to explain she "just couldn't" bring herself to come and see him if he was dying.

"What would I say to him?" she asked.

I said it would be nice if she would visit him even once but she said her son needed her at home.

We could do nothing more, except prescribe painkillers and wait for him to die. We saw him twice a day on rounds. One day on morning rounds Brent Hoéchst, the chief resident, marched by Mr. Grenville's room without stopping.

"That's one surgical bed tied up uselessly. No wonder we have a long waiting list."

I was outraged. I left rounds and went in to speak to Mr. Grenville. I asked him how he felt, if he had been able to sleep, if the medicine was enough for the pain, and if there was anything we could do for him.

"Thank you, Dr. Morgan," said Mr. Grenville hoarsely, spitting into a tissue. "I'm all right. Thanks for stopping by."

After that, twice a day, I dropped out of rounds when Brent marched us by Mr. Grenville's room. Brent turned purple every time. It was the ultimate insubordination. The first day, he stiffened.

"Elizabeth, you must keep up with us on rounds. We have a lot of work to do."

I glared at him.

The next day Brent proceeded to the next patient's door, not noticing that I had left the group. Through the wall I could hear him say, in his penetrating voice, "What is your recommendation? Dr. Morgan?" By the time I emerged into the hall a few moments later he was waiting for me.

"Dr. Morgan, the integrity of a surgical unit depends on the cooperation of every member. I cannot lead morning rounds, and discuss every patient properly, unless every member is present and adding their mite, no matter how small."

"I'm sorry, Dr. Hoechst," I said quietly. "I was making rounds on Mr. Grenville because you forgot."

"I have always found mavericks to be detrimental, Dr. Morgan. Remember that. Now give me your treatment plan on Mr. Wilson."

Brent and I had much the same conversation every day for the two weeks that it took Mr. Grenville to die. Our conversation was so predictable that Sean knew he could slump against the wall and get twenty seconds of extra sleep every morning outside Mr. Grenville's room.

At the end of two weeks Mr. Grenville weighed fifty pounds. His skin was so loose, it folded on his bones like a sheet of paper. His lips were dry and crusted. He was incontinent, but the nurses kept him clean. He died at four in the morning; I was on call, and I pronounced him dead. He had no money and had a pauper's burial funded by the city. There was no autopsy. There were no next of kin to give permission for one, and I had refused Brent's advice to make Mr. Grenville sign a permission form before he died. I told him to ask Mr. Grenville himself, which he never did.

Recovery Is Better
If You Don't Need the Surgery

Although Brent and I got on better after Mr. Grenville's death, I noticed I had an increasing tendency to quarrel with people and criticize them, especially my chief residents and the attendings. Both of my brothers complained to me that I wasn't as agreeable as I used to be.

"It's not my job to be nice," I agreed. "I'm a senior surgical resident and my job is to see that things get done, and done right."

"You don't have anything else to talk about, except surgery," Rob complained. "And you're very hard on people."

"I have to be critical of everyone. I'm critical of myself, too."

"I know, I know," said Rob, and he changed the conversation, but my mother told me later that he thought surgery was bad for me.

Snappish as I was, I loved the attending surgeons at the V.A. Like Dr. Sutherland and Dr. Berenson, the doctors on the V.A. service were doing some of the best work of their careers. Dr. Egilson the chief had three other full-time attendings, and three excellent surgeons in private practice to teach us and to operate with us. In addition, he had lined up two plastic surgeons from the General to come whenever we needed them. Somehow Dr. Egilson worked around the cumbersome V.A. bureaucracy to build a first-rate service. The medical service referred us a patient with a bizarre disease of the pancreas and Dr. Egilson and I wrote a paper on his case, which turned into another bibliographical nightmare for me.

Although the work was hard, the teaching was wonderful, and I was sorry to leave for Jones Memorial Hospital, my last rotation as a fourth-year surgical resident. The three months at Jones were designed to give me technical experience in a busy private hospital, but commuting to the suburb where it was located was an experience in itself. Two residents at Jones assured me that the rotation was worth the commute.

"You can cut to your heart's content. The volume of surgery is unbelievable. You may not agree with the way they manage patients, though. Their approach is different from a teaching hospital."

Jones had a full-time chief of surgery who had given up practice after a heart attack and devoted his time to building up the surgical service. The medical department was affiliated with a university and had residents, a strong teaching staff and an excellent training program. Surgery was not "academically oriented," the chief of surgery told me, but he added, "You'll do plenty of cases. You'll have done enough to pass your Boards after you finish here."

I was chief resident at Jones. The residents working with me were a Korean man who worked hard but spoke no English, and a Venezuelan who spoke English but did no work.

The busiest surgeon by far was Dr. Kerwin. The money his operations brought in kept the hospital running, according to the nurses. I decided to operate with him as much as I could. The first time I did, he was removing the stomach of a patient with a bleeding stomach ulcer.

"Could you point out the ulcer to me?" I asked when I looked at the x-rays. "I can't seem to find it."

"Oh, you can't see the ulcer on the x-ray. A gastroenterologist saw ulcerations that he thought were bleeding when he 'scoped her. Her bleeding may have been from aspirin, but I thought we should be on the safe side and cut out the ulcer for her."

He opened her abdomen, removed half of her stomach, and cut the vagus nerves that control stomach acid secretion, a standard operation for gastric ulcers. We opened the stomach after it was out. There was no ulcer.

"It must have healed," he said and shrugged.

The next day we operated on a lady with intractable ulcer pain. Again I could not see the ulcer on the x-rays.

"You can't see it on the films we have here," Dr. Kerwin said, "but the radiologist saw it when he fluoroscoped her." He removed half of her stomach and cut the vagus nerves. I asked him to open the stomach to show me the ulcer. There was none.

"It's healed," said Dr. Kerwin. "You can see the scarring. Her pain must have been from the scar tissue."

I could not see the scar tissue.

The next day I met with Dr. Kerwin to do a cholecystectomy on a patient with gallstones. The x-rays had been done by a private radiologist, but Dr. Kerwin did not have them with him. As we scrubbed, he said, "You know, I went out to buy myself a stereo system yesterday. Now me, I can spend twenty thousand on a stereo system and not notice the difference, but you should have seen this character in the store. He couldn't have been over thirty. Long hair, blue jeans, dirty. He walked in and ordered a speaker, a turntable—it must have cost him ten thousand. Now, where do people like that get the money to spend?"

I hadn't the slightest idea. We began to operate, and he removed the patient's gallbladder. There were no gallstones.

"You can see the inflammation around the gallbladder," said Dr. Kerwin. "Acalculous cholecystitis, present in ten percent of patients."

The gallbladder did not look inflamed to me. Five normal gallbladders and five normal stomachs later I had learned that Dr. "K" earned $1,000,000 a year, and that he was not the surgeon to teach me when to operate. If a patient was present in his office, he took that as a good sign he should operate. I hurt his feelings when I chose to start operating with the other surgeons instead of him, and he often stopped me in the hall to tell me about the good cases he had lined up for the next day. Of course, some of his patients did need surgery, and he was technically competent. He liked to hold philosophical chats with me.

"Elizabeth, being a surgeon is very hard."

I agreed.

"The decisions can be very hard. Look at a surgeon's indications for operations. When there's money in the bank, you'll find you operate less. When you need a car, want to go to the Bahamas, there's a psychological instinct to operate. You find you do more surgery at those times."

He also advised me on how to avoid malpractice suits. "Elizabeth, let me give you a piece of advice. In twenty years I've never been sued. There's a lot of malpractice suits going on around here. Other surgeons I know don't talk to their patients. Always remember to talk to your patient, explain things, hold his hand. They'll worship you like God. You can do anything you want to them; they'll believe anything you say."

This, of course, is not true. Doctors who are absolutely honest, scrupulous and talk to their patients are sued every day, often because of unforeseen, unavoidable complications. But Dr. "K" had an advantage. Most of his patients did well postoperatively because they were normal. Patients without disease recover more quickly and with fewer complications than patients who have actually needed surgery.

Working with Dr. Kerwin was depressing. On top of everything else, he had connections and advised insurance companies about how much to reimburse local surgeons for their operations. A doctor whom Dr. Kerwin did not like might suddenly find that he was earning much less.

While I was at Jones I still went to our own Grand Rounds in Boston. Dr. Anjou was now the chief of surgery, and had made Surgical Grand Rounds mandatory for all attendings and residents. They were held on Saturday morning at 8:30. After one Grand Rounds, I asked Mark what he thought about Dr. Kerwin.

"He's a creep, Elizabeth. Not a high-class character at all. Stay away from him. Listen, speaking of far-out surgeons, did I ever tell you what happened to me once? I was an intern, and operating with this surgeon. He seemed a normal enough guy. One day I happened to be operating with him on some simple case, I think it was a hernia. He cut through the skin. Once we were through the skin, he poked around with a clamp and didn't do anything. I didn't know what was going on, so I said nothing, and waited. Then he walked across the room and sat down on a stool. The anesthesiologist asked him if he was all right, and he said, 'I can't do this case. It's too hard.'

"Another surgeon happened to walk in, looking for some sutures, and he scrubbed in and did the case. It was frightening. And did I

283

tell you the one about the mad orthopod who thought the CIA was trying to get him through his patients? He put his patients in full-length body casts, came to see them at night when they were helpless in bed, turned the lights on and interrogated them. They had to lock him up.

"Kerwin's crazy, too, but just crazy about money. Look at it this way, though. In July you'll be chief, and I'll be chief, and this nonsense will be over. All the rotations will be good. I don't go to the Third Service. Which one do you miss?"

"I miss the Second, so I don't work with Dr. Baker."

"You don't work with Sharman, either, you lucky bum. Listen, when I'm chief on the Second Service, Sharman won't know what hit him. I've told Anjou he's a bad egg. He may be a good surgeon technically, but I think he has to go. Wait and see, Lizzie. There will be fireworks."

Of the hundreds of surgeons I have worked with, Dr. Kerwin was the *only* surgeon who operated for money alone. It is the few surgeons like him who give surgery a bad name.

All My Buddies Drink at Pat's Bar

It was a relief to leave Jones. Among other things, the on-call room was infested with cockroaches that would run all over you while you slept.

In July 1975 I started back at the V.A., this time as chief. I had struggled four years for this, but it was frightening suddenly to be in charge. I made every surgical decision and was responsible for teaching the medical students, too. I wrote up a "ward manual" for all the routines we were likely to forget: the medicines for patients before x-ray studies, the preparation needed before colon surgery, before vascular surgery, and emergency medicines needed if a patient developed blood clots in the leg. I had a good team to work with— Phil Bundy, an excellent senior resident, my old friend Sean, and a very good intern. As senior resident Phil was also in charge of the chest service as I had been six months before.

Shortly after July first, I got a consult from the medical service to see a man who was a heavy drinker and had had some stomach bleeding earlier in the week. He had lost about five units of blood. Cirrhosis of the liver, the well-known effect of heavy drinking, consists of scars in the liver which block blood flow. As a result, blood builds up in the veins of the stomach and esophagus. If one of these swollen veins (varices) becomes irritated or inflamed, an alcoholic can bleed massively into his stomach or throat. If he bleeds once, he is likely to bleed again and die within a year. Surgeons believe that an operation, or "shunt," should be done to divert the blood away from the swollen veins, but shunt operations can result in delirium from waste products collecting in the blood after they are shunted away from the liver. Some internists regard a shunt as last-ditch surgery for a patient who will die anyhow, and when I arrived to see Mr. Callahan on the medical service I learned that his doctor had decided against a shunt. Mr. Callahan was packing to leave the hospital. He was about fifty-five, gray-haired and pot-bellied. He wore a threadbare pin-striped suit much too big for him, probably a gift from the Salvation Army.

Mr. Callahan was fussing with the buttons on his shirt. He could not fasten them quickly, because his fingers shook from years of drinking. When he realized that I had come to see him, he became self-conscious and had even more trouble with the buttons. I offered to help him, but it was the wrong thing to do. He muttered angrily that he could button his own shirt. I said I would go away and come back. He said he might be gone by then. I sat down to wait, and started to talk with him, so he would not think I was sitting and staring. I told him who I was, and that his doctors had asked me to see him.

"I'm leaving," he said with great conviction. "I'm off the stuff. I'll never drink again. I don't need surgery. My doctor said it was all right."

"Yes, you can go home today. I didn't come to make you stay, but I thought you might be willing to come and visit us occasionally in clinic, when you come to see your other doctors."

"I don't need to see my other doctors. They told me I'm all right as long as I don't drink."

"Do you think you can stop?" I asked. "How much were you drinking when you were drinking heavily?"

He looked at me incredulously. "I was never a heavy drinker. I never drank at home, ever. And now I've stopped altogether. I'm never going to drink again. I know I can do it. My doctors let me go out on pass yesterday evening, to see if I could do it, and I could. I went down to Pat's Bar. All my buddies and friends drink down there. I sat around and I didn't have a single drink all evening. I know I won't drink again, if I can do that. You can't stop me from leaving."

I didn't try. I was sure that he would drink again, and bleed again, so I pressed him until he agreed to make a surgical clinic appointment so that we could keep in touch with him. I talked to his medical resident and explained our surgical viewpoint, that a shunt operation should be done before the patient is beyond salvage. The resident already knew this. He explained to me the medical viewpoint, which was to keep the alcoholic from major surgery until the bleeding was so severe that surgery was the only recourse. I already knew this. We exchanged journal references supporting our respective views, and quoted the opinions of our professors. We agreed we ourselves did not have enough experience to know which was the better thing to do, and we parted amicably. Mr. Callahan shuffled up behind me to thank the resident for "saving his life" and promised never to touch a drop of the stuff again.

He did not keep his surgical clinic appointment. He did not keep his promise to the resident either. A week later, when we were trying to see sixty patients in clinic, I was called by the emergency room. The E.R. doctor said he didn't think that I would want to see this patient, who was complaining of hemorrhoid pain, but the patient was asking for me by name. I stamped my foot in frustration. How could he be such an idiot as to call me for a hemorrhoid patient when we were trying to finish a huge clinic? Some patients had already been waiting two or three hours, and they were going to have to wait even longer because I had to go and advise an unknown man about his hemorrhoids. I apologized to Phil and walked down the hallway while the patients looked at me reproachfully.

When I got to the emergency room, I was glad I had come. Poor Mr. Callahan was sitting in a heap in a small examining room. The whole room smelled of unwashed body and stale liquor. His clothes were filthy.

"I can't stand it any more, Doctor," he said hoarsely. "I had an awful time with my hemorrhoids. Will you let me come into the hospital?"

"Yes," I said. "But what happened?"

"I went out of the hospital, the day I saw you, remember. It was yesterday, wasn't it?"

"It was a few days ago. What happened?"

"I went back to my apartment, see. Was it yesterday? No, I don't remember when it was. I'm all confused."

"It doesn't matter. Just tell me what happened."

He finally told me his saga. He had been late in paying rent when he entered the hospital, and his landlord had threatened to throw him out if he didn't pay as soon as he got out. He lived in a battered third-floor apartment in an old house in a run-down part of the city. After leaving the hospital, he went to the welfare office and collected his overdue monthly check of several hundred dollars for unemployment or medical disability, he could not remember which, and left the welfare office with every intention of paying his landlord at once. When he got back to the apartment, it was dusk. He tried to get in, dropped his key, poked in the grass around the house looking for it, but couldn't find it. He shouted outside for someone to let him in. His landlord shouted back that the door was locked to keep him out, told Mr. Callahan to pay his rent immediately or go away, and threatened to throw his belongings out the window. Mr. Callahan kept searching in the grass, but finally gave up. He decided not to pay his landlord after all because he had been so rotten to him, and wandered away. After he had walked around Boston for a while, his hemorrhoids began to burn. He went to a bar—not Pat's Bar—just to sit. After sitting a while, he had some beer. He then went in search of a place to sleep. He had plenty of welfare money so he went to the Holiday Inn in the center of Boston, checked in, paid cash in advance and had a very soothing bath. He went there because the "Inns" and "Detox Centers" for alcoholics do not all provide baths. The next night he got drunk. The following morning, after another bath, he felt awful and went to church. He tried to get the priest to help him, but the priest was not interested in his hemorrhoids because he was still drunk.

He was asked to check out of the Holiday Inn, which he did. He wasn't sure if he paid for the second night. He spent the rest of the five days, which he had more or less forgotten, drinking in bars and sleeping in the street. I agreed to readmit him to hospital, and he in turn agreed to have an x-ray study to examine his liver.

Before the intern examined Mr. Callahan, the nurses put him in the bathtub. He had lice. I thought how appalled the Holiday Inn would be if the next occupant of that room caught his lice.

The next day Mr. Callahan wanted to leave the hospital and pay his landlord. Instead we had the social worker deliver the money for him. We treated Mr. Callahan with soaks for his hemorrhoids and a nutritious diet. Two days later he bled massively after drinking some alcohol smuggled into the hospital by a friend, and vomited blood all over the floor. We poured blood back in through his veins and rushed him off to Dr. Dobson for a special x-ray study, to find the bleeding vein and inject the drug Pitressin directly into the vein to make it stop bleeding. An emergency shunt operation has a very high mortality, so we did not want to operate while he was bleeding.

The Pitressin stopped the bleeding and I left the hospital at seven. At eight, Phil called me. He had to rush a chest patient back to the operating room after lung surgery, and at the same time, Mr. Callahan had begun to bleed again. I came in to cover and spent the next four hours in the I.C.U. Four of the eight beds were occupied by our surgical patients. One was another alcoholic, also bleeding from varices. Mr. Callahan was vomiting blood all over the floor while Helen, the head nurse, pumped blood into his intravenous line. As I came into the unit, the ward nurse called to me to come immediately to see a Mr. Brown, who had just gone into shock. I could not leave two bleeding alcoholics, so I asked them to ship Mr. Brown to the I.C.U. at once. Next, the second alcoholic became agitated and pulled apart the catheter Dr. Dobson had placed in his artery to infuse Pitressin. Blood spurted out, and I leaped over to reattach the catheter. We tied the man down. Then Mr. Callahan pulled out his intravenous line, announced that he was going home, vomited some more blood and passed out. Helen and I tied him down. He began to thrash around. With great trouble I inserted a large I.V. needle into his arm and a second one into his neck, so we could give him blood transfusions. The blood bank called to ask how much blood we would need for him. I estimated twenty units. He vomited again. The blood bank called back to say did we really need that much blood? They would have to call in emergency donors and didn't want to. I asked the secretary to tell them that our patient was bleeding to death.

At this moment, Mr. Brown was wheeled in the door on a stretcher. He looked agitated and sweaty. I put a large I.V. neck line in him, and poured in some fluid. His temperature was 105°. A fever after an operation is usually from an infection. I checked him everywhere for an abscess, and found none. He had had his appendix removed three days before. His wound was perfectly normal, and there was no sign of infection. I took cultures from everywhere and started him on massive doses of antibiotics. I turned back to Mr. Callahan, who was still vomiting blood out while Helen pumped it in. Mr. Brown's blood pressure improved rapidly with fluids, and his pulse slowed down. Mr. Callahan needed a Sengstoken tube—a huge red-rubber tube with an inflatable balloon. When the tube is in the stomach, the pressure of the inflated balloon stops the veins from bleeding. Helen was waving the balloon, ready for me to put it down his throat, but first I had to put a tube into his lungs so he could breathe easily while the Sengstoken was at the back of his throat.

Usually the anesthesiologist puts in lung tubes, but he was in the operating room with Phil. Helen handed me the tube and Mr. Callahan tried to climb out of bed. I explained to him what I would be doing, and he vomited more blood. Helen held him down but he shook his head and vomited some more. I gave him an enormous dose of sedative. This, too, was dangerous because the sedative could make him stop breathing, but he would bleed to death if I couldn't insert the balloon.

Finally, I put the lung tube in without trouble. Helen and I hooked it to a respirator and she handed me the Sengstoken tube. Mr. Callahan's blood pressure suddenly dropped, but more blood arrived from the blood bank. We pumped it in, and his pressure improved. I had the Sengstoken ready when the I.C.U. door swung open and three elderly men walked in. Two stayed by the door. The third walked toward us. He swayed slightly, and came over and looked at me sympathetically.

"How's he doing, Doctor? I'm his brother and I'm here to make sure he does everything you say."

Before I could say anything, Mr. Callahan became violently agitated and Helen grabbed his lung tube to keep it from being dislodged.

"Harold," shouted the man. "This is Henry. You're being a damned fool. You drink too much. Now let the doctor do what she has to do. It's a nice lady doctor. Be polite."

Harold became more agitated. Henry shouted more. With the secretary's help, I guided him from the unit.

"If you think he's drunk," said the secretary, "you ought to smell the other two. They've been out there all evening."

Mr. Callahan's brother swayed back into the I.C.U.

"You're a very nice lady," he told me. "I was in the Army in '42 and . . ."

"I have to go. Your brother is bleeding to death."

"Harold!" he shouted. "Behave yourself or I'll kill you." He swayed out.

I gave Mr. Callahan another massive dose of sedative. He was still thrashing around. An alcoholic can take staggering doses of sedative without noticeable effect. I pushed the Sengstoken down his throat and it stuck. I tried again. No success. The Sengstokens are not always easy to insert. This one had to go in quickly. Helen was pumping some blood and whispered to me: "Would you be very insulted if I gave you some advice? I was a M.A.S.H. nurse in Vietnam, and I used to do this all the time in Da Nang. Take the tube in your hand and put your entire hand down the throat, holding the jaw up with the other hand. Remove hand, shove down tube."

It worked. Impressed, I peered into his mouth to see if blood was coming up the tube. Mr. Callahan suddenly vomited again, in a projectile fountain into my face. I was sprayed from face to foot with blood, and so was the curtain drawn by the bed. Helen pumped in more blood. I inflated the Sengstoken with my eyes closed to keep out the blood but I kept getting it in my mouth as the secretary wiped my face with a wet towel.

At 1:00 A.M. all the action suddenly stopped just as Phil got out of the operating room. The second alcoholic went to sleep and stopped bleeding. Mr. Callahan did the same. Mr. Brown's temperature fell to normal. When Phil walked in, wheeling his patient back to the unit, he saw a quiet room and a chief resident covered with blood. Empty blood transfusers, intravenous bottles, dressings, and instruments were all over the floor and the trash bins were overflowing.

"Been busy?" he asked.

"A zoo," I said wearily, but I didn't mind. As chief resident, I spent little time working with patients and most of my time supervising the team, in conferences or the O.R. This night had been like a practical examination in surgical emergency care, and in a perverse way I had enjoyed the challenge. I went to my on-call room and fell asleep without even bothering to change.

At the next afternoon's surgical conference, Dr. Dobson showed us Mr. Callahan's x-rays. The veins throughout his abdomen were hugely dilated, because blood flow to his liver was completely blocked. No wonder he had painful hemorrhoids; all the blood in his lower intestine was flowing in a reverse direction into enormous hemorrhoid veins that were taking 20 percent of his whole circulation. There was nothing we could do for him surgically because his stomach veins had already done what a shunt operation would do— bypass the blocked liver. I made a note in red ink in his hospital chart after the conference: "Mr. Callahan's enlarged hemorrhoids are the result of a blocked portal vein. Hemorrhoidectomy is contraindicated—uncontrollable bleeding will result." The following morning on rounds, Mr. Callahan was sitting on the edge of the bed, gesturing that he wanted to go home, while his nurse struggled to keep him from pulling all the tubes out.

I had no surgery till the afternoon, and I came back after rounds to reason with him. As I came in, I saw him jerk out both his lung tube and his Sengstoken when the nurse was not looking. I ran over.

"Mr. Callahan, what are you doing?"

He tried to hit me.

"I want to go home. You can't keep me here."

He grabbed the intravenous line in his neck and pulled it out.

"You're a sick man," I said soothingly. "We are here to help you. You almost died."

"That's what you say. Women. Liars."

He pulled out his other intravenous and croaked, hoarse from the tubes. "You try to keep me here and I'll call my Congressman. He's a powerful man."

"Who is your Congressman?"

"Don't try to confuse me. Don't get smart." He smiled furtively. "Trying to get me to talk, aren't you?" He jumped out of bed, naked, his bladder catheter trailing beside him. "I'm going home."

"If you wait, we'll send for your clothes."

"Promise?"

"I promise."

While he waited, he suddenly grabbed the bladder catheter.

"Don't pull," his nurse and I called out together. She deflated the balloon attachment that kept the tube in his bladder, and I removed the tube.

Dr. Egilson walked in. He was always mild and friendly, but as Phil said, he never missed a trick. Without appearing to watch us, he knew how we were managing every patient. He didn't often tell us what to do, but when he did, we never questioned him because he always turned out to be right.

"Mr. Callahan has made a remarkable recovery," Dr. Egilson said. "Isn't this the man who got fifteen units of blood two days ago?"

"And now he wants to go home," I said despairingly.

Dr. Egilson smiled. "Mr. Callahan, I hear you don't like staying with us."

"I'm leaving. You can't keep me. It's against the law." He smirked. "You can't make me talk. I know secrets, but I won't talk."

"That's very interesting." Dr. Egilson pulled up a chair and sat down next to him. "Are you sure you can't stay for a day or two? You have been seriously ill. You almost died. You have made a rapid recovery, but Dr. Morgan had to give you fifteen units of blood."

"I can leave. You can't keep me. It's illegal."

"You're right. We can't force you, but we can advise you."

"I'm leaving." And he did.

"Elizabeth," said Dr. Egilson, "I don't want you to be concerned about this. There is nothing surgery or medicine can do for this man. Wouldn't you rather he spent his last days enjoying himself?"

Mr. Callahan seemed almost indestructible. He drank steadily for another year, but when I had gone and Phil was chief resident he returned to the hospital and bled to death.

Flash

Shortly after Mr. Callahan signed out of the hospital, I did too. A severe cough which I had had since April turned out to be due to a paralyzed vocal cord from a virus infection, and on top of that I got a strep throat. I had a fever of 102°, and my throat was so painful I dreaded each swallow.

I had not missed a working day since my first year of residency, but now Dr. Egilson sent me home, despite my hoarse objections. I was not allowed in the operating room because a strep infection in an operative wound can be rapidly fatal.

Feeling sick and guilty I dragged myself home and spent a week in bed unable to talk. My air conditioner broke down, the temperature in Boston went to 110°, and my apartment reeked of sweet-and-sour pork from the Chinese restaurant below.

On my third day in bed Phil called.

"Elizabeth, on O'Toole in the I.C.U., could you have left a rubber drain inside him during surgery?"

"What?" I croaked.

"It's an awful question to ask you, but his x-ray shows a rubber drain inside him. I know you did his surgery when you weren't feeling very well."

"God. I couldn't have. I mean, it's possible to do anything. But I don't remember even using a drain."

"There's one in him now. I'm sorry to bother you. I really am." He hung up and I staggered back to bed, distraught at the thought of having left a drain in someone's abdomen. The phone rang again.

"Elizabeth, it's Phil again. Good news. The medical student tucked a drain in his open wound and the skin had hidden it so we couldn't see it. Sean found it. Don't worry about coming back to work in a hurry. The service is very slow."

Phil was wonderful. I staggered back to bed again.

The service was busy when I returned. We had a lot of vascular reconstruction surgery on patients with atherosclerosis, which meant replacing the diseased arteries with vein grafts. Dr. Egilson assisted me at the surgery of my most difficult patients, one of whom was Mr. Putrovski, fifty years old. He had been an army cook for a few weeks but he just wasn't smart enough to help in the kitchen so the army discharged him honorably, after which he smoked and drank happily for years. Now he was a permanent psychiatric inmate at another veterans' hospital where he had been committed by his brother. His diagnosis was Korsakoff's syndrome, mental deterioration from alcohol. I was never sure whether Mr. Putrovski actually had Korsakoff's or whether he was just a pleasant, slow man who let his brother run his life, but in any case he needed blood vessel reconstruction on his leg. One toe was dead and without surgery he could not walk because of the pain. We needed his brother's permission to operate, since he was the legal guardian, and I called his brother two days before the operation.

"Who is this calling me?"

"I'm Dr. Morgan at the Veterans Hospital."

"Who gave you permission to call?"

"No one, sir, but your name is in the chart as your brother's only living relative and guardian."

"Take it off the goddamned chart. I don't want my name on his chart."

"Then how can we reach you for permission, sir? You are his guardian."

"I'm not his guardian. I don't want anything to do with him."

"Will you at least give us permission to operate on him?"

"You call me one more time and I'll sue you for invasion of

privacy. Get off the phone, whoever you are. You do whatever you want to him, but don't ever call me. I don't know anything about him."

Dr. Egilson suggested the brother might be afraid that the Veterans Hospital would bill him for his brother's care or discharge his brother home to him. As a result Mr. Putrovski became a legal ward of the Veterans Hospital.

He loved the hospital. He loved us. Pals on the ward brought him presents of cigarettes from the canteen. He would sit on the side of his bed dangling his gangrenous leg, smoking the cigarettes that had led to the gangrene, laughing at everyone's jokes. He almost never spoke. We did not want to amputate his leg unless infection made that necessary, because we did not think he was smart enough to learn to walk with a wooden leg.

The surgery Dr. Egilson and I decided on was a "jump graft"—using a vein to bring in blood from his thigh to his calf, thus bypassing the diseased arteries, bringing in more blood, and possibly stopping the gangrene from spreading. Once we'd decided, I spoke to Mr. Putrovski in simple terms about the surgery. He smiled and nodded. He signed the permission slip, which also had to be signed by the hospital administrator, since Mr. Putrovski was mentally incompetent. I asked him to tell me what I had explained, to see how much he had understood. He laughed and shook his head. The next day I brought Dr. Egilson to see him. Dr. Egilson explained the surgery in even simpler terms and Mr. Putrovski's eyes widened with interest. It all seemed new to him. I asked him if he remembered my discussing it with him the day before. He thought for a while and said hesitantly, "Operate?"

"Yes, operate." We felt we had done our best.

Operating with Dr. Egilson was always a pleasure. He let me work my own way, at my own speed, unless I asked him for advice.

We started at eight o'clock and Sean and the intern removed the vein from the lower leg while Dr. Egilson and I dissected the femoral artery in the abdomen. The artery was blocked from the abdomen down to the knee, and the vein graft, sewn in above and below the block, would replace it. It was a long, often tedious operation, but worthwhile if it saved a leg.

Sean handed me the vein, and I handed it to the scrub nurse. She wrapped it in a saline-soaked sponge, and Dr. Egilson and I started to dissect the knee. Dr. Petersen came in to watch.

"Why don't you scrub out and have some lunch?" I suggested to the intern, "then come back and relieve Sean." I tried to remember to let my assistants leave for a break during a long operation.

"That's probably not a good idea, Elizabeth," said Dr. Petersen. "The essence of surgery is training your team to work without a break."

Before I could speak, Dr. Egilson did. "Elizabeth is very thoughtful. She runs a service differently than we do, and I don't think hers is a bad way. Now we'll have to pay attention to the knee dissection. It's very delicate."

It was nice of him to intervene because I didn't like to argue with Dr. Petersen. I tried not to run a rigid service. I let Sean and the intern go home early when they could, and I tried to see we all got breakfast and dinner, when it was possible. I was evolving my own style of being a surgeon—considerate of my team whenever that was possible.

I knew Phil didn't approve. He never said anything but a look of disapproving impatience would come over his face whenever we started rounds at 6:45 instead of 6:30, or when I let the intern go home an hour early on Friday. I relied on Phil and we got on well together, but he clearly didn't like to see a woman in charge. Like Dr. Petersen, he obviously thought I should run the service in the "Die in the front line of battle" warrior tradition.

At four o'clock, Dr. Egilson and I had sewn the vein into the popliteal artery in the knee. There was a pulse for the first time in years in Mr. Putrovski's foot, and the skin was pink, not dead white. We ran an x-ray check to be sure the vein was not twisted under the skin between the abdomen and the knee, and Dr. Petersen's volume Doppler showed that the volume of blood flow was adequate to keep the leg alive. Mr. Putrovski's leg was alive again, and Dr. Egilson and I felt the pride of achievement.

After the operation, we put Mr. Putrovski in a private room, so he could get better care. He was strictly forbidden to walk—it would endanger the graft—and he was to stay in bed, without cigarettes.

The morning after surgery most patients are happy to be left alone with some morphine for the pain, but when I walked onto the ward at

6:00 A.M., I saw Mr. Putrovski standing in his doorway, his intravenous bottle on the floor at his feet, his bladder catheter looped casually around his neck. He was puffing on a cigarette and watching with great interest as the cleaning man mopped the floor.

I gasped and ran to him. He cheerfully got back into bed without a word, gave me his cigarette, and pointed to a hidden pack in his top drawer. I replaced his intravenous infusion, straightened his bladder catheter so it did not drag on his penis, and anxiously checked his feet. The new pulse in his foot was still strong. So far the surgery was still successful.

I sighed in relief, and we started rounds. At eleven I brought Dr. Egilson to see Mr. Putrovski. I had checked him first but he was still in bed, smiling sweetly. I raised the bedrail to make sure he stayed there. Fifteen minutes later I was telling Dr. Egilson with pride how I had persuaded him to stay in bed. We walked into his room. Mr. Putrovski had flung his bladder catheter onto the floor, through the bedrail. His intravenous line was wrapped around his leg. He was halfway through the bedrail, carefully maneuvering his newly operated leg through, while puffing on a cigarette. We gave up. Before the surgery the pain of the gangrene had left him unable to walk. Now, scuffling around in slippers, smoking and visiting friends, he was happy.

Once back on the open ward, however, he discovered a new trick to entertain his pals. On morning rounds every day we would examine his leg, say "Hello" and move on. One day Mr. Putrovski muttered "Hey, Doc." When I turned around, he yanked down the sheets for a second, then quickly covered up again, grinning broadly. Mr. Putrovski was flashing me.

"I don't think this guy is as stupid as he pretends ," said Sean the first time it happened. The men in the other beds laughed. From then on, Mr. Putrovski flashed on morning, evening and attending rounds. He then started to walk around the other wards, flashing during visiting hours. We had no choice but to send him back to the psychiatric ward.

Death of the Count

At the end of four months at the V.A., I returned to our main teaching hospital in the Danger Zone. I had been away for over a year—at the V.A., at Jones Hospital, and with Dr. Sutherland—and there had been many changes. The biggest was that Dr. Anjou was now chief of the surgery department.

I was now starting at chief resident on the First Service—vascular surgery with Dr. Mulveney. Mark Lehman was starting on the Second Service with Doctors Baker and Sharman. On Mark's first day as chief of Second, Dr. Sharman asked if Mark could see a patient for him.

"Dr. Sharman, will you be making the surgical decisions, or am I taking care of the patient?" Mark asked.

"I will, of course. You're too ignorant," huffed Count Maligno.

"Then you go and see the patient," said Mark.

War was declared.

One Monday, vascular clinic finished early. Sean Stewart, who was with me in the First Service, had been on call that weekend and after clinic we met in the coffee shop for lunch. All morning in clinic, Sean had nudged me as we passed from room to room.

"Elizabeth, have I got news for you! No, no. I can't tell you here.

I'll tell you at lunch. It's incredible. I can't believe it happened. No, I can't tell you. Wait till later."

Even at lunch, Sean wouldn't speak until he had finished a double order of French fries and a cheeseburger. I had a bacon-lettuce-and-tomato and listened.

"Now, Elizabeth, you know how much Mark hates the Count? You know that. And you know how much the Count hates Mark. Well, Sunday morning, I was at the nurses' desk on Ward Four just checking the lab data. Percy Fitzgerald, Mark's intern, was making rounds with the Count. Mark swore to me Friday that if the Count ever spoke to him again, he would kill him. This Sunday, the Count ordered Mark to join him for rounds. Mark did, very controlled and polite, not looking for a fight. As they were going to see the first patient, Mark's beeper went off. He went to the phone in the hallway, answered his page, went back to the Count. His beeper goes off again. He's on call for the emergency room, so what can he do? He has to answer his page. He apologized to the Count and left again to answer it. I'm standing there next to the phone at the nurses' station. Mark takes the phone, answers the page and hangs up. Then I see the Count coming out into the hall, looking for Mark. He is really angry. The Count backs Mark against the wall and says, 'If I ever left an attending on rounds when I was a resident, I'd have finished my training at Angel Memorial Animal Hospital.'

"Mark pushes the Count away and says sweetly, 'But Dr. Sharman, I thought you *did* train at Angel Memorial Animal Hospital.'

"Percy took one look at Mark and backed away. He's got an instinct for survival, that boy. The nurses scattered. I'm just standing there with my mouth open, and Sharman says, 'Mark, you're the worst doctor I've ever met, and I'm going to ruin your career. I'll write to every member of the American College of Surgeons, and you will never practice surgery.'

"Of course, Mark is so rich, he could buy up Sharman, or the hospital, or the whole city, if he wanted to. Mark says, 'Dr. Sharman, what I've always liked about you is your credibility. You don't have any.'

"'I'm going to see you fired right now,' says Sharman.

"'Not before I knock your fucking head off,' says Mark, clenching his fist. Sharman grabs Mark to hit him, but now Mark's got him by the collar, up against the wall. Elizabeth, I thought I was going to see a dead man. Mark was wild. You remember the time he picked the medical resident up and shook him—the guy who was trying to explain why he had almost killed one of Dr. Mulveney's patients? Mark looked like that—Godzilla's Revenge. At this point, I see the nursing supervisor coming down the hall. She was watching Mark, watching Sharman, and not believing what she was seeing. One of Sharman's patients was watching from his room, laughing, and cheering Mark on. Suddenly the elevator door opens, and out steps Dr. Baker, the world's greatest pacifist. You could see he was walking with his head in the air, thinking thoughts about calcitonin and Sipple syndrome, a thousand miles away.

"Baker took one look at Mark and Sharman, and literally flung himself between the two, just as Mark is winding up his punch. Sharman is trying to grab Mark by the throat, Mark is trying to punch Sharman in the face, and in the middle is Dr. Baker, saying, 'No, no. Not here, not on the ward. Kill each other downstairs,' and he yells to the nursing supervisor to hold the elevator button. The elevator comes, and he maneuvers them both into it and they disappear.

"Mark told me later that they burst into Anjou's office, Sharman screaming that Mark should be fired. Anjou threw Sharman out of the office. Then he turned on Mark and asked him if he thought he could be recommended for Surgical Boards if he killed another surgeon. Then he says, 'Mark, there's more than one way to skin a cat. I've been looking at certain members of the surgical staff, and I don't like what I see. That is what I keep trying to get into your thick head. I'm running this department. You take care of the patients. You let me do the firing.'

"But, Elizabeth, that's not the end of it. Sharman's secretary told Mulveney's secretary today that the Count is looking for a new job. Can you believe it?"

The duel between Mark and Count Maligno was not the only violent confrontation to take place on the surgical service. One night a crisis over a patient led Karl "The King" Kingsley—a fourth-year resident and chief resident on the transplant service—to influence a medical intern by strength rather than reason.

During the night medical interns had the power to ask the on-call surgical residents for consults, without asking the medical senior resident first. One medical intern became notorious for calling often, and always for ridiculous reasons. One night he called me at 1:00 A.M. for an emergency consult on a patient who had been mildly constipated for the last twenty years. He suspected she had rectal cancer and wanted me to operate. What added to the absurdity was that the patient had had a heart attack that day and would not have been well enough for a rectal exam for several days.

Another night the same intern called Mark Lehman at 3:00 A.M., asking him to see an 80-year-old woman dying in the I.C.U. At the family's request, nothing was being done for her except to keep her free from pain. She was about an hour away from death when the medical intern summoned Mark to examine her abdomen—he thought it seemed more tender than it had that morning. Mark explained that examining her would be uncomfortable for the patient and was of no possible importance. The intern said he wanted her abdomen examined "for teaching purposes." Mark then told him he was crazy, refused to disturb the dying woman, and went back to bed.

Mark Lehman and I both pegged the intern as not very bright, probably disturbed and let it go at that. It was worse for Karl Kingsley; somehow the medical intern really got under his skin. It may have been the man's attitude—he clearly felt that The King was tall, but he, the medical intern, was smart.

His second night on call, Karl was called at midnight by the same intern, who wanted him to check out "a bit of stomach bleeding." The senior medical resident was tied up with an emergency, and the intern was in charge of the patient. The King told me about it the next day as we ate breakfast before morning rounds.

"Liz, the guy was ankle-deep in a pile of blood-soaked sheets. The poor lady was vomiting blood through and around a tiny stomach tube. I staggered back, astounded, and said, 'Your patient's having a massive hemorrhage. Look, you have to put down a big tube, like a Ewald tube, to empty her stomach. Then call in the angiographers and gastroenterologists. You're going to have to look into her stomach, x-ray it to see where the bleeding is, and inject Pitressin before she bleeds to death.'

"The wimp just said to me, 'I make my own decisions.'

"Then I pulled him aside and said, 'You're an idiot to have waited so long already. Don't you have any sense?'

"He just smirked at me and said, 'Thank you, Doctor Kingsley, for your consult. In fact, I disagree, and will not call anyone. I simply wanted your opinion as to whether surgery was needed at the moment.'

"'Wait a minute, you cretin,' I said. 'You could kill this lady if you don't get the angiographers to stop her bleeding. You've got a dying woman on your hands.'

"And this flea intern says to me, very snippy, 'Doctor, you are merely a surgical consult. This lady's care is my responsibility, not yours. Thank you for your advice, but I choose not to follow it. I haven't been impressed by your opinion in the past, so I'm not going to follow your advice now.'

"These guys just don't listen, Liz. His patient vomited another basin of blood. I couldn't stand there and watch her die, so I grabbed the intern up by his shirt, both feet off the floor. I carried him out of the room like that, held him against the wall in the hallway, and I said, 'You do what I tell you, you insect, or I'm going to beat you up so badly they'll just send you to pathology in a bottle. I mean it.'

"Finally he agreed to do what I told him to do. She stopped bleeding with Pitressin but she took twenty units of blood after that."

Karl Kingsley was proud that he had saved her life, but we knew the medical service would be furious. There was a long conference that day between Dr. Anjou, chief of surgery, and Dr. Bliss, chief of medicine, along with the intern, and later, the intern's lawyer. The intern wanted to sue The King for assault and battery.

The following week, over coffee and doughnuts between cases, a group of surgical residents were gossiping about the latest rumor that Dr. Anjou was going to throw Karl out of the program. Just then The King himself walked in and told the story of the famous night from his own point of view.

"This voice gets me on the horn about midnight, just as I'm racking out. Wants my advice on a little bit of blood. Blood! I had to take a canoe because the elevator was flooded out with blood. I needed a snorkel to get to the patient's bedside, and this eunuch tells me it's all right with him if the lady dies. He's just a carpet, and I walk on carpets, so I beat him up a bit, to make him listen to me. I saved the lady's life and now he wants to sue me for assault and battery!"

Dr. Anjou scowled every time "Dr. Kingsley" was paged on the loudspeaker system that week. After Grand Rounds on Saturday morning, he told all the surgical residents to stay for "a little chat."

It was a one-sided chat. Dr. Anjou did all the talking.

"I went into surgery because I wanted to be a good surgeon, and I hope you did too. I didn't want to be an internist. There are many internists I respect, and some I don't. I also played football in college." He hunched his shoulders. "Tackle. But football is football and surgery is surgery. It is a sad day for me when one of my surgeons can't talk to an internist about a patient, and uses physical force to decide on patient care. Any resident of mine that does that in the future can consider himself fired. Such behavior is illegal, unethical and disgraceful. If a resident of mine can't handle a medical resident"—a pause"or intern"—long pause"who is willfully neglecting a patient's welfare, call me. I'm either home or in the hospital. You guys are masculine, aggressive men but physical force against another doctor is sad. This has been a sad week for me, and I hope for all of you." He walked out.

We all felt ashamed and left the conference room in silence to make rounds.

"You know," The King said to me as we walked up the stairs, "the Old Man is right. I shouldn't have done it. I really feel rotten. I should live and let live. I bet you never beat up a medical intern, did you, Lizzy? It's easy for you. You just smile sweetly and ask an internist to do something and he runs off to do it. It's not fair."

In a way he was right. Like Karl, I could not have stood by while the intern let his patient hemorrhage to death. But if I could not coax the intern to do it my way, I would have immediately sent for someone he *would* obey—the chief of surgery, the medical chief resident, or an attending. Both Patsy Glover, the other woman surgical resident, and I had had our advice refused by medical residents, but we didn't take it as a personal affront or an invitation to fight. Nor did we inspire in other doctors the urge to fight. If I disagreed sharply with another doctor, he might disagree and say so loudly, but his ego would not feel challenged. As a woman I was not tempted to use physical strength to assert myself. The tempering influence of women was, I thought, a good change for surgery.

I never could have threatened to send anyone to pathology in a bottle, but I often felt violently frustrated as a resident. Internship and residency were a fight for survival, and out of fatigue and indignation I was often rude and quarrelsome. Surgery taught aggressiveness, and abrasiveness, and I had acquired my share.

As chief resident, I had three colleagues. One was Mark Lehman, with whom I had worked through medical school and five years of residency. We admired the same surgeons and shared the same complaints, and had the same impatience with our last few months of residency. Patsy Glover and Arnie Coleman were the other chief residents for our year. Patsy had refused to go to the Veterans Hospital as a chief resident because she didn't like the five-mile commute, so Arnie was there for the last six months of the year, while Patsy, Mark and I were the chief residents downtown.

Patsy complained about things in general, and was a bit of a joke among the residents on the surgical service. Most surgical residents, male or female, become toughened by residency, but it seemed Patsy survived less by being tough and struggling through, and more by depending on chivalrous men to come to her aid when she felt tired or overworked.

"Liz, have you ever cried?" Mark asked me one day at lunch.

"Of course."

"At work, I mean, as a surgeon."

"Never."

"Then why does Patsy? Every time she has to work past five o'clock she gets upset about going home late to her husband and asks me to do her work for her. If I say I'm too busy, she cries."

"That's never happened with Patsy and me," I said. "She's never asked me herself, although the other day Dr. Mulveney told me to see her consult patients for her. I refused. I did my time with him, and I don't see why I should do it again."

The next day I found three consult slips addressed to Patsy lying on my desk. I thought it was a mistake and put them back on her desk. They were back on mine in the evening and since I was on call, I assumed they had been addressed to her by mistake. But when I visited the patients I discovered that all three had been seen and treated by Patsy the day before. None needed surgery, but all needed a surgeon to check on them every day or two while they were in the hospital, and they were Patsy's patients.

The next morning I handed the slips back to Patsy, saying, "I saw these for you last night but they're your patients."

"Can't you see them for me?" she asked.

"Why?"

"I'm so busy, I didn't get home for dinner last night."

"I never do," I said in astonishment. "I take care of my patients, Patsy. You can take care of yours."

She pouted and turned away. For the next two weeks she put her consult patient slips on my desk and I put them back on hers. She wasn't ill, she wasn't having problems at home and she was overworked but had had an easy year so far by avoiding the Veterans Hospital. At the end of two weeks I found a pile of consult slips on my desk, with a note from Dr. Mulveney. "See these patients!"

They were all Patsy's. I walked into his office.

"Dr. Mulveney, what does this mean?"

"It means see them."

"Why? They're Patsy's patients."

"She told me you and Mark were not being nice to her." His voice softened. "Elizabeth, she came to me in tears last night. We've been very busy on this service, and she was going to get home late for dinner, and she hadn't been able to go shopping and clean her house and I told her you would see them."

"You mean I work hard on your service and when Patsy finds out she might have to work hard, I get to do her work for her?"

"Don't speak to me like that," said Dr. Mulveney sharply.

I closed the door of his office slowly and turned back to face him. I was ready to kill him, but I was going to do it in private. I threw the consult slips on his desk.

"You see them. I went into surgery because I thought I was as good as any man. I'm a good surgeon. I'm proud of it and I can take it. I didn't get through surgery by crying when things got tough. I don't have time to do my shopping and house cleaning either and neither does any other surgical resident, but I don't ask Patsy to do my work so I can go home early to sweep the floor. If it's too tough for her, assign *all* the surgical patients to Mark and me and we can pretend we only have two chief residents instead of three. I don't mind the extra patients; I've cared for too many patients at one time before. But I won't do someone else's work because they don't happen to feel like doing it. No male surgeon has ever asked me to do his work for him, and I'm ashamed that a woman has. And don't you dare give those consult slips to any resident on my team because I'll tear them up."

There was a long pause.

"I think I understand," said Dr. Mulveney.

"Another fight, another enemy," I said to myself as I left his office. "Why can't I keep cool?"

There was no more said about consults and Patsy looked after her own patients, but a week later George Woodruff, a surgical attending from Germany, took me aside.

"Elizabeth, I need to talk with you. Patsy came to me today and wanted me to go with her to Dr. Anjou to demand that you be fired."

I stared at him in amazement. Fired? For what? A horrible fear came over me. If Dr. Mulveney was behind this, there was no question I could be fired. His political power was far-reaching.

"She said that you've been neglecting your patients, and that she has to do your work for you."

"Not true!"

"Let me finish. What she told me didn't sound like the Elizabeth I know, and I refused to have anything to do with it. But I think you'd better mend some fences. You're a hard worker, you look after your patients and you get on with most people. But you are getting hard, impatient and critical and it's going to hurt you. You're making enemies."

I was not on call for a few days so I had time to think about what Dr. Woodruff had said. I thought of nothing else all weekend, in fact, and on Sunday I called my mother.

"Am I getting hard, impatient and critical?" She hesitated. "Mother, I need to know the truth."

"Then the answer is yes."

"Masculine?"

"Definitely not, but less feminine."

And for the first time in a long, long time I started to cry. When I could speak again I told her about Patsy and Dr. Mulveney and George Woodruff, and the possibility of being fired.

"Five years of killing myself—for this?"

"You won't be fired, I'm certain, but you might stop and think about yourself. Being a woman in surgery is much harder than you like to admit. Patsy has adapted by not fighting, and letting men feel sorry for her. It makes a lot of men feel noble and grand and protective. You've adapted by making things as hard for yourself as possible. Now you're being seen as a hard woman who won't even help out another woman. Do you want to be seen that way?"

"No, of course not. I'm *not* that way."

"Then from now till the end of your residency, don't criticize anyone and don't fight with anyone. Apologize to Dr. Mulveney, and offer to do the work Patsy won't do herself."

"Oh, God. But Mark wouldn't do the work either, and he's not in trouble."

"He's not a woman. Don't you see, Patsy's turned many of the men against you. She behaves the way they expect a woman to behave, so when you demand that she behave like any other surgeon, as you do, they take her side." She sighed. "I'm afraid surgical residency hasn't been good for you *or* Patsy. But don't take it all so seriously. Try to relax and bend a little."

My mother was right. In my determination to be as tough as the other surgeons I had forgotten how to get along with people and had lost much of my sense of humor. It was very hard for me to loosen up, but I tried. Dr. Mulveney accepted my apology with a cynical smile but Patsy happily let me do her consults. I had the time; her service really was much busier than mine. When The King asked me why I had changed my mind I just said: "Why not? We're women in surgery, and we help each other."

The End of the First Road

By the time spring came, I was looking forward to starting my plastic surgery residency, but I did each operation in general surgery with some regret, saying to myself, "This could be the last time I ever take out a gallbladder. This is the last time I take out a colon cancer." I loved general surgery, with the challenges of a difficult diagnosis and pulling a sick patient through an emergency operation. Still, I was tired. In some ways I felt beaten, and I looked forward to the change. I hated hearing the phone ring at two and three in the morning. When I was a junior resident, it could mean something minor like a sleeping pill order. As a chief, it meant an operation and being up the rest of the night. We all made mistakes as chief resident, and I made my share.

One patient had colon cancer, and the colon on the right side was scarred to the gallbladder from previous gallbladder attacks. His cancer was on the left side and was removed without trouble, but I thought he needed a temporary colostomy to divert the stool to an outside opening in the abdomen. The attending decided not to do the colostomy, and although I disagreed, I said nothing.

A week later the patient had an infection around the operation and needed an emergency colostomy. The attending did not come to the operation, and I was in a hurry to finish, so my dissection was not as careful as it should have been. The next evening the colon in the colostomy was swollen and blue-black. I called the surgeon who was on call for the night.

"Dr. Carter, I have a patient on whom I did a colostomy yesterday. His colon is dead and I need to take him back to the O.R."

"Are you sure? That's a strange complication."

"I'm sure. His colon was scarred to his gallbladder, and I didn't do a good dissection. I must have torn off the blood vessels to the colon. At any rate, the colon is dead."

There was a long pause. "Well . . . go ahead and get him ready. I'll be over as soon as I can. Do you want me to speak to his family, or are you happy talking with them?"

"I can talk with them. I know him and his wife."

I told his wife the bad news; her husband was very sick, because dead colon is always accompanied by severe infection.

At surgery I found that two feet of colon, the scarred part around the gallbladder, was dead. In doing the colostomy the day before, I had injured all the arteries and veins that kept that part of the colon alive.

"You were right," said Dr. Carter. "I wouldn't want to let this stay inside him all night. What a mess."

We cut out the dead colon and did a new colostomy. To my immense relief, the man recovered rapidly. Six months later, when Karl Kingsley was chief resident, the patient was well enough to have the colostomy closed so that he was normal again.

Another mistake I made was to misdiagnose a thirty-year-old alcoholic who lived on the streets. He was admitted to the medical service for abdominal pain, which I thought was pancreatitis from his drinking. I reexamined him several times during the day, but I could not decide whether to operate. After evening rounds I went home, and later that same evening Sean had to do an emergency operation on him with Dr. Mulveney. The patient's intestines were dead from stomach to rectum and probably had been for several days. He was dead by morning. He would almost certainly have died regardless of any treatment, but I had made a serious error of judgment in not operating earlier.

I began to understand dead intestine. My last emergency room patient during my final week as chief resident was an eighty-five-year-old lady who lived with her eighty-year-old brother. She did not look ill but came into the emergency room with a mild heart arrhythmia and mild stomach pain. She was admitted to the I.C.U. because of her heart.

At four o'clock in the afternoon her heart was fine. She had no fever, her abdomen seemed normal, but she still had stomach pain. I was worried because, as I had learned, stomach pain can mean dead intestines. Dr. James, the attending, called me after I examined her for the second time.

"What do you think of that old lady? I was thinking of leaving early today to see my children. I don't think she needs surgery, do you?"

"Yes, I think she might. I'm worried about her abdomen. I think there's something going on."

"Like what?"

"Dead bowel, perhaps? She has a heart arrhythmia, and a blood clot in the heart could have broken off and blocked the blood vessels in the intestine."

"It sounds far-fetched, Elizabeth, but if you think she needs the knife, let's get going. I don't want to be here all night."

At six o'clock we opened her abdomen.

"Yuch." It was Sean, holding retractors for me. He got the first whiff of the stink of dead intestine. Her intestine was black, completely dead, except for a foot of living intestine beyond the stomach.

"I don't think there is much we can do for her, do you?" I said to Dr. James. "She's eighty-five. She won't be able to live with so little intestine."

"Give her a chance. If she's lived this long, she can probably survive anything." I cut out the yards of bloated, black intestine that smelled like rotting garbage, and sewed the one foot of living intestine to the colon, which was still alive. The lady lost some weight, but she had been fat to start with. She went home two weeks after surgery, and Dr. James told me a year later that she was still well.

At the end of the year Dr. Anjou rented the Museum of Science for an evening and gave a going-away party for his four chief residents. We had cocktails in the Dinosaur Room and dinner in the rooftop restaurant. Except for one resident, and a surgical attending assigned to stay in the hospital, and the resident on call at the V.A., the whole surgical staff and their wives were there. It seemed impossible that my five years of general surgery residency were done. Toward the end of the party, Dr. Anjou called for silence.

"It is a pleasure for me to be chief of surgery of this department," he said. "It is a pleasure for me to have the chief residents we have had this year. They have, all four, been outstanding surgeons, and outstanding people. Two of them even fought with the attendings as much as I did as a resident.

"I never thought I would say I enjoyed training women surgeons. It was two against one," he pointed to Patsy and to me, "and I still enjoyed it. It gives me pride and pleasure to present certificates to our four departing chiefs. I'll see you four at the national meetings, so I won't say good-bye. But if any of you fail the General Surgery Boards, I'll come looking for you. You can't hide from the chief. Good luck and keep in touch."

I would never again be working with Sean, or Mark Lehman, or Karl Kingsley, Dr. Baker, Dr. Egilson, or any of the surgeons I had worked with for three years. After knowing Mark Lehman for eleven years, through medical school and the whole residency, it seemed odd that tonight might be the last time we would talk with each other. I would be a plastic surgery fellow at another hospital. Mark would stay on an extra year with Dr. Mulveney as a vascular surgery fellow before moving to California to practice. The longest struggle was over, but I knew I would miss the companionship and camaraderie that is found only in general surgical residency (and, I have been told, in troops under enemy attack).

At eleven o'clock the party broke up. I walked to the garage in a steamy rain and got into my 1968 Dodge. It was so battered that even in Cambridge, where the car theft rate is the highest in the world, I had not locked the car for three years. I drove off to a new teaching program, a new apartment, and a new career. I had been a general surgeon for five years. I was eligible for my Surgical Board examinations. I was no longer the chief. Now I was a junior resident again, this time as a plastic surgeon.

Puffing and Pale

My new apartment was modern, but I discovered on the first night that it had cockroaches. In my old apartment, there had been a mouse that kept cockroaches away. I planned to kill it with a mouse trap, but I did not have the heart. It lived under the stove and I fed it cheese at night so that it would not eat my books and clothes. There was nothing to keep the roaches away in the new apartment. It was an inauspicious beginning.

I made rounds the first day with Helen Bell, the outgoing chief resident of the plastic surgery service.

"If you survive this," she said, "you'll amaze me. I'm leaving you sixty patients, including six major burns in the I.C.U. You have three clinics a week, with thirty to fifty patients each. You operate all day on elective cases. You operate all night on emergencies. None of the general surgery residents are interested in the face, hand, neck, or any wound, so you will take care of every cut and scratch on the face and hand in the emergency room. The attendings are not interested in teaching and they don't like women. Good luck. You'll need it."

"Who is on the team with me?" I asked.

"You are the team, except for the intern. Good-bye."

I spent the first night in the emergency room, taking care of cuts, scrapes, face abrasions and a girl who had bitten her cheek while eating hard candy. The physicians' assistant in the emergency room told me to see her, so I had to.

The first week I enjoyed the surgery, which was interesting, but I was awake almost all night, every night, for the next three months. I had four hours of sleep the whole first week, and slept one hour the next week. In two months, I averaged twenty minutes of sleep a night. The third month, things improved and I averaged an hour a night.

Four of the five attendings were dissatisfied with my work, and told me I was irritable and lazy. I had never worked harder, and I had never had so little credit for my work.

"It's a game to the attendings," Helen had told me. "Cat and mouse. They want to see if they can break you. I wish I could help you, but they did the same to me. All you can do is hang on."

The rotation lasted three months. Every night I was called out, I prayed a car would hit me, so I would go in as a patient, and be able to sleep. I developed rectal bleeding, but I survived. After that rotation, I had two rotations of three months each during which I read a textbook a week and slept. On none of the three rotations was there any plastic surgery teaching. My last rotation of the year was on the private service with four plastic surgeons; Dr. Mendelssohn, Dr. Delio, Dr. Marion and Dr. Bunting. They were anxious to teach me, and showed me how to do surgery to correct deformities in children, reconstruct cancer defects, and repair head and neck injuries. I began to think I should be a plastic surgeon after all. After my first six months I had planned to finish out the year, then go back into general surgery, but working with these four plastic surgeons made me decide to stay.

Not only did these three men teach me, but they accepted me as a surgeon. I spent a day with each of them in their offices; they brought me references and reprints on unusual cases, and except for Dr. Bunting, they each took me to dinner or asked me to their homes. At the end of the three months I had learned how to take out a parotid tumor, repair a lacerated tendon and nerve in the hand, remove tumors from the face, repair scars and do cosmetic surgery of the face and breast.

As a going-away gift, Dr. Mendelssohn presented me with the new, seven-volume edition of the most important plastic surgery textbook. It was a wonderful rotation and I was sorry when it ended.

At the end of that year, I had a week's vacation. I moved to a new apartment, without roaches, and went to see Dr. Baker about my rectal bleeding. I had hoped it was from hemorrhoids, and that it would go away, but after nine months of bleeding and increasing abdominal cramps, I knew it was something more serious. Being a doctor doesn't make you braver about consulting one, and I was nervous.

Dr. Baker examined me and referred me to a gastroenterologist, who confirmed my fears that I had ulcerative colitis. This can be a minor problem or a catastrophic illness, with colon rupture, massive bleeding and sudden death. As soon as he said the words "ulcerative colitis," I decided to write a will. Would it be better to sell my old Dodge, or should I leave it to Jimmy or Rob? Would they want it, or would it be trouble for them? It needed a lot of body work. The gastroenterologist interrupted my thoughts.

"It doesn't look very bad, about grade three out of five. You need to take Azulfadine. Chances are it will get better quickly."

I filled the prescription, started taking the pills and the bleeding stopped two days later. He had told me to take the pills for three months, but after a few weeks I felt tired, and I thought I was turning into a hypochondriac. It was hard for me to get up in the morning and I began to sleep an extraordinary amount. I was a senior plastic surgery resident and did not take many emergency calls, but all I did in the evening was go home at seven and sleep until seven the next morning. Soon I was too tired to run up stairs. Walking up one flight was an effort, and made me short of breath. I decided I was out of shape and went to a ballet lesson, but I dragged through the class and danced badly. The next day a nurse told me I looked pale. I felt pale. I went home at four, went to bed, and slept until seven the next morning. I decided I was losing my mind. I went to work.

"Dr. Morgan, you look like a ghost," said a nursing aide. "Are you anemic?"

"Me? Anemic? Why?" I panted. I was very short of breath.

"You look anemic. Your skin is white."

"My skin always looks white."

"It looks whiter. You ought to check your blood count."

It seemed like a silly idea. Feeling more like a hypochondriac than ever, I tottered into the hospital laboratory and asked the technician to draw a blood count.

"How long have you been anemic?" she asked me.

"I don't know that I am," I said irritably. "An aide told me I looked pale, and I'm humoring her."

"You ought to check your pulse."

"Check my pulse? I'm not anemic." All the same, I took my pulse. It was 120, double my normal rate. "Maybe I am anemic."

The technician took a blood sample. My blood count was 21, half of what it had been three weeks before in the gastroenterologist's office. Twenty-one is low. I would not operate on a patient with a blood count of twenty-one, until he had had two or three blood transfusions. No wonder I felt tired and out of breath. I stopped the Azulfadine pills for two days, and my blood count rose to twenty-nine. Two days later, it was thirty-five. I called the gastroenterologist to ask if I should stop taking them permanently.

"Twenty-one? That low? That's a very rare and dangerous complication. Your body reacts to Azulfadine by destroying your own blood cells. No, you shouldn't take the pills again. Next time you might not recover. How is your colitis?"

"My colitis is fine. It's the anemia that's destroying me."

It didn't keep me from working, but I worked slowly. It wasn't until January that I had the energy to take another ballet lesson. There is nothing like the firsthand experience of being a patient.

Man Beats Bus

My second year in plastic surgery was like being welcomed home. I loved plastic surgery and wanted to learn more. The word plastic is derived from the Greek word "to mold," and plastic surgery includes reconstruction of all kinds—putting together hands and faces damaged in accidents, treating burn damage, building breasts after cancer surgery, and repairing birth deformities, like the cleft lip. It also includes cosmetic surgery, from the face lift to breast augmentation. Plastic surgery appealed to me because the results are visible. Plastic surgeons always take before and after photographs of their patients, and if you have done a good—or a bad—job, you can see it and study how to do an even better job the next time. I also liked the fact that this was a broad field. Every operation is different, no deformity is exactly like any other and a new operation has to be planned for each patient. Also, the psychology of plastic surgery fascinated me. I liked to try to understand why one patient might be obsessed with a minor scar and another patient not troubled at all by a deformed ear or grotesquely crooked nose.

I spent much of that second year studying in Cambridge with Drs. Fitzhugh and Sinclair, but I also spent time in Boston with Dr. Sutherland, the professor of plastic surgery, and Drs. Berenson, Revere and Potter. Dr. Revere happened to live near me, and often drove me in on Friday mornings to Sunshine Serenade, the 7:00 A.M. plastic surgery Grand Rounds.

When I was a general surgery resident I had written a short paper with Dr. Revere on a patient with tuberous sclerosis, a rare inherited disease of the skin, and I had hoped someday to know as much as Dr. Revere did. By now, I had learned never to expect that. No one had a memory like his. If someone at Grand Rounds said, "I think that syndrome was reported six years ago in the *Plastic Journal*," Dr. Revere would wrinkle his brow in thought, and then remark, "I'm fairly sure it was in Volume 62, on page 354, but actually von Grafelin reported it first in 1811." He was especially interested in medical history and knew the lives of most of the famous surgeons, and also of many less well-known plastic surgeons of the 1800s.

Plastic surgeons are specialists in making wounds heal. In Cambridge, where I spent much time during my second year in plastic surgery, we saw the most difficult wounds in men over eighty.

One such patient was a retired architect. He burned the top of his head when he fell asleep with his bed against a hot radiator. He refused skin grafting, but after several weeks of treatment in our clinic his burn healed. In gratitude he braved a snowstorm to deliver to us six bottles of champagne.

My most amazing older patient was Mr. Kushnikoff, who had been born in a part of Russia where people live to be one hundred and fifty years old. During the First World War he had walked out of Russia into Italy; during the Second World War he left Italy and settled in Cambridge. He had had surgery for atherosclerosis when he was eighty and now, at eighty-five, he was healthy enough to go to work every day in his own cobbler shop even though at five feet eight, he weighed two hundred and fifty pounds.

One morning at the shop he wanted gefilte fish for lunch and walked across the street to buy it. In the middle of the street he was hit by a bus. I first saw him when Dr. Kurz, the chief of general surgery, called me to the operating room. No bones were broken, but all the skin of his right leg had been sheared off, and most of it had been destroyed. He was bleeding heavily from his leg and his upper arm, where the skin and muscle had also been torn off. I worked on his leg with Dr. Fitzhugh, the chief of plastic surgery, while Bill Jedder, a junior resident, helped the anesthesiologist keep him alive with intravenous fluids, blood and oxygen. Everyone was covered in blood. We did our best, but we all agreed that poor Mr. Kushnikoff could not survive such a dreadful injury.

Mr. Kushnikoff survived his operation, and when I came to see him on morning rounds, he told me about his flight to Italy from Russia.

"It was a long walk, a very long walk, but I was young and strong, not an old man." He raised his bushy white eyebrows and smiled happily. One morning, he greeted us politely, but was obviously feeling worse. He was too tired to talk, and had trouble breathing. His skin was pale and he was sweating. Blood clots in his legs were breaking loose and moving to his lungs. At noon, Dr. Kurz was doing an emergency operation on Mr. Kushnikoff to tie off the veins from his legs to his lungs to block the blood clots.

Two days later, Mr. Kushnikoff had largely recovered from his second surgery, and was cheerfully calling the head nurse "Sweetheart." When I asked him how he was, he said he would be better if I gave him a kiss.

Three days later, Mr. Kushnikoff's wound was badly infected. I helped the general surgeons cut away hunks of black gangrenous muscle and skin from his leg. It took us three hours, and he was in shock during the operation, from blood loss and severe infection, with a blood pressure far below normal. This seemed like the end. He looked very sick, and was unconscious for three days. He desperately needed skin grafts on his leg wounds to prevent them from getting infected again. I scheduled his skin graft surgery for a Monday, but on Sunday night, when I was in the hospital, Dr. Fitzhugh called me.

"Our old friend Mr. Kushnikoff apparently is moribund. Dr. Kurz doesn't think he'll survive the night. Keep him on the operating schedule, but I'm reluctant to put him through surgery, even if he is alive. I don't want him to die with a bunch of plastic surgeons slicing skin grafts off him."

I agreed, and went to say good-bye to Mr. Kushnikoff. He was lying in bed, unconscious. His breathing was slow and heavy. I spoke to him, but his only response was an occasional twitch. I stood watching him, thinking that it was kinder to let him die in peace. As I was leaving, he snored, and sighed peacefully.

Dying people don't usually snore. I checked his medicine sheet. An hour earlier he had been given a huge dose of morphine for the pain in his leg. Perhaps, I hoped, he was sedated, not dying. A little old woman dressed in black came in to ask how he was doing. She was his wife. I explained how sick he was and that we might postpone surgery as we did not want him to suffer. She said she prayed he would come back home again. They had been married for sixty-seven years, and she found it hard to be without him.

The next morning Mr. Kushnikoff was much better. He asked how long the graft surgery would take, and was anxious to have it done, so I went ahead.

I did the grafting with Bill Jedder, teaching him how to use the dermatome to take grafts. Mr. Kushnikoff had no skin on his right leg or buttock, one of the usual sources of skin for grafts, so we had to take it from his back and abdomen as well as his left leg and buttock.

His leg wound was enormous and the operation took us four hours. The grafts we did that day covered about half his wound. For two weeks after the surgery he lay in bed, hallucinating and refusing to eat. His skin grafts healed slowly, and he ran a fever of 102° every night. We could find no infection, and the fever burned up calories as fast as we poured them intravenously. His hands had to be tied to the bedrails to prevent him from picking off the skin grafts in his delirium, but he rattled his hands against the bedrails so violently we were afraid he would hurt himself.

After two weeks most of the grafts had taken and his wounds were getting better, but he stayed confused, speaking garbled English mixed with Ukrainian. I scheduled a second operation to skin graft the remaining open wounds, under spinal anesthesia this time. I was afraid he might die under general anesthesia, which takes longer to recover from than a spinal, and Mr. Kushnikoff now also had pneumonia as well as kidney failure from antibiotics given for the infected wound. His condition, bad as it was, necessitated the second skin grafting. A large raw wound constantly oozes out protein; the body burns up calories trying to heal the wound; bacteria settle on open wounds. Until Mr. Kushnikoff's wound was covered with skin and healed, his body would be constantly depleted of protein. Although he was desperately ill, the surgery could not be postponed or he would never recover.

Bill Jedder and I rushed through the surgery. A week later, the grafts had healed beautifully. Mr. Kushnikoff began to eat and to talk coherently, although he tired quickly and his voice would trail off in mid-sentence. He could sit in his chair and take a few steps, but he was terribly weak. He had lost seventy pounds.

Five days later he started to vomit and ran a high fever. He had acute diverticulitis—inflammation in his colon—and had to be treated with a tube in his stomach, antibiotics and nothing to eat or drink. It was almost more than I could stand. It seemed silly to pretend he would ever go home. His wife visited him every day, but she never said anything to us. She would walk away sadly, with her daughter or granddaughter helping her.

Two days later, on morning rounds, I found Mr. Kushnikoff sitting up in bed, thoughtfully patting his stomach and shaking his head. The tube through his nose flipped side to side with each shake of his head.

"I feel much better today," he said. "I have been very sick. I don't want any food."

The next day on morning rounds, Mr. Kushnikoff was arguing angrily with the girl from the kitchen because she wouldn't give him a breakfast tray. He was indignant, but she just shook her head and said it wasn't ordered.

"Are you hungry?" I asked him.

"Hungry!" he said, as though the word was inadequate. "I want to eat a horse."

He was allowed only Jell-O and juices by Dr. Kurz. In retaliation, he pulled out the stomach tube from his nose. The next day when I made rounds, he was sitting on the edge of his bed. A nursing aide was pouring sugar and milk over his oatmeal and he was supervising it all very closely.

A week later Mr. Kushnikoff was cruising the hallways unsteadily, with an orderly supporting him on either side. His legs were stiff from being in bed. He looked very old and the hospital bathrobe was loose on him. It was the last time I saw him before leaving Cambridge for a rotation at another Boston hospital.

Three months later I returned, and my first day back I went to the plastic surgery clinic at 8:30 in the morning. A nurse grabbed my arm.

"Mr. Kushnikoff is in a great rush. Could you see him right away?" He had been home for a month and was thin, but fit. He proudly showed me his right leg. It was healed, but there were some stitches that I wanted to remove.

"No, Doctor Jedder said the sutures stay in for another week," he announced firmly. I didn't argue. His arm had healed so well the scars did not show.

Not a Lucky Lady

One of the advances in plastic surgery has been reconstruction of the breast for women who have had a breast removed for cancer. In my second year of plastic surgery, I learned how this is done; the breast is rebuilt with a silicone implant, or by moving in skin and muscle tissue, depending on how much has been removed in the mastectomy. Five percent of American women develop breast cancer and ninety percent of the cases caught early can be cured with surgery, so there are an increasing number of women interested in reconstruction.

Muriel Spitzer was happily married when she got breast cancer. She had only one child, a mongoloid whom she had raised at home, although he was so severely retarded that at fourteen his mental age was five. She was determined not to send him to a state home. Her husband divorced her after her breast was removed because, he said, he did not want to look at her any more. Her cancer had spread to the lymph glands and after the mastectomy she had six months of drug therapy to try to arrest the cancer there. The drugs made her hair fall out and caused her to bruise easily and feel tired and nauseated.

After her drug treatment was over, Mrs. Spitzer came to Dr. Fitzhugh and requested a breast reconstruction, saying, "I know it's a new thing, but all the women at home where I live are having it done after mastectomy. Besides, my husband left me because I looked deformed. I was never a great beauty, but I can't go on looking this way."

Her surgery had to be done in two stages, three months apart. There was enough skin and muscle left on the chest, so in the first operation a silicone implant could be put under the skin, to make a breastlike fullness. The second operation was to create a new nipple. I met Muriel when she came to the hospital for the first stage and I assisted Dr. Fitzhugh with the surgery. Tests before her surgery showed no sign that the cancer had returned. She wore a blond wig to hide the hair she had lost during drug therapy. Her hair was growing back, but it was frizzy, a common side-effect of the drugs. She healed without complications, and three months later the day for her second operation was approaching.

The day before the surgery her insurance company called Dr. Fitzhugh's secretary to say this second operation was cosmetic and they would not pay for it. Dr. Fitzhugh called the insurance doctor back immediately.

"What do you idiots over there in your ivory tower think you are doing? Cosmetic? You said it was fine to do the first operation. It wasn't cosmetic then. Now all of a sudden it is. You're just trying to save money off a poor lady who's had breast cancer. What are you guys doing with all the money you steal from people? Hiding it in a Swiss bank account? You call yourself an insurance doctor? I call you Scrooge."

Within an hour, the company changed its mind, agreed to pay and called Mrs. Spitzer to tell her she could have her surgery. She arrived late at the hospital, about 7:30 in the evening. She had put her mongoloid son in a nursery, and the dog in a boarding kennel, and had driven frantically through traffic jams. She was eager to have her surgery, and exultant about the insurance.

"You'd understand," she said to me, "as a woman. I wanted this operation so much, I would have paid for it myself, even though my husband didn't leave me with much. I wasn't going to tell *them* that, of course. I'm so happy with my new breast shape. I can wear a bra, and feel normal again." She lowered her voice. "These men," she said in disgust. "Cosmetic. If it was their penises, it wouldn't be cosmetic surgery."

The next morning, her laboratory tests from the night before showed that her liver enzymes were abnormal, suggesting that the cancer had returned and spread to her liver. Dr. Fitzhugh postponed her stage two operation to do more liver tests. If she had cancer in the liver, breast reconstruction was pointless. She would not live long enough to enjoy it.

The liver scans showed huge cancer pockets in the liver. She was destined to die, and soon. She refused further treatment. She wanted to be left alone.

"You're very kind, but I'm not a lucky lady. I'm sorry to disappoint you, but no more drugs and radiation for Muriel. I have more important things to do." She started to cry. "You just don't understand. I have no family, except a lovable fourteen-year-old son who is going to have to be put away in a state home, because Mommy won't be around any longer. It's going to be very hard on him."

She wiped her eyes. "I don't want to leave him. I know they won't treat him as nicely as I do, and he won't be happy. He's been very happy at home. It will take me at least two months to find a good place for him. I just pray I have those two months."

She drove home and never called back. When I called to see how she was, a recording told me, "service has been permanently disconnected."

Plastic surgery deals less with life and death than general surgery, and in spite of the statistics Muriel Spitzer's recurrent cancer was a shock to me. Dr. Fitzhugh was upset, too, particularly about the behavior of her ex-husband, who had refused to speak to her or visit her in the hospital. "I'd like to get my hands on him," was all Dr. Fitzhugh would say, but it was just as well the two men never met— Dr. Fitzhugh was the fourth generation of a family of professional and amateur boxers. As a chief resident he had been attacked in the hospital parking lot and had beaten his assailant to a pulp without meaning to do him much harm.

The memory of Muriel Spitzer cast a pall over the service for several weeks until we were distracted by Mr. Malinowski. I was asked to see Mr. Malinowski for a hand infection which he had had for several months. When I went in to see him the first time, the nurse warned me never to turn my back.

"He's likely to pinch you."

"Does he make a habit of that?"

"The man is absolutely impossible. Several women patients have complained that he won't leave them alone. He creeps up behind us on rounds and pinches us, too."

Mr. Malinowski spoke no English. He had a swollen but painless finger which, according to the interpreter, he wanted us to cut off. The x-rays looked as though the bone was infected but the abnormal swelling of the finger suggested it might be a tumor and his doctor had asked us for a second opinion.

Another patient of mine was in the same room and I talked to that patient first, while Mr. Malinowski gazed out of the window looking at nothing. Then, as I talked, Mr. Malinowski walked over to stand beside me, nodding his head wisely. I pulled the curtains shut around my patient's bed to exclude him. Afterwards I went to examine him. His right index finger was badly swollen and he could not move it. When I left him, Mr. Malinowski followed me into the corridor. He made a chopping action against his index finger, nodded his head vigorously and followed me to the nurses' desk. I sat down to read his chart. He looked bored and set about emptying the wastepaper baskets onto the floor. According to the interpreter, who had interviewed his wife, Mr. Malinowski had had a severe brain infection several years ago and had behaved peculiarly ever since.

The next day I returned with Dr. Fitzhugh to decide whether to operate on the infected bone. We could not find Mr. Malinowski in his room but, following a sudden cry of distress, we found a nurse pulling him away from the bed of an elderly lady. Mr. Malinowski had watched the intern put a feeding tube into a patient's stomach through the nose. Intrigued, he found a discarded tube in the trash, and had tried to push that into the elderly lady's nose as well. The nurse was dragging him off.

"He's always causing trouble," she grumbled. "I don't mind when he plays janitor with the trash, but last night he tried to climb into bed with a lady."

Mr. Malinowski followed us back to his room and had a passionate discussion with the interpreter. At the end, the interpreter told me Mr. Malinowski wanted his finger cut off. I explained that surgery and six weeks of antibiotics might cure the infection. There was another passionate discussion. Mr. Malinowski agreed to the surgery and antibiotics. The interpreter left, and Mr. Malinowski walked to the nurses' desk and gathered all the pens on the desk into a pile.

The operation I planned was to clean out the abnormal bone, and have it examined by pathology to make certain the bone was merely infected and not cancerous. I had planned to do the operation with local anesthesia and Mr. Malinowski agreed. In the operating room he was most cooperative and lay quietly while I injected Novocaine around the finger, and then placed sterile drapes around his arm. His arm was stretched out on a side attachment to the operating table, and I sat down to operate.

"Marking pen," I said. The nurse handed me the blue ink marker and I marked out my incision. Mr. Malinowski tried to sit up to watch me, but the anesthesiologist told him, in Spanish, to lie down. He seemed to understand.

"Scalpel," I said. The nurse handed it to me, and I made the incision along the side of his finger. I spread the skin apart. I pointed to a skin hook. The nurse handed it to me, and I placed it so that it would hold the skin away.

"Hold the hook for me, please," I asked the nurse.

"Me! Me! I want to!" announced Mr. Malinowski in his own language and he sat up and grabbed at the hook. With a struggle, we persuaded him to lie down again, but not until he had shaken off the sterile drapes and thrown the instruments on the floor.

"Dr. Morgan, may I make a suggestion?" asked the anesthesiologist.

"Yes. I think I know what it is." The anesthesiologist injected Pentathol.

Once Mr. Malinowski was asleep I scrubbed and draped his hand again, and in fifteen minutes had cleaned out the infected bone, sent it to pathology and was sewing up the skin.

Mr. Malinowski needed six weeks of antibiotics intravenously to cure his infection, but two days after the surgery he disappeared. The night before, he had told Bill Jedder through an interpreter that he was going home in the morning to make love to his wife. We found his intravenous antibiotic bottle hidden in the wastepaper basket. We called his family but he had not arrived home. We sent the police to look for him. I called his family again later in the day. Mr. Malinowski had returned, but disappeared again. Two days later he reappeared on the ward. As he climbed back into bed he told the

The Next Generation

One afternoon I was sitting in the O.R. lounge eating lunch with the nurses when Dr. Kurz came in, sat down next to me and groaned. "Elizabeth, what are you doing?"

"Eating lunch. Do you want half a tuna sandwich?"

"No. What are you doing to Dr. Fitzhugh? First he lets you come here and now he tells me a woman surgical intern is starting here tomorrow."

"I didn't know that. That's terrific."

"Terrific indeed. Yesterday you suggested flowers in the operating room and today you'll want pink scrub suits."

"Dr. Kurz, I thought you liked me."

"You're all right but women in general don't belong in surgery."

"I don't know what to suggest. I know a lot of women surgeons, and pretty soon there won't be any men."

He laughed, ate the rest of my sandwich, and went off to help his chief resident to remove a stomach cancer.

The woman intern, Melissa Smith, was pretty, friendly, and enthusiastic. She worked hard, complained about the work like every intern and reminded me of Leslie and me during our internship six years before. Three weeks later Dr. Fitzhugh, Dr. Kurz and I were in the surgical office getting ready to go home when Dr. Kurz suddenly said, "We have to do something about Melissa Smith."

"What's wrong with Lis?" I asked in surprise.

"She's nice all right," said Dr. Kurz. "She's a very nice girl but she's not like a surgeon. She told me the other day that there should be a special I.V. nurse to do the I.V.s instead of the interns. I don't think she likes to work. I'll have to toughen her up."

"You'll regret it," I said. "I was tough when I was a general surgery resident and I was perfectly horrible."

Dr. Kurz laughed. "I don't believe it. I bet you just batted your eyelashes and soon nice men did your work for you."

Two weeks later there was an edge to Melissa's voice, and a week after that I heard her on the phone. "We want that blood and we want it stat, so set it up and no excuses." She hung up and turned to me. "Those fools in the blood bank. Dr. Kurz needs the blood for this case and they don't have it ready."

"Take it easy," I said. "Dr. Kurz is a good surgeon and a good teacher but he's leaning on you a bit because you're a woman. Don't complain. Don't get mean. It's the worst mistake you can make. Just do your work and he'll back off." She didn't believe me. I could only hope that she would learn, sooner than I had, and with less struggle, how to be a surgeon and a woman at the same time.

Genghis Khan vs. Attila the Hun

Halfway through the year I made a major decision about my life as a doctor: when my residency was over, I would go into private practice. I was not cut out for the maneuvering for political power and federal grants that is necessary in academic medicine and surgery. In private practice a doctor must work hard to pay his bills and support himself but is otherwise independent. In academic medicine a doctor gives up individual freedom in exchange for status, a fixed salary, time and opportunity to teach and do research, and payment by the university of all business expenses such as office rent, secretarial salaries, and malpractice insurance. These expenses run around $40,000 a year for a plastic surgeon in private practice. In some areas, where the malpractice rates are $30,000 or higher, the overhead goes up accordingly.

To succeed in academic practice a surgeon must be capable of making and breaking alliances with other surgeons in order to get voted the promotions, pay and committee memberships he needs to advance professionally. It had become clear that politics was not my gift and besides, after seven years of residency, what I wanted most of all was not to be told what to do by anyone and not to work as a subordinate for another surgeon.

In spite of my desire to be on my own, I did have my doubts at times about whether I could succeed in private practice. I thought I might postpone it for a year or two by doing research, possibly even working for a Ph.D. But when I asked Dr. Berenson for advice he shook his head firmly. "Women in surgery, to my disappointment, tend to end up in laboratory research or lower paid teaching positions simply because they're afraid of striking out on their own. You are competent, well-trained, and all you need is the courage to leave the protective nest, go out into the world and work." Dr. Fitzhugh, Dr. Sinclair and Dr. Berenson were in private practice and I began to watch them to learn how they made things work. The most important element of their set-up, I learned, was a good secretary.

At the moment Dr. Fitzhugh was being driven frantic by his secretaries. He had had a wonderful secretary for years, but she ran off with a married doctor to live in Ohio. After that he hired Flora. She was enthusiastic, cheerful and friendly, but not very well suited to a medical office. The office, to Flora, was a chance for behind-the-scenes drama. She particularly enjoyed the drama of calling Dr. Fitzhugh out of the operating room.

"Dr. Fitzhugh, I'm sorry to call you out of surgery, but I think this is urgent. It's a man from the drug company, and he says it's an important business matter."

"It sounds as though he is trying to sell me a new drug."

"Oh, really? He didn't sound like a salesman."

"Did you ask him why he was calling?"

"Oh, naughty Flora. Bad girl. I forgot to ask him that. I asked him everything else."

"Like what? I'm trying to operate and you call me out to speak to a drug salesman?"

"Dr. Fitzhugh, I'm terribly sorry if it was wrong, but it was with the best intentions. If I slip his phone call down to you in the operating room, you can give him a teeny bit of your time, to make him happy. I promised him he could speak with you. It might be urgent."

It is sometimes difficult to know whether a doctor's calls are urgent or not. The first time it happened, he was patient.

"She's new," he said. "She'll learn."

The third time, his eyes glared over his operating mask. The fourth time, his hair stood on end. The fifth time, he exploded.

"Is there no peace? Are you the KGB or the CIA? I'm trying to earn my living as a surgeon. How can I operate when you call me every five minutes. What is the call?"

"Mrs. Langley. You did a face lift on her three weeks ago."

"I know I did. What does she want, an appointment?"

"Oh, no. It sounded like an emergency. She's desperate to talk with you."

He sighed. "All right. Transfer her call to the operating room. I'll speak with her."

A nurse tapped him on the shoulder. "Dr. Fitzhugh, your patient is waiting."

"Yes, thank you. I have to take an urgent call, and I'll be right in."

The call came through.

"Dr. Fitzhugh, it's Mrs. Langley. I'm sorry to trouble you, but is my appointment today for three o'clock or four?"

His eyes narrowed but his voice was calm. "It's four, Mrs. Langley. Couldn't my secretary answer your question?"

"She didn't ask why I was calling. She said I had to speak with you."

The last straw was the hamburger. Dr. Fitzhugh was operating when Flora called him out of surgery for an emergency.

"Yes, Flora. What is it now?"

"Dr. Fitzhugh, you wanted a hamburger for lunch?"

"Yes."

"Or was it roast beef? I don't want to make a mistake."

"You're fired."

"What?"

"You're fired."

"Why?"

He hung up.

"That woman is Genghis Khan, the scourge of the West."

Flora was well-intentioned, but belonged on stage, not in an office. The next month when I was in Boston with Dr. Sutherland again, I found his office struggling to recover from Maybelle, a secretary-typist hired in November to help his regular secretaries, who were superb. Lisa, Dr. Sutherland's head secretary, was away when Maybelle was hired and another secretary recommended her for the job. Maybelle was thirty and a good typist. Her first day at work, she wore a see-through black dress and an Afro bleached-blond wig which made it hard for her to answer the telephone. Lisa told

Maybelle to type some letters, and to check Dr. Sutherland's file for patients who had missed appointments, then send out a standard letter suggesting they call for a new appointment. Among the letters dictated for her to type were answers to doctors applying for residency positions.

At the end of the first week, Lisa asked Maybelle to pick up the mail in the mail room.

"I'll do it this time," she said, "but I really couldn't do it again. It would impair the dignity of my position."

"Dr. Sutherland, I think Maybelle is very odd," said Lisa, later on. He agreed, but had to leave town for two weeks of surgical meetings.

At the end of her second week on the job, Maybelle wore hot red polyester pyjamas to work. The third week she wore an emerald green jumpsuit slit to the waist, and a red beehive wig. She typed frantically. Lisa reminded her that Dr. Sutherland read and approved all his letters before they were sent out. Maybelle agreed, and kept a letter pile for Dr. Sutherland but refused to let Lisa see it.

"You're not my boss," said Maybelle, "you're just jealous of my superior office work."

On Friday of the third week Maybelle arrived at work with a case of root beer. "I am the Christmas spirit," she announced, "and next Monday there will be a magnificent Christmas party for everyone!"

She spent that day trying to make urgent collect telephone calls to famous politicians, but the other secretaries had too much work to do to pay attention to her, and couldn't control her anyhow. Dr. Revere, Dr. Downing and Dr. Potter were too busy operating.

On Monday, Dr. Downing had an 8:30 interview with an intern applicant from a Midwest medical school. Maybelle came early to open the office for him.

"By the way," she told him, "I mailed all of Dr. Sutherland's letters this weekend. They couldn't wait any longer." She started to type more letters.

Dr. Downing and the applicant went into the inner room, a library-office with wall-to-wall books and a large desk with Dr. Sutherland's lecture notes in the drawers. Five minutes after Dr. Downing started to interview the intern-applicant, Maybelle walked into the inner room.

"I'm sorry. I'm looking for some papers. I looked for them out there, but I can't find them."

"Please leave us alone until we are finished," asked Dr. Downing.

He was trying to put the shy intern-applicant at ease. Five minutes later, Maybelle came in again.

"I'm sorry," she said, "but I need something." She opened one of the desk drawers, looked inside and left it open. She took off her sweater and put it on the floor.

"Please," said Dr. Downing, "we would like not to be interrupted."

Maybelle walked out, leaving her sweater, but came back.

"I'm leaving you alone from now on," she said.

Two minutes later she walked in, and said nothing. She took some books out of the shelves, and walked out again. Before she left, she kicked her shoes off, and left them behind. Dr. Downing tried to pretend he did not notice. Immediately after that, Maybelle returned. She said nothing, but removed two drawers from the desk and put them on the floor. She sat on the floor, and put the papers from the first desk drawer into the second one. She took off her necklace and her hair ribbon, and put them in the first drawer. She left, but returned almost immediately and took out two more drawers, and put them on the floor. She also took some books out of the bookshelves, and put them on the floor. She moved five books from a shelf on the left to an empty shelf on the right. She put her earrings and her belt on the empty shelf. The intern-applicant was looking nervous.

"This is absurd," said Dr. Downing angrily. "Please leave us alone."

She said nothing. She was gone for five minutes but came back again. She put the books from one bookshelf on the floor. She removed two more drawers from the desk and put them on the floor. She took two drawers from the desk and shoved them into the wrong slots of the desk. They stuck halfway and she left them like that. She took the papers in the drawers and scattered them on the floor. She put her necklace on the desk, and unbuttoned her blouse. As soon as she left, Dr. Downing jumped up and locked the door, and then continued the interview as calmly as he could.

"Let me in," shouted Maybelle, when she found the door locked. She rattled the handle. "You can't lock me out. All right, now I've locked you out. Joke! Joke!"

He could hear her laughing on the far side of the door. The medical student was looking shell-shocked.

At nine o'clock Lisa and the two other secretaries arrived.

Maybelle had locked the main door to the office so they could not get in. Dr. Downing could hear her laughing, and heard file cabinet drawers pulled open, and slammed closed. He could hear furniture bumping around. Lisa called a psychiatrist from a phone in another office. For forty-five minutes Dr. Downing and the intern-applicant were locked in the office, listening as the psychiatrist talked to Maybelle and she just laughed at him. Another hour later, she agreed to accompany him to a psychiatric hospital.

"You understand, this is for a summer vacation," she explained, as she left. "I will be back to resume my position as chairman of the department as soon as vacation is over."

She had rearranged the office. Every drawer was on the floor. All the papers from the drawers were on the floor. In every empty drawer and in every file cabinet was a bottle of root beer. Dr. Downing led the intern-applicant through the chaos and closed the interview. For the next month, Lisa received phone calls from Dr. Sutherland's patients.

"You've just sent me a letter saying that Dr. Sutherland can never see me again. I canceled my last appointment because something came up at my job and I couldn't keep it. What does this mean?"

Maybelle had mailed out letters that read:

> Dear Patient, You failed to keep your last appointment.
> I am much too busy and important to waste my time with
> the irresponsible or the forgetful. This is good-bye. Sin-
> cerely, Office of Dr. Sutherland.

The letter to the residency applicants informed them that Dr. Sutherland's residency was filled completely for eight years in advance and advised the applicant to lower his aspirations and apply elsewhere.

Lisa also received calls from Maybelle. She was in a psychiatric ward, but had a phone at her bedside. She called the office each hour.

"Listen, Lisa, I have a fantastic new idea on how to organize the office. Now, just listen one minute and I'll explain. It's something new and different."

"I'll bet it is," said Lisa. "Good-bye."

The psychiatrists disconnected Maybelle's telephone, but she called from a pay phone in the hallway. Besides calling the office, she called her Congressman, her Senator and the White House. She was not able to get through to the Pope. She was then transferred to a locked ward. Dr. Sutherland's office had to hire two new secretaries, one to help Lisa, and one to send out letters to explain the ones Maybelle had mailed.

"She sounds like Attila the Hun, Scourge of God," said Dr. Fitzhugh. "Thank God I only had Flora."

If Lisa had been around when Maybelle applied for the job, she would never have been hired. Male surgeons are very careful when evaluating residents. When it comes to a secretary, despite repeated disappointments, they hire the first one who looks the part.

Tummy Lift

Plastic surgery includes cosmetic surgery and I learned from Dr. Fitzhugh and Dr. Sinclair how to do face lifts and nose operations, breast enlargements, breast reductions, and how to choose which patients should have the surgery.

From what women read in the newspapers, a face lift will make her younger, breast surgery will make her sexier and nose surgery will make her beautiful. What people forget is that an operation may change the way you look, but it isn't a magical transformation into a different personality. There are possible complications and it is expensive. One of the most difficult decisions is whether the patient really will benefit from cosmetic surgery, or has unrealistic or downright bizarre ideas of what it will do for him or her.

The plastic surgery clinic where I worked did not do much cosmetic surgery, although occasionally patients would come to the clinic to see if they could have cosmetic surgery for a reduced fee. I could arrange this, depending on the case, but cosmetic candidates were unusual at the clinic.

One afternoon a girl came in to ask me about having an abdominoplasty, or tummy lift, which removes loose skin over the abdomen. The girl was thin, pretty and twenty-five. First I examined her. She had some stretch marks on her abdomen, but not much loose skin. I explained surgery would make her tummy tighter, but the stretch marks would remain. She began to cry, and I sat down to talk with her.

"Why do you want to get rid of the stretch marks?" I asked.

"Because they remind me of when I was pregnant."

"Why do you want to forget being pregnant?"

"Because it makes me feel horrible. I feel so guilty."

"Why do you feel guilty?"

She did not answer at first, but finally told me that she was the younger and more attractive of two sisters. Her mother was an alcoholic, and had never liked her. Her father was also an alcoholic. When her father paid her attention when she was young, her mother became angry. When she was eight, her father used to fondle her sexually. Her mother discovered it, and her father went away and never returned. When she was fourteen, she and her mother and sister were living with an uncle and his son. A nineteen-year-old friend of the son raped her in her home, and she became pregnant. Her mother made her marry the boy when she turned fifteen. She developed the stretch marks during that pregnancy. Her husband drank and never worked, and she and her husband and the baby lived with her mother and her sister at her uncle's house.

Her sister married two years later and moved away. After that, her husband started to beat her up in front of her mother, who watched. Afterward, her mother would say that if she behaved properly her husband would not have to beat her. Her husband began to beat the child, and she ran away with the baby to her sister, but her mother and husband found her and came after her. They wanted the child for the child support from welfare. She refused to come or give them the child. Before they left, her husband threw her onto the floor and kicked her, and her mother told her that she should have died before being born. She never saw her mother again.

She stayed with her sister, worked and earned enough to move to an apartment of her own. She was then eighteen. Three years later, she met her present lover. They were not married, but had lived together for four years. This man had a steady job, bought a house and supported her and her daughter, who was now ten. My patient wanted to return to school, take the high school equivalency exam, and go to a community college to study art and design. She did freelance art work for local companies, but they would not hire her full time unless she had more formal training. Her lover had two thousand dollars in a savings bank. Part was for his grandmother, who needed an operation. The rest was saved for her education.

"Exactly why do you want the tummy lift? Does your lover want you to have it?" I asked.

"No."

"Why do you want it done?"

She started to cry again.

"My lover is so good to me. He is such a wonderful man. I look at my stomach when I wake up in the morning. I see those stretch marks, and I feel ashamed that I belonged to any man before him. I feel disgusted with myself."

"You understand that even if we charge you nothing, the cost of the hospital and the operating room will be close to two thousand dollars?"

She nodded.

"You understand that you will still have the stretch marks. You will also have a surgical scar that goes across the lower abdomen, from hip to hip. It may not be obvious, but you could see it."

She nodded again.

"If you have the surgery, will you be able to take the high school equivalency exam?"

"No. The exam is given in a month. If I have the surgery, I'll be in the hospital during the review course for the exam."

"If you have the surgery, will your lover have any money to give to his grandmother?"

"No."

"When you wake up in the morning after your surgery and you see stretch marks, and the surgical scar, will you feel guilty that you asked your lover for money for your operation, when he wanted to give some of it to his grandmother?"

She looked horrified.

"I hadn't thought of that. That would be awful. I know I would think that way. I don't think I could live with that. What should I do?"

"Why don't you postpone your surgery? Let your lover pay for his grandmother's operation, and for your education. Take your high school equivalency exam. Enroll in community college next semester and get a design job."

340

She nodded. "I can probably get a part-time job as soon as I'm enrolled."

"After you get the job, and you've saved some money, if you still want the surgery, come back and talk with us about it."

She shook her head. "I don't know what got into me. It was a crazy idea, having surgery. If I earned that much money, I could spend it on my daughter. I'm very grateful for your talking with me for so long. Sometimes I get confused about where I'm headed."

"Elizabeth," said a clinic nurse after the girl left, "I know it's late, but a psychiatrist called and wants you to see a patient for him. He thinks she needs cosmetic surgery. Do you have time?"

"What time is it?"

"Four-thirty, but clinic closes at five. Will you be through by then, with a cosmetic patient?"

"I'll try."

"Let me explain," the psychiatrist said over the telephone, after thanking me, "I've been seeing the lady for several weeks. She has a complicated psychiatric history, but she is on the way to rehabilitation. She's concerned about her body image, and I know you plastic surgeons do a lot of body-image surgery. I thought you might be able to help her."

The psychiatry patient was a wild-eyed middle-aged lady. She was very fat and looked angry.

I brought the lady into the examining room after I introduced myself. She sat down, and looked around suspiciously.

"You're the doctor?"

"Yes."

"A lady doctor?"

"Yes."

"I don't like lady doctors."

"I'm sorry. I'm the only plastic surgeon here to see you."

"I don't like lady plastic surgeons. You make me feel funny."

"I'm sorry. Perhaps you can tell me about your problem, and see if I can help you."

"You'll just laugh at me." She looked around again. "I want you to cut my stomach off."

"Really? This is very interesting. Why don't you show me exactly what you want us to fix."

She undressed. She was very fat. Plastic surgery cannot change

341

that. The person has to lose weight before the surgery, which removes skin, not fat.

"And I want you to fix me up in general."

"How do you mean?"

"Well, fix me up in general. You know what I mean. Don't act dumb. You know, everything."

She had a wide scar running across one breast, and a disfiguring scar across one eye.

"Do you want us to try to improve the scars on your face, and your breast?"

"Them? No. They don't bother me."

"Why don't you put your clothes on, sit down and tell me more about yourself."

She dressed and sat down.

"Do you have a job?"

"No."

"Where do you live?"

"With a friend, but she's going to throw me out. I have to find a place of my own soon."

"Are you married?"

"No. I was once, but not now."

"When?"

"A long time ago."

"How old were you when you got married?"

"It was before."

"Before when?"

"Before they locked me up. I spent twenty years in the state mental hospital. They sent me there when I was twenty-two or something. I had a baby, and I had a husband, and my husband didn't like what I did to the baby. He made the court give the baby to him. I went after him to get the baby back. I heard voices and things telling me to kill him. I thought it was God but in the mental hospital they showed me that it was the devil. I thought that I had to kill the baby to save my soul, but I couldn't make my husband understand. The mental hospital drugged me for twenty years, to brainwash me."

"Why did they release you?"

"They passed a law that the community has to look after me and they can't keep me in a state hospital. It's not just me, it's a law for everyone. I don't understand it, but they said I had to leave, and they would look after me here."

342

"Did they give you any medicine to take?"

"Yes."

"Do you take it?"

"No." She laughed and looked around suspiciously. "They're trying to control me, I know that, so when they give me the prescription, I get it filled. I know they'll check on that, but I walk around, and I drop the pills on the street so they can't find me and control me. I get a lot of help."

"Who helps you?"

"People."

"What sort of people?"

"A man."

"Is he a friend?"

She smiled.

"Where does he live?"

She laughed. "He lives inside my brain, right here," and she tapped the back of her head. "They taught me in the mental hospital that I'm not supposed to say these things. The man tells me what to do, and I listen. I think he's the devil. I'm scared." She looked up at the ceiling. "They might reach down from up there," and she pointed at the light. "I can see them hiding, and they could take me away. Do you see them? They have long fingernails. I don't like them, so I listen to the devil inside my head. That way they can't control my mind."

"Isn't that interesting," I said. "Now about this surgery you wanted."

"I want it. You have to do it."

"What I want to do is to help you."

"I want you to cut everything off, so I will look different. The psychiatrist said you had to."

This was alarming. My past experience with surgery on disturbed patients was that surgery solved nothing, and often made them much worse, even violent.

I didn't want to offend the psychiatrist and I didn't want to operate on his patient. She was fat and out-of-shape, and to a normal patient I would recommend exercise and dieting, so I gave her the same advice.

"You need to improve your whole body," I told her. "Do you like to dance?"

"Yes."

"Do you like to take walks?"

"Yes."

"You can improve your whole body by losing some weight, eating regular meals of mostly meat and fruit and vegetables, and taking a walk every day. There are dance lessons at the community center. You could take dance lessons. Dance makes your body feel better."

"I like that. He's listening." She whispered and tapped her head. "Shhh. If I lose a hundred pounds and am fit and everything like you say, could I have surgery?"

"When you have lost fifty pounds, you can come back and see us," I promised. She might need surgery to remove loose skin, if she lost that much weight. The lady nodded happily. I called her psychiatrist and told him that I would like to see his patient again after she had spent several months sculpturing her body-image.

The patient was happy and the psychiatrist was happy. I liked to operate, but not unnecessarily, and I had spared two women unnecessary surgery, so I was happy, too.

Eleven Years for This

I had now been a resident for six and a half years. I had hoped to finish my plastic surgery residency in another six months, in July, but it did not look possible. I had had a disagreement with one of the plastic surgeons in the first few months of my residency a year and a half ago. I knew that he had tremendous political power and had recommended to the Plastic Surgery Board that my time with him not be approved. I would have to take an extra, unforeseen, eighth year of residency, if the Board denied me credit for my time with him. I sent in my application for approval with letters of recommendation from other plastic surgeons, but I did not think my application would be approved. I had enjoyed my training, but an eighth year of residency seemed too much to take. Some days I became quite depressed. From the time I was twenty, I had been in medicine. I was now thirty, and although I had known various men who liked me, and whom I liked, I had been too busy for the past six years to become involved in anything permanent. I was not as tired as in the preceding six years. I was treated well, I had more time free from scut work and did more teaching, but I still spent most of my time working in the hospital. I began to feel socially stunted, deprived of the company of anyone except surgeons, and I wanted my residency to end. I began to resent the time I had given to my residency, and I wondered if I had wasted the entire decade of my twenties. Some days I was tempted to take the next plane out of Boston and get a job in D.C. as a grocery store checkout clerk. I had had enough.

Small wonder that when patients encounter a surgeon after residency they may sense that he is, to some degree, out for himself. The use of surgical residents to do mindless labor is a shocking waste of surgical talent. I didn't go into medicine to make money. I went into medicine to be a doctor, but after fifteen years of education, including seven years of surgical residency, I felt that I had been used. Surgical programs make every surgeon slightly bitter about the hundreds of hours wasted doing the routine scut. Many are permanently cynical and feel entitled, after what they have endured, to make as much money as possible, with the least effort. If America is not happy with its surgeons—or other doctors—it must change the training system.

I had passed my general surgery Boards, and as a Board Certified General Surgeon, still spent my nights on call in the hospital doing the same mindless chores I did as an intern. How much training do you need to call a hospital laboratory? I wrote preoperative test results in patients' charts. The secretaries wrote the same results on a different chart. The nurses wrote the same results on yet a different chart. Nevertheless, it was a rule that, before surgery, laboratory results had to be recorded by the residents on the patient's chart.

One night I had seven preoperative patients, and they took me three hours, as they were on seven different wards. As soon as I arrived on each ward, a nurse wanted me to write out an order to verify verbal orders given earlier in the day. The nurse cannot go off duty until verbal orders are verified. Also, in six of the seven cases, the lab had not sent back the laboratory results. I called the laboratory technicians, explained what tests I needed, and waited.

"That test has not been done yet," I was told.

I said nothing.

"That test never came here. It may have been lost. It was not delivered."

I said nothing.

"Here it is! Do you want to know what it is?" I had to call six times because the laboratory technician will not give out more than one patient's results at one time. Once I went to the laboratory for the results, thinking that would save time.

"You can't look in the book, Doctor. You have to call."

On this particular night, between calls to the lab, my beeper would ring. I called the page operator who gave me the extension to call.

"Dr. Morgan, you must come right away to see Marcia Stevens!"

"I don't have a patient by that name."

"Sorry. Good-bye."

My beeper went off again. The emergency room wanted me. A medical student, a woman, answered the phone and demanded that I sew up a laceration over her eye. Immediately! There were three surgeons in the emergency room, but she wanted a plastic surgery resident. I explained that I had things to do, but would come as soon as I could.

"How long will it take you?"

"Perhaps twenty minutes."

She sighed. "I suppose that will be all right. My point is that I'm trying to save myself a trip across town to the university hospital. But if it takes you longer than twenty minutes, it won't save me much time. So hurry up!"

When I arrived in the emergency room, the nurse said that the medical student was sleeping in a back room. She was not there. Five minutes later, the girl strolled back into the emergency room with a soft drink. It was now 10:30 P.M. I had had no dinner. Lunch had been an Oreo cookie and two Fig Newtons. I had not sat down once. I had answered my pages standing on one foot, avoiding secretaries, nurses and swinging doors, while I wrote orders and waited for the page operator to answer.

"Hi, Elizabeth. I'm Cynthia," said the medical student. "I was playing squash with my boyfriend this evening and his backhand chopped my eyebrow. Do a good job." I removed a large bandage from over her eye. She needed a Band-Aid, not a plastic surgeon Surely a third-year medical student like Cynthia, who had done a surgery rotation, should have known when a cut needed a Band-Aid.

"You don't need any sutures."

"You're only the resident. You don't know. Sew it up or I'll call the Dean."

I had better things to do than argue. I put in four tiny sutures, which she did not need.

"If it's not any good, I'll sue you. Do it right."

The next morning Dr. Revere told me that in the medical school it was well known that Cynthia was seriously disturbed. Yet she had not been asked to discontinue her training. Medical schools have a misguided loyalty to the students they accept. Once in medical school no student is dismissed, no matter how disturbed or ill-suited for medicine. The reluctance on the part of medical schools to dismiss their students is strongly reinforced by the lawsuits against them for "discrimination" whenever a student, male or female, is dismissed. It's cheaper for the school to keep the student, but it's bad for patients, and for medicine.

I finished sewing Cynthia up and returned to the ward to do paper work. I had to get operation permits signed for ten patients. It took ten minutes for each patient. I had to find the form, fill it in, take it to the patient, read it to him and have him sign it. This is what you get to do when you are a Board Certified Surgeon. The last two patients had signed their permits earlier in the day in Dr. Sutherland's office. I loved him. He had just given me twenty more minutes of sleep. I was paged again.

"Dr. Morgan. We have a late admission. Mr. Warren. Are you coming? This is the third time we have called." I had answered each of their three calls, and let the phone ring for five minutes, but the nurses on that ward did not answer the phone unless it rang fifty times. They said it kept the nursing supervisor from bothering them.

All three of the nurses were young and competent, and the nursing supervisor, who was close to retiring, was interested only in how they made a bed or how neat their uniforms were. She called them every half hour or so to "check" on them, and they could only get their work done if they left the phone unanswered.

I went to examine Mr. Warren and on the way stopped to look at preoperative chest x-ray films. Mr. Warren had been on the ward since two in the afternoon. The intern ought to have examined him before he went home, but the intern was very sick with the flu and had gone home early. As an outpatient, Mr. Warren had had a biopsy taken which showed that he had cancer of the mouth. He was a six-foot, elderly man with grizzled hair and a wide smile. I introduced myself. He roared with laughter.

"You're a cute little girl I'd like to get to know. Do I call you Girl, Miss or Ma'am?"

"Just call me Doctor Morgan."

He laughed again. "Call you Doctor? Yes, Ma'am." He laughed uncontrollably.

My friendly façade faded. My face froze. "Why did you come to the hospital?"

"I came to be resurrected by the New Jesus Christ." Mr. Warren laughed again.

"Why have you come to the hospital?" I repeated patiently, not amused. "What is your problem that you have come to get our help?"

"I have come, I have come to find and love the Son and Savior, the New Jesus Christ." Mr. Warren widened his eyes, waved his arms emphatically and broke into a loud laugh.

"How much did you smoke?"

"Less than I used to."

"How much is that?"

"Well, look." He waved a half-empty pack of cigarettes.

"How long does it take you to smoke a pack?"

"Since Christmas. They spoke to me then, and I set them aside. I said, I set these aside, and I take an ounce every day."

There were ten cigarette stubs in his bedside ashtray.

"How much do you drink?"

"I used to drink. I used to be an alcoholic. Now, I drink only beer. Only beer and brandy. Only beer and brandy and sherry. Only one drink a day."

"Do you have any allergies, Mr. Warren?"

"Yes, I have a lot of them."

"What are you allergic to?"

"Wine, whiskey and liquor, and brandy and beer and sherry."

"How many children do you have?"

"I could keep a lot of women happy."

"How often have you been married?"

"Nine times."

"Really?"

"No, maybe I was married once, but I have nine children.

349

Anyhow, Doctor, I don't have nothing that isn't from Mother Nature."

"How do you mean?"

"I told you. I don't have no problem that isn't from Mother Nature."

I had finished the physical, except for the rectal exam. I couldn't explain to this crazy man in the middle of a ward of sixteen men at 11:30 at night why I wanted to examine his rectum. The intern could do it for me in the morning.

It was clear from his chart that Mr. Warren had had mental problems for eight years, possibly from heavy alcohol drinking. He had last been seen in the emergency room, hallucinating that it was World War II and he was back in Italy fighting the Nazis. I wrote my note on Mr. Warren and the plan of treatment. He needed surgery for his cancer. I left the ward and walked to the other end of the hospital to see postoperative patients. I was paged by Mr. Warren's nurse.

"You have to return immediately."

"Why?"

"Mr. Warren is shouting and swearing. We tried to give him the sedative you ordered, but he is uncontrollable. I think he's going to attack someone."

"Don't count on me to control him. He's six feet tall, and I'm five feet five. He weighs two hundred and twenty pounds, and I weigh a hundred and twenty."

"You might talk to him."

"No, I don't think talking to him will help. You need to call the security guards, and give Mr. Warren a choice: He can leave the hospital, or go to sleep, or have a sedative and go to sleep."

"I really think you should come to see him, Doctor."

I walked all the way back to see Mr. Warren, pausing on the way to examine another postoperative patient. When I arrived, the nurse looked surprised to see me.

"You didn't have to come. He calmed down and went to sleep."

Eleven years of medical training for this?

The next morning we made attending rounds with all the plastic surgery professors. Everyone wore a white coat for these rounds; even I did, occasionally. There were eleven doctors, including four residents. Each patient was presented briefly. Dr. Sutherland was introduced, the case discussed, and we moved on. The eleven of us in white walked across the open ward to see Mr. Warren. Mr. Warren flung himself onto his knees on his bed, leaned forward and grasped Dr. Sutherland's hand.

"Jesus, Oh, Jesus Christ!" he shouted. The fifteen other patients turned to watch. "I knew I would find you if I came to the hospital. God, the One and Only, the Almighty." He gestured to the intern. "And Jesus Christ, sitting on His right hand in all the power and glory. Lord be praised." He kissed Dr. Sutherland's hand affectionately.

Solemnly, Dr. Sutherland patted his hand and turned to the intern.

"I would like you to bring Mr. Warren to my office this afternoon to be examined. I don't think a proper exam can be done on the ward."

We left the ward to the sound of Mr. Warren's laughter.

As a plastic surgery resident in Cambridge I missed working with a team, as I always had in general surgery. But in Boston I was back with a team. Adrian Sherlock, Dr. Sutherland's chief plastic surgery resident; Joseph Moore, an oral surgery chief resident from the General; and our intern, Paul Montgomery.

We did good work together. I especially looked forward to the operations on children with birth defects because the differences, before and after, were so dramatic. I did my first cleft lip and cleft palate operations in Boston. These deformities are now fairly uncommon and they are seldom seen except in large teaching hospitals. I did my first cleft palate with Dr. Godfrey, and although I knew how it was done, when I actually began it seemed incredible. The child was only a year and a half old and its mouth seemed tiny, the palate even smaller, and the scalpel much too large and awkward.

"Go ahead," said Dr. Godfrey and I cut through the palate tissue down to bone and lifted it off, until the tissue was freed up enough to sew together. Before the operation you could look from the mouth directly into the nose. Now the hole was closed, and the palate was reconstructed. It was miraculous. I was always exhilarated after an operation went well.

Snow Rounds

One Friday, Boston had twenty inches of snow. It started at six in the morning and by noon, after our first operation, my car was buried under snow. The buses stopped running. So did the cabs. It didn't rain, or get warmer, so the snow didn't melt, but we had no more snow that week.

The following Monday, it began again. The winds blew up to a hundred miles an hour, all transportation ceased, the electricity failed and the Governor declared a state of emergency. Fortunately none of my patients was in critical condition, and the junior resident had been snowed in at the hospital. But after two days at home I was stir-crazy, and hiked the five miles to the hospital, feeling like an Arctic explorer.

When I arrived, everything was quiet. The National Guard was bringing in nurses and taking home the ones who had been there for three days. All the general surgery residents had been snowed in at the hospital. I had escaped on Monday just in time. The roads had been impassable by 7:00 P.M., when the general surgeons finished rounds. During the snow days, there had been only one emergency—a college student who had jumped into the snow from his second-floor window and injured his back. A neurosurgeon had been brought in by snowmobile to operate on him. The total accumulation of snow was thirty inches.

In the spring the snow finally began to melt, to everyone's relief. We were all tired of looking at and fighting through dirty black snow. One Monday, Joseph and I met Dr. Downing for Monday morning rounds. Dr. Downing, the newest member of the plastic surgery attending team, was in a good mood. He was in charge of hand surgery and had only been an attending for nine months. He liked being in charge and this morning was a delight for him. Dr. Sutherland was away at an important spring surgical meeting and Dr. Revere was at the same meeting, as a guest speaker. Adrian Sherlock had gone as the professor's guest. Dr. Potter was at another meeting and Dr. Downing had been left behind, in charge of plastic surgery.

Spring was coming and life was looking up. An eighth year of residency didn't look quite so bad. I had been off for the weekend and had flown to Washington to visit my family, and to see the D'Oyly Carte Company perform *H.M.S. Pinafore*. Joseph had also been off, and the two of us met outside Dr. Downing's office, where he was finishing some dictation.

"Let's go," said Dr. Downing. "We'll meet the intern on D3." Almost everyone was away, we had no emergency surgery, and except for clinic, rounds and Dr. Downing's surgery, there was little to do.

The three of us left the office and set out for the pediatric ward. Joseph was still in a daze from his weekend off and I had not had enough coffee to be quite awake either. The office is on the third floor, and opens on a walkway by a stairwell. It is a wide, old-fashioned stairwell, with a wrought-iron balustrade from which you can look three floors down to the foyer. I walked out of the office, past the stairwell. Dr. Downing walked out of the office, past the stairwell. Joseph walked out of the office, past the stairwell and stopped suddenly.

"What's the matter?" I asked.

Dr. Downing frowned. He did not like unforeseen interruptions of morning rounds when he was in charge. Joseph shook his head and looked worried.

"I know it's Monday morning, and I'm not quite awake, Elizabeth, but I think I just saw a chicken. It may have been a duck."

"Joseph," I asked, "are you sure you're not having the D.T.s? Could it have been a pink duck?"

Dr. Downing and Joseph and I walked back to the stairwell. Joseph pointed down to the first floor foyer. There was no chicken, and there was no duck. There was the elevator, a large plastic trash basket and a nurse, crouched on her hands and knees clucking to the wastebasket. We looked at one another.

"She doesn't look like a chicken," said Dr. Downing.

We kept watching the nurse. From behind the trash basket appeared a small white feathered head, then a large white feathered body and a pair of large yellow feet.

"It's a duck," I announced firmly.

"Elizabeth," said Dr. Downing in surprise, "it's not. It doesn't have webbed feet. It *is* a chicken." Without my glasses I could not see the details of the feet. I put on my glasses. It was clearly a chicken. A fat, white chicken in excellent health, with a large yellow crest and bright yellow feet to match.

The chicken started to follow the clucking nurse, who had coaxed it out of hiding behind the trash basket. The chicken paraded proudly up and down in front of the elevator, delighted to be the center of attention.

"How did it get here?" Joseph asked me.

"It escaped from a laboratory, probably," said Dr. Downing.

"There aren't any in this building," said Joseph. "But it may have a dental clinic appointment." He leaned over the balustrade. "How did it get there?" he asked the nurse.

The chicken looked at Joseph, flapped its wings and ran back behind the wastebasket, clucking. The nurse looked up at us. She was still on her hands and knees.

"I don't know how it got here. I just found it when I came in to work. It doesn't belong to you, does it?" she asked hopefully.

"No, it is not a member of the plastic surgery department," said Dr. Downing.

The nurse sighed. "I didn't know what to do, so first I called the nursing supervisor. She told me to call the hospital police, because the chicken must have gotten past the hospital security check. You should have heard them on the phone when I called. 'Lady, you say you have a chicken by the dental clinic? I never heard of a lady having chickens. Ladies just have babies. You say it's not your chicken? Well, we don't need any chickens today. Thanks for calling.' They finally promised to come to help."

We stayed by the balustrade, waiting to see what happened when the police came. The nurse resumed clucking to the chicken, which finally condescended to strut out from behind the trash basket. The chicken listened to the nurse's clucks appreciatively, and then clucked back in a gentle compassionate manner. Up the stairs from the basement, two men appeared with a large cardboard box, the kind used to ship a gross of paper towels.

"We're coming. We're the police," the two men shouted as they walked up to the first floor.

The chicken looked at them disapprovingly, but walked up to the balustrade to inspect them. The nurse headed the chicken off when it tried to retreat, and the police popped the cardboard box over it. The balustrade prevented the box from coming down flat. The chicken nipped out from beneath the box and fluffed its wings indignantly. The nurse grabbed at the chicken. It jumped up the stairs. The police lunged at it with the box again. The chicken flew up two more stairs. The nurse lunged again. The chicken flew up another step, and the police chased it with the cardboard box. The chicken tried to avoid the box by flying sideways. This was a tactical error, and the chicken flew into the nurse's arms. The chicken looked surprised, but still sat in her arms, looking quickly left and right. The nurse carefully put the chicken in the large cardboard carton.

The police carried the chicken back downstairs to headquarters. We could see the chicken turn around in a circle, shake its head, peck the cardboard and then sit down, nodding. As soon as the police and chicken disappeared, a dental school professor walked into the foyer, nodding his head, just like the chicken, while he talked to a dental clinic nurse. He turned around, startled, when we laughed.

When we arrived at the ward we found the intern talking to a young man I'd never seen before.

"This is our new medical student. He's visiting us from Minnesota," said the intern, introducing us.

"Hello, how are you?" said Dr. Downing, absent-mindedly. "We're late because we were watching a chicken." Without further explanation, he started rounds.

Are You a Real Surgeon?

In the spring I was the plastic surgeon for the Veterans Hospital. I operated there one day a week, and spent the rest of the time in Boston or Cambridge. At the V.A. I operated on my own, but could ask for help if I needed it. The Plastic Surgery Board had not replied to my request for approval of my first-year residency. It seemed hard that a disagreement with a plastic surgeon in the first three months of my residency would force an extra year of training on me, but that was the way it was going to be. It helped to spend one day a week at the Veterans Hospital, because there I operated on my own. Every surgeon does things his own way. In plastic surgery, there are infinite variations in what instrument, what sutures, what retractors and what dressings you use. I had reached the point where I did not want someone to tell me what suture to use any more.

On my first day at the V.A., I arrived to do one operation and did three more as well. They were all skin cancers on the face. These cancers were usually curable but cutting out a circle of facial skin requires some skill and planning to keep from deforming the patient. Sewing up a poorly planned excision can drag the lower eyelid onto the cheek, pull the upper eyebrow into the hair, or drag the mouth down toward the chin.

356

The first cancer I removed was easy. The second was on the eyelid, but was small and did not take much time. The third was an enormous tumor on the nose and the cheek. The patient had recently had a stroke and a heart operation. His speech was slurred from the stroke and was hard to understand. I thought he was senile, until I realized he was asking me how bad the cancer was, and if he would look all right afterward. To cut out the cancer meant cutting out all the skin on the left side of his nose and cheek. Because of his heart surgery, it was safer to work under local anesthesia and I had to operate fairly quickly. I decided to use a small flap from his forehead to replace the skin lost from the nose and cheek.

I explained this to my patient, wheeled him into the room and helped him onto the operating table. The anesthesiologist monitored his heart rhythm, and started an intravenous. I took photographs of the cancer, scrubbed my hands, washed my patient's face with antiseptic soap and draped sterile towels and sheets around him. I was ready to inject the anesthetic, with epinephrine, which decreases the bleeding.

"You can't use epinephrine," the anesthesiologist said in an agitated voice. "You'll kill him. He's just had a coronary bypass. You can't use it."

"I can't possibly operate without using epinephrine. I won't be able to see through the bleeding."

"Then you can't continue."

"Wait a minute," I said. "He hasn't had a coronary bypass. He had a valve replaced. His heart arteries are in good shape. Besides, the epinephrine is a dilute solution, only one to four hundred thousand. It should be quite safe."

The anesthesiologist brightened.

"You're absolutely right. I'm sorry to interrupt you."

"Is everything all right, Doctor?" asked the patient.

"Everything is fine," I said. "We were discussing the best medicines for you." I started to inject him. "After these injections, nothing will hurt. You can sleep if you like." Two minutes later he was snoring.

I had no trouble cutting out the tumor. I measured around the cancer. It was a lot of tissue to cut out and a relatively harmless type of skin cancer, but as Dr. Sutherland liked to say, "It's still a cancer. Inadequate resection on the first operation and a later cancer

357

recurrence can mean losing half your face. First you cut the cancer out. Then worry about deformity."

I cut out the left side of the patient's nose, and the skin over his cheek down to his mouth. I passed the tissue specimen to the scrub nurse, a man who in turn passed it to the circulating nurse, also a man, who looked from me to the patient's face and back again. The nurse cleared his throat, and whispered to me, "It looks as though a hand grenade went off in the guy's face. What the hell are you going to do?"

The circulating nurse took the specimen out, and after that a steady stream of nurses tiptoed into the room, peered over my shoulder at the sleeping patient, gasped and tiptoed out. The anesthesiologist looked at him, said, "Jesus," and walked out.

I measured the skin flap on the patient's forehead and injected more anesthetic. The patient woke up.

"How much longer, Doctor?"

"It's going very well," I said. "The cancer is out. I just have to put things back together again."

I raised the flap down to the skin and blood vessels near the eyebrow, dissecting slowly. I looked at the clock, and realized that I was operating too slowly, considering the anesthetic. I turned the skin flap to fit it into the defect in the face. For a horrible moment I thought I had designed it backwards, i.e., for the right side of the face, not the left. I could hear Dr. Fitzhugh saying, "If this operation goes wrong, take a one-way ticket to Argentina. They'll never find you in the jungle." Then I realized it was fine but I had to cut the skin more, so the flap would turn onto the cheek. It fitted beautifully.

The anesthesiologist came in again.

"What the hell are you going to do with his forehead?" he whispered and went out shaking his head. I knew the forehead would not be a problem. The skin was loose, and would slide back together with some well-placed sutures. I finished the operation. The anesthesiologist bounded in.

"Are you done?" He looked at my patient's face. "It looks good!" He bounded out again.

My patient woke up. "Doc, I'm hungry. Are you done?"

I was. The orderly wheeled him back to the room. I wrote the orders, dictated the operation, had a cup of coffee and went down to see my patient. He was arguing with the nurse. He wanted coffee as well as Jell-O.

The next day I came to see him again. He leaned forward eagerly. "You did a nice job, Dr. Morgan," he said. "I don't want to seem rude or fresh, but tell me—do you do this sort of thing all the time? Are you a real surgeon?"

You're Our Consultant

One Wednesday, in late May, the Board sent me a letter:

> Dear Doctor Morgan, Your application for examination
> has been received and approved. Your name has been
> added to the list of Candidates who plan to take Part I of
> the Plastic Surgery Board Examination this year. You will
> receive further information as to the exact location and
> time of the examination.

I read it again. My two years had been approved. My residency
would end on July 1. I was Board-eligible! I told Dr. Fitzhugh the
next day. He said, "Congratulations!" and then, "You know that Dr.
Berenson spent a lot of time arranging for you to work with him
starting in July. You can probably work with him as an assistant
instead of a resident, and take your Board exams. You had better ask
him what arrangements he wants to make."

I would have been happier to leave for Washington in July, but a
year with Dr. Berenson would be a great year. He was not only a
remarkable surgeon, but able to inspire people. I was worried about
my status, though. If I worked with him as a resident, I automatically was not eligible to take Boards. If I could not work with him as

an assistant, I would be a resident once again. Dr. Berenson was away and I did not see him until the following Friday at plastic surgery Grand Rounds. He was sitting with his associate, having coffee and doughnuts, and waiting for the speaker to arrive.

"Elizabeth, how are you? I haven't seen you for weeks."

"Dr. Berenson, I'm fine. I got the news that I'm Board-eligible." He sat up in his chair.

"Excellent. Now what are you going to do?"

"I thought I would talk to you about it. I would like to take the Board exams this year."

"You should."

"I won't be able to take them if I am still a resident, so I was wondering about this coming year with you. I would prefer not to be a resident, if I don't have to."

"Of course not. Where are you hoping to set up practice?"

"I have been planning to return to Washington, but I don't mind putting that off for a year while I work here with you. I would love it, but I just don't want it to be as a resident.."

"I see. You're feeling guilty. Stop it. You've been a resident for seven years, and that's quite enough. It is time for you to leave the nest, Elizabeth. If you are no longer a resident, I don't want you to spend a year studying with me or anyone else. You are a qualified plastic surgeon. I want to see you out of town by July."

I leaned back, overwhelmed. "It seems sudden, to fly off to open my own practice."

"I won't let you put it off any more. You can't be a resident forever. It's time to become a responsible person, a real doctor, and to work for your living for a change."

"He's absolutely right," said Dr. Seeton, his associate, watching the jelly ooze out of his doughnut. "You go on being a resident for so long that it seems impossible to be anything else. Doing it suddenly like this is the best way. Go home, study for Boards, and open an office. It sounds exciting."

"You notice that we're anxious to get you out of town," said Dr. Berenson, avoiding the jelly falling from Dr. Seeton's doughnut. "It's the sure sign of a good plastic surgeon, when all the other plastic surgeons try to get rid of you. You'll do very well. Let me know if there's anything I can do to help."

Now that I had what I wanted, I was frightened. It seemed a

staggering step to go to a state where I had not lived for eighteen years, to open an office and hope to make a living. I could see myself, sitting alone behind my desk for two years, unknown and starving, deeply in debt and living on eggs and stale bread.

"It's easy," said Dr. Fitzhugh. "A lot of hard work, but easy. This is what you do. Decide where you want to practice. Apply for privileges to the hospitals in the area. Your credentials are excellent. You shouldn't have trouble.

"Go around and introduce yourself. Take emergency calls. Give lectures, if the other departments ask you to. You'll make a living within a few years and then you'll be able to pay off your debts. You have to go into debt to get started."

"How much?"

"These days, it will take you at least fifty thousand for the office, the secretary and the minimal equipment, but don't let it bother you. All I ask is that you pass Boards first."

Before I left Boston, Dr. Berenson offered to help me, and had called the plastic surgeons he knew in Washington and asked them to help too. Dr. Fitzhugh did the same, calling the plastic surgeons he knew, and writing letters of recommendation to the hospitals. Dr. Mendelssohn called to congratulate me and to see what he could do to help. He called his friends in Washington, too. I was touched and grateful for their help, given out of the kindness of their hearts. Without it, I could not have started my practice.

I flew out of Boston on July 1. The movers had taken my things the week before. I carried nothing but my sleeping bag onto the airplane, and arrived an hour later in Washington, an about-to-be private plastic surgeon. I studied for Boards for two months, and passed the written exam. The oral exam, on my own cases in private practice, would come in a year or two. I took two weeks of vacation in France and England and came back home. The agony of being a resident and going sleepless for a week at a time had already faded. Since July, I had spent an enormous amount of time sleeping, ten, often twelve hours a night.

In November I stopped sleeping so much, and needed only seven or eight hours a night. Obviously I had been sleep-deprived for seven years, and my body had been catching up.

I was working on office arrangements one afternoon at four o'clock when the telephone rang in my temporary office. My regular office and my practice were scheduled to open January 1.

"Dr. Morgan, this is National Hospital. We have a patient with a lacerated face. How long will it take you to come?"

"I don't understand."

"You are on our emergency call list, as the consultant plastic surgeon."

"Since when?"

"Starting in November, when we opened the new, expanded emergency room."

"They didn't tell me," I said, "which is why I sound so surprised."

"Can you come?"

"Of course. It's the rush hour though, and it will take me twenty minutes. Can you explain to the patient that I'm coming, but there will be a delay?"

"Certainly. I look forward to meeting you. Good-bye."

I rushed around to grab my camera, my prescription forms, my doctor's bag, cards and a few instruments, and set off. I was a Real Doctor.

Epilogue

My greatest fear when I opened my own office was that I would "sell out" to cosmetic surgery. Less than a hundred years ago, cosmetic surgeons were often charlatans or, at best, doctors of doubtful ethics. The "face lifts" they did gave only a short-lived "lift" to the lower face. Modern plastic surgery did not begin with these disreputable men, but with a group of European and American surgeons in World War I who developed new surgical techniques for soldiers and civilians who suffered burns and gunshot wounds that left their faces and hands hideously deformed and disabled. After World War I these skilled and innovative surgeons returned to private practice and many of them began doing cosmetic surgery as one aspect of reconstructive surgery.

During World War II, new advances were made. Plastic surgeons improved the treatment of facial fractures, burns, and hand injuries and began research on transplantation. Since World War II, plastic surgery has attracted surgeons who want to develop new methods of reconstruction, especially after cancer surgery. At the same time, as more plastic surgeons are trained, more people want cosmetic surgery, from face lifts and eyelid surgery to rhinoplasty to breast enlargement and reduction. Cosmetic surgery fees are high, paid in advance, and surgery can be scheduled at the doctor's and the patient's convenience—the surgeon does not have to get out of bed in the middle of the night as he does in cases of severe trauma.

It is tempting for a plastic surgeon to concentrate on cosmetic surgery, and plastic surgeons who limit their practice to cosmetic surgery may become wealthy, often famous. They are in the cosmetic surgery business, not the practice of medicine. I had often thought that cosmetic surgery tended to be done at the patient's request, with too little attention paid to why the patients wanted cosmetic surgery and if the results for them would be worth the time and expense.

Everyone's face loosens with age and most people have a less-than-perfect nose. People who want cosmetic surgery to change their appearance *may* do so because of psychological problems or worries, like a woman who wants a face lift so she will not be rejected by her husband or lover. Yet, when they walk into a plastic surgeon's office, such patients say they want a "face lift" and don't mention psychological problems that contribute to their dissatisfactions with the way they look. In my practice, I have found that many women who asked about a face lift decide against it if I spend time encouraging them to talk about what else is happening in their lives. One woman, for instance, had not had a vacation in twenty years. She did not need a face lift to look rested and younger, she needed a vacation, and I persuaded her to take one. Not all women were so ready to listen to advice. One woman, Mrs. Kenneth, asked me to do a face lift. I explained the fee, how the surgery was done and the possible, though unlikely, complications. She nodded vigorously but did not smile. She looked distraught, and stared out the window without ever looking at me.

"Why do you want the surgery?" I asked.

"I just want to feel better about the way I look." She was fifty-eight, and her face would be tightened by a face lift. There is nothing magical about it—the operation repositions the skin of the neck, jaw and lower face, giving a tighter, though not always more youthful, appearance.

"What made you decide to have it done now?" I asked.

"I had planned to retire, but my husband is suddenly no longer able to work, so I have to go back to work as a language teacher in high school." She looked down at the floor and I thought she was going to cry.

"If you have to go back to work for financial reasons, it may not be wise to spend several thousand dollars on cosmetic surgery."

"I have the money. I've saved it."

"Why is your husband no longer able to work?" I asked. I thought he might be seriously ill and if so, she might need the money.

"I didn't expect to discuss my life with you, Doctor. I had hoped you would tell me about the surgery. I am very anxious to have it done." She spoke like a teacher dealing with a problem student.

"I'm not sure why you want it done," I said.

"I want to feel good about myself before I go back to work. I need to look young to get on with the school kids these days." She was indignant.

"The surgery won't necessarily make you look any younger," I pointed out, "and children in high school are teenagers. There is no way they'll look on you as one of them. Even if you were thirty-five, you would seem old to a teenager."

"I don't want to look young," she said abruptly. "I'm not stupid. I understand what you're saying."

"Tell me more about your husband," I said. "Is he ill? You don't want extensive surgery if you have to look after him."

"Doctor, really, it's a very personal question, and I'm not going to discuss it. If it's the money you're worried about," she said, "I have it. My husband is not the problem. I want a face lift. That's what a plastic surgeon is for, isn't it?"

I agreed to consider doing a face lift if she would come back to talk to me a second time before I decided finally for or against the surgery. I thought about Mrs. Kenneth a lot during the next week. I felt increasingly certain that she was struggling with a psychological problem of much more importance than a face lift. I thought perhaps her husband had died and she wanted a face lift to help her over the sorrow. We know that it is not wise to do cosmetic surgery at a time of emotional turmoil because it may depress the patient even more. The second time, I was more direct.

"I've been thinking about you since you were here, Mrs. Kenneth," I began. "You must be honest with me. I can't do a face lift to make you look better if there is something in your life that makes you so unhappy that you cannot smile. Cosmetic surgery will not solve a problem for you. It will only tighten your face."

366

Her eyes welled with tears. "Doctor, I am being honest with you. All I want is a face lift so I can go back to work."

"You have a job," I objected.

"I have to look young," she said angrily, and glared at the rug. I shook my head.

"I cannot operate on you. I'll give you the names of several excellent plastic surgeons who may not feel the way I do."

Mrs. Kenneth burst into tears, ran out of my consulting room, slamming the door, dashed through the waiting room and disappeared. Two weeks later, I was in a hospital operating room and another surgeon was there, drinking coffee with the nurses.

"What an awful experience last week," he said. "That nutty neurotic, Mrs. Kenneth."

"What happened?" I asked. He didn't know I knew her.

"I was doing a face lift on this Mrs. Kenneth, a perfectly normal cooperative woman, and halfway through she starts the dry heaves and vomiting. She said the operation was making her nervous. I almost couldn't finish. She was heaving the entire time. Fortunately, she's healed all right. When she came back to have her stitches out, she told my nurse that she had just had her husband put away in an institution. Apparently he's a hopeless alcoholic." So that was what she wouldn't tell me. Perhaps the face lift gave her the strength to lock her husband up, but it would have been cheaper, and more help to her, to see a psychiatrist rather than a plastic surgeon.

Sometimes surgery does seem to help a patient's emotional problems, at least at first. One young man wanted his nose straightened. It had been crooked ever since a football injury in high school. He was a twin, less successful than his brother, and he said before surgery that he was tired of people calling him "the twin with the funny nose."

"It makes me feel inferior to my brother," he said, "and I hope once my nose is straight, that won't happen any more."

He was happy after the surgery, and not only recovered quickly, but flew out to California and got a job he had wanted but hadn't dared to apply for before the surgery. He also got a new girl friend. I saw him in my office six months later when he came back East on a visit. His nose looked good, but he had gained about forty pounds. I wondered why he wanted to see me.

"Dr. Morgan," he said in the examining room, "could you prescribe some amphetamines for me?"

"Why?"

"Ever since you operated on my nose, I stopped running and keeping fit. I'm much fatter than my twin brother, and it bothers me when people call me 'the fat twin.' It makes me feel inferior."

His nose was straight, but now he was fat. I wondered how much I had helped him.

Plastic surgeons who let their patients tell them what operation to do abdicate their roles as physicians and become instead highly skilled providers of technical services. As a doctor, I don't let my patients tell me what to do, but give them the best advice I can. Often when I advise a woman to spend her money on something that she needs more than a face lift, she is happy, and I am too.